# The Philosophy of Film Noir

# The
# Philosophy
# of
# Film Noir

edited by
Mark T. Conard

Foreword by Robert Porfirio

THE UNIVERSITY PRESS OF KENTUCKY

Publication of this volume was made possible in part by a grant from the National Endowment for the Humanities.

Scholarly publisher for the Commonwealth,
serving Bellarmine University, Berea College, Centre
College of Kentucky, Eastern Kentucky University,
The Filson Historical Society, Georgetown College,
Kentucky Historical Society, Kentucky State University,
Morehead State University, Murray State University,
Northern Kentucky University, Transylvania University,
University of Kentucky, University of Louisville,
and Western Kentucky University.

*Editorial and Sales Offices:* The University Press of Kentucky
663 South Limestone Street, Lexington, Kentucky 40508-4008
www.kentuckypress.com

10  09  08  07  06    5  4  3  2  1

Library of Congress Cataloging-in-Publication Data

The philosophy of film noir / edited by Mark T. Conard with a foreword
by Robert Porfirio.
    p. cm.
  Includes bibliographical references and index.
ISBN-13: 978-0-8131-2377-6 (hardcover : alk. paper)
ISBN-10: 0-8131-2377-1 (hardcover : alk. paper)
  1. Film noir—History and criticism.  I. Conard, Mark T., 1965-
PN1995.9.F54P55 2005
791.43'6552—dc22
2005030639

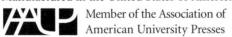 Member of the Association of
American University Presses

To Bill Irwin, Pepper Landis, John and Linda Pappas, Read Schuchardt, and Aeon Skoble—movie lovers all, *and the best friends a guy could have*

# CONTENTS

**Part 3: Six Classic Films Noirs**

# FOREWORD

In the fall of 1976, when I wrote the article "No Way Out: Existential Motifs in the *Film Noir*" for *Sight and Sound* (vol. 45, no. 4, pp. 212–17), little would I have expected that some twenty-five years later a collection of essays under the title *The Philosophy of Film Noir* would be published. Yet here it is, a welcome indication of how far we have traveled in terms of public awareness and scholarly respectability. Indeed, in 1976, the term *film noir* was little known beyond a coterie of French and American cineasts and derided by some as a specious classification created in a post hoc manner and not worthy of serious critical attention. By now, the ontology of film noir seems to be settled in its favor, although epistemological argumentation rages on. Anyone interested in tracing the course of this argumentation over the past quarter century would be well advised to consult the appendices in *Film Noir: An Encyclopedic Reference to the American Style* (ed. Alain Silver and Elizabeth Ward, with Carl Macek and Robert Porfirio, 3rd ed., rev. and expanded [Woodstock, N.Y.: Overlook, 1992]) as well as the *Film Noir Readers* (Alain Silver and James Ursini, eds., *Film Noir Reader* [1996; New York: Limelight, 2001], *Film Noir Reader 2* [New York: Limelight, 1999], and *Film Noir Reader 4* [New York: Limelight, 2004]; and Robert Porfirio, Alain Silver, and James Ursini, eds., *Film Noir Reader 3* [New York: Limelight, 2001]), which, taken together, cover virtually all the controversies surrounding the field of film noir scholarship and evidence the debt that such scholarship owes to Alain Silver.

That the essence of film noir is yet to be distilled is implicit in the excellent essays contained in this volume, each of which sees film noir through a slightly different lens. The essays here go well beyond my earlier, somewhat simplistic effort to extract a "philosophy" of film noir in terms of an outlook on life that these diverse films seemed to share—an attitude toward existence that was akin to modern existentialism, particularly as it evolved in postwar France. Perhaps that is why it was the French cineasts who were the first to identify the cycle. But, if I may be allowed to indulge myself a bit here, I would like to take issue with their assertion (and that of other critics following in their wake, myself included) that what was surprising in these early films noirs was the degree to which they went against the grain of that native-bred optimism that seemed to define the American character (so well articulated by Alexis de Tocqueville in the early nineteenth century). If we take an extensive historical look at this American character, we can detect a dark side implicit in it from its very beginnings, one that predated those vaunted attributes of self-reliance and individual enterprise associated with "Yankee ingenuity" and those virtues inherent in the Jeffersonian agrarian ideal, the yeoman farmer.

That dark side can surely be seen in the culture and lifestyle of our Puritan ancestry, a heritage quite at odds with the new breed of "American" exemplified by Benjamin Franklin (at least as he presented himself in his *Autobiography*, a work that itself went a long way toward papering over those differences). Nathaniel Hawthorne's fiction in turn dramatized this dark side by showing how it worked itself out in the psyche of nineteenth-century America. Yet the distinctively American bias given to transcendentalism by Emerson and Thoreau—the faith in the natural world and the emphasis on self-reliance—should have purged America of its darkest inclinations. Walt Whitman, writing before, during, and after the trauma of the American Civil War, is an exemplar in this regard. For, despite the dislocations engendered by that war, he retained his belief in the power of the individual spirit to overcome all odds. Emersonian transcendentalism, however, did not fare as well in the fiction of Melville and Poe. The "voyage" into nature could end in disaster, as in Melville's *Moby Dick,* just as the Yankee entrepreneurial spirit could degenerate into the crass materialism of *The Confidence Man,* a prophetic work given the excesses of America's Gilded Age, and one that questioned the validity of any sort of faith.

The work of Edgar Allan Poe is particularly relevant to anyone tracing the antecedents of American film noir. Short tales such as *Ms. Found in a Bottle* and *The Narrative of Arthur Gordon Pym* left the outcome of the transcendental voyage quite problematic. But it was Poe's arabesque tales that called into question the power of human reason. These "grotesque" stories harked back to an earlier tradition of gothic literature, yet, more often than not, they eschewed the supernatural in favor of such themes as murder, revenge, betrayal, and entrapment, and they were frequently centered around the figure of a fatal woman. And they paved the way for such future practitioners as Cornell Woolrich. As if in an effort to maintain his own sanity, Poe also wrote his stories of ratiocination and, in so doing, created the prototype for the classic private detective, an agent of order both moral and social. In reaction to this classic detective, Dashiell Hammett helped create the modern "hard-boiled private eye," whose allegiance was only to a highly personal and private code, whose style was virtually everything, and who attempted to survive in a universe as chaotic as anything in Poe.

At the turn of the century, the pragmatism of William James, with its emphasis on radical empiricism, proved to be the philosophic death knell for Emersonian transcendentalism. And as America moved into the twentieth century, it was beset with a variety of "isms"—Darwinism, determinism, Freudianism, Marxism—all of which challenged the integrity of the individual. Social Darwinism went so far as to provide a rationale for an abusive variety of capitalism that, unchecked, placed the plutocrat at the top of the social ladder. Not that the works of Spencer, Nietzsche, Schopenhauer, or Freud were part of the mass culture of that era. Few beyond the well educated would have even been familiar with them. But their influence on American fiction, especially on those writers who felt a kinship with literary naturalism, was profound. And large numbers of Americans did read authors like Frank Norris, Theodore Dreiser, and Jack London, who, along with others of their ilk, reduced the human being to a monad, little more than Dreiser's "waif amidst forces."

By the twenties, the publishing industry was changing, and fiction became increasingly accessible to an increasingly literate American public. Pulp magazines began to replace the older dime-novel format as a mass outlet for fiction. Priced from ten to twenty-five cents, pulps were printed on coarse newspaper stock with glossy, colorful, and often lurid covers. More important, they provided a medium for those "penny-a-word" writers who were at the center of the hard-boiled school, among them Hammett, Chandler, and Woolrich. With the introduction of the paperback in the thirties, the pulps had a competitor in the marketplace (and one that would completely displace them in the fifties). Now both lowbrow fiction (e.g., Cain, McCoy) and high-brow fiction (e.g., Hemingway, Steinbeck, Faulkner) could be purchased for well under a dollar, and American authors could achieve a popularity that was unthinkable in the nineteenth century. In a very real sense, the films noirs of the classic period represented Hollywood's attempt to capitalize on the public taste for crime, violence, and sexuality, a taste already made palatable by the publishing world.

As Hollywood turned increasingly during the thirties to themes of crime and violence, films moved well beyond the clean parlors of the classic whodunit to deal with gangsterism and other social issues. Yet, by making the environment the main determinant of aberrant behavior, these films displayed a greater affinity for literary naturalism than for the hard-boiled tradition (see *The Public Enemy* [William A. Wellman, 1931], *Dead End* [William Wyler, 1937], *Wild Boys of the Road* [William A. Wellman, 1933]). It wasn't until the forties that a confluence of factors, many of which are discussed in the essays contained herein, allowed Hollywood to capture the essence of that literary tradition expressed through a series of films that we have come to call *film noir.*

I do not wish to ignore the social and historical dimensions of this confluence, however, since culture does not exist in a vacuum. Certainly, the rapid succession of two world wars punctuated by a depression propelled the evolution of the hard-boiled tradition, while its social consequences may have conditioned audiences to accept the bleak view of the world expressed in both American literature and American film. Nor do I wish to underestimate the effect of the foreign influence. Throughout the thirties and forties, America became the major refuge for a group of artists, intellectuals, and writers that I have elsewhere termed the *Germanic émigrés.* Many of these settled in southern California; some, quite naturally, gravitated to the film industry. Most were fleeing fascist Europe. It seems evident to me that they contributed much to that expressionist style of Hollywood filmmaking as it evolved from the gangster and horror films of the thirties to become a defining motif of the films noirs of the forties and fifties. What seems questionable to me is that their morbid sensibilities, quite explicable in the light of their experiences in their homelands (many were of Jewish descent), somehow explain the pessimistic trajectory of film noir. More likely, perhaps, is that they were drawn to the dark strain of American culture that I have been tracing here, a strain for which they had an understandable affinity. In any case, no one can accuse them of failing to do justice to the cinematic equivalent of that dark strain as it worked its way through the culture of America in the thirties, forties, and fifties.

The atmosphere of fear and paranoia that pervades film noir was familiar enough terrain for those Germanic émigrés, given the precariousness of their existence in war-ravaged Europe (recall Professor Warren's admonition to the heroine of Robert Siodmak's *The Spiral Staircase* [1946]: "Don't trust anyone!"). And, while the life experiences of most Americans were far less precarious, the psychological effects of World War II and its aftermath (the loss of insular security, the Red Scare, the nuclear threat) would have made such an atmosphere something less than foreign. If such be the case, one might speculate on what contemporary filmmakers, filling the void left by film noir with today's neo-noir thrillers, will produce in the wake of 9/11.

*Robert Porfirio*

# Acknowledgments

First, I'd like to thank the contributors for all their hard work and patience, both of which are clearly evident in these terrific essays. Many thanks are also due to Steve Wrinn at the University Press of Kentucky, with whom it's been a real pleasure to work; and I'd like to thank Paul Cantor for introducing me to Steve. I'd also like to thank Bob Porfirio for his willingness to write the foreword and for the wonderful job that he did. Last, for all their love and support, I want to thank my family and friends.

# INTRODUCTION

A drifter, driven purely by desire, is convinced by a beautiful woman—a femme fatale—to murder her husband. A whiskey-drinking, chain-smoking detective becomes involved with a gang of ruthless criminals in pursuit of a priceless artifact, for which they're all willing to kill. An insurance salesman is lured by a restless, avaricious housewife to murder her husband for the insurance money. Another detective, this one sleepy eyed and trench coated, is hired by a gangster to find a woman who tried to kill him and then absconded with his money—except, when the detective finds her, he takes up with her himself, only later to be betrayed by her. The claustrophobic settings are awash in deep shadows, the streets are rain swept, it always seems to be night, and the atmosphere is charged and angst ridden. We know the stories; we love the noir style, at once romantic and pessimistic; we sympathize, maybe even identify, with the doomed antihero; the anxiety and sense of alienation are uncomfortably familiar. All true enough—but what does any of this have to do with *philosophy*?

Actually, quite a lot, as it turns out.

First, what *is* film noir? (And immediately we find ourselves on philosophical ground: questions both about the essence of a thing, what makes it what it is, and about definition are philosophical in nature.) Critics tend to identify the classic noir period as falling between 1941 and 1958, beginning with John Huston's *The Maltese Falcon* and ending with Orson Welles's *Touch of Evil*, two masterpieces of noir. This period, not coincidentally, lasts from America's involvement in World War II through the postwar era. We can easily identify classic film noir by the constant opposition of light and shadow, its oblique camera angles, and its disruptive compositional balance of frames and scenes, the way characters are placed in awkward and unconventional positions within a particular shot, for example. But, besides these technical cinematic characteristics, there are a number of themes that characterize film noir, such as the inversion of traditional values and the corresponding moral ambivalence (e.g., the protagonist of the story, who traditionally is the good guy, in noir films often makes very questionable moral decisions); the feeling of alienation, paranoia, and cyni-

*1*

cism; the presence of crime and violence; and the disorientation of the viewer, which is in large part accomplished by the filming techniques mentioned above. Some paradigmatic examples of classic films noirs are *Double Indemnity* (Billy Wilder, 1944), *The Postman Always Rings Twice* (Tay Garnett, 1946), *The Big Sleep* (Howard Hawks, 1946), and *Out of the Past* (Jacques Tourner, 1953).

These classic noir films have their roots both in the hard-boiled literature of the thirties and forties (think here, e.g., of James M. Cain, Raymond Chandler, David Goodis, and Horace McCoy) and in the German/Austrian immigration during and after the war, given that a number of very important writers, directors, and other film technicians were German or Austrian émigrés.

In addition to these classic noir films, there are more recent films that are often identified as *neo-noir* since—while falling outside the classic time period and (typically) not in black and white—they share the inversion of values, the alienation and pessimism, the violence, and the disorientation of the spectator. *Reservoir Dogs* (Quentin Tarantino, 1992), *Blue Velvet* (David Lynch, 1986), *Taxi Driver* (Martin Scorsese, 1976), and *Memento* (Christopher Nolan, 2000) are often considered to be examples of neo-noir.

Now, French existentialist philosophy was contemporaneous with classic film noir and shares some of its themes, if not its outlook and tone. While most critics agree that there wasn't a direct influence of the existentialists on the films, those philosophical themes are clearly present in the movies, themes like moral ambiguity, reason versus passion in human decision making and action, the meaning of life, and pessimism.

The present volume, then, investigates the philosophical themes and underpinnings of these films and also uses the movies as a vehicle for exploring and explicating traditional philosophical ideas. It comprises thirteen essays from scholars in both philosophy and film and media studies. The essays are written in nontechnical language and require no knowledge of philosophy to appreciate or understand.

In part 1, "The Essence and Elements of Noir," my "Nietzsche and the Meaning and Definition of Noir" gives a history of the attempts at defining film noir and then—using Nietzsche's claim that God is dead—makes a modest proposal for seeing and understanding film noir in a new light. Jason Holt, in "A Darker Shade: Realism in Neo-Noir," claims that the real heart and essence of noir is realized only after the classic noir period is over, in neo-noir films. In "Moral Clarity and Practical Reason in Film

Noir," Aeon J. Skoble contends that, contrary to the common view that noir films depict and perhaps promote a world without ethics and values, these movies actually present significant moral lessons. Read Mercer Schuchardt claims next, in his essay "Cherchez la Femme Fatale: The Mother of Film Noir," that *The Jazz Singer* (Alan Crosland, 1927) should be considered the first film noir since it is the first film to announce or acknowledge the death of God. In "From Sherlock Holmes to the Hard-Boiled Detective in Film Noir," Jerold J. Abrams argues that the hard-boiled detectives of film noir follow the detective logic of their non-noir predecessors (like Holmes) but that they inhabit a significantly different reality than those predecessors do—one in which there is no escape from the maze of the world.

Part 2, "Existentialism and Nihilism in Film Noir," begins with "Film Noir and the Meaning of Life," in which Steven M. Sanders explores film noir's (largely pessimistic) ideas about life's purpose, meaning, and value. Next, in "The Horizon of Disenchantment: Film Noir, Camus, and the Vicissitudes of Descent," Alan Woolfolk contends that the noir antihero lives in a disenchanted world, one that is "not so benign," and one that he can neither fully escape nor fully embrace. And, last, in "Symbolism, Meaning, and Nihilism in Quentin Tarantino's *Pulp Fiction*," I argue that Quentin Tarantino's neo-noir classic *Pulp Fiction* (1994) is really about nihilism and the principal characters' attempts at finding or reclaiming meaning and value in a nihilistic world.

In part 3, "Six Classic Films Noirs," Paul A. Cantor asserts, in "Film Noir and the Frankfurt School: America as Wasteland in Edgar Ulmer's *Detour*," that the classic noir *Detour* (1945) offers a vision of American life that is strikingly similar to that of the Frankfurt school theorists Horkheimer and Adorno and that, because of the influence of German émigrés, film noir is less of a purely American phenomenon than previously thought. Next, in "Knowledge, Morality, and Tragedy in *The Killers* and *Out of the Past*," Ian Jarvie asks why noir films, full of violence, angst, and treachery, are successful and entertaining and whether they might fit Aristotle's definition of tragedy and thus engage the viewer by means of the catharsis that they provide. R. Barton Palmer argues, in "Moral Man in the Dark City: Film Noir, the Postwar Religious Revival, and *The Accused*," that there is an important subgenre of noir films that emphasizes spiritual redemption and eschews the typical noir angst-filled despair, and he takes as his paradigm case William Dieterle's *The Accused* (1949). Then, in "On Reason and Passion in *The Maltese Falcon*," Deborah Knight discusses the traditional philosophical treatment of the relation between reason and passion, using John Huston's noir masterpiece to demonstrate that rational action usually has some underlying emotion associated with it and that, while the femme fatale is in this case motivated by reason alone, the detective displays a proper balance between reason and emotion. Finally, in his "*Ride the Pink Horse:* Money, Mischance, Murder, and the Monads of Film Noir," Alain Silver claims that Robert Montgomery's classic *Ride the Pink Horse* (1947) contains interesting parallels to the philosophical and aesthetic principles of Arthur Schopenhauer.

At the heart of this volume are our abiding fondness for and appreciation of these wonderful movies. We sincerely hope and believe that our analyses will deepen and enrich your respect for and understanding of them, not merely as works of art, but as philosophically interesting texts in their own right, especially if you love them as much as we do.

# PART 1

## THE ESSENCE AND ELEMENTS of NOIR

# Nietzsche and the Meaning and Definition of Noir

*Mark T. Conard*

*The Postman Always Rings Twice* (Tay Garnett, 1946) was adapted from a novel by the writer of hard-boiled fiction James M. Cain. Interspersed throughout the movie is voice-over narration by the protagonist, Frank Chambers (John Garfield), indicating that he is recalling events in the past. Frank is a drifter who takes a job at a remote diner owned by an older man, Nick (Cecil Kellaway), after getting a look at Nick's stunning young wife, Cora (Lana Turner). There is a strong sexual attraction between Frank and Cora, and, after one aborted attempt, they succeed in killing Nick and making it look like a car accident in order to be together. A suspicious DA, however, hounds them and finally tricks Frank into signing a statement claiming that Cora murdered Nick. Cora beats the rap, and the lovers are bitterly estranged for a short period. In the end (after some other twists and turns), they come back together, knowing that they're too much in love to be apart, knowing that they're fated to be together. Ironically, they have a car accident in which Cora is killed. The DA prosecutes Frank for Cora's murder, and Frank is convicted and sentenced to death. We learn at the end that he has been telling the story to a priest in his prison cell, awaiting execution.

*Postman* displays all the distinctive conventions of film noir—the noir look and feel as well as a typical noir narrative, with the femme fatale, the alienated and doomed antihero, and their scheme to do away with her husband. It has the feeling of disorientation, pessimism, and the rejection of traditional ideas about morality, what's right and what's wrong. Further, a great many noir films were either adapted from hard-boiled novels or heavily influenced by them. Finally, *Postman* is told in flashback form through Frank's voice-over, another noir convention. Indeed, *Postman* is considered to be a classic film noir.

But what does that mean? What exactly *is* film noir? Is it a genre (like a western or a romantic comedy)? Is it a film style constituted by the deep shadows and odd scene compositions? Is it perhaps a cycle of films lasting through a certain period (typically identified as 1941–58)? Is noir a certain mood and tone, that of alienation and pessimism? Each of these answers, among others, has been given as an explanation of just what film noir is. And, given that there is widespread disagreement about what film noir is, there is likewise disagreement about which films count as noir films. Clearly, *Postman* is a noir film, but is *Citizen Kane* (Orson Welles, 1941), for example? Or, perhaps more pointedly, is *Beat the Devil* (1953) or *The Treasure of the Sierra Madre* (1948)? Like *The Maltese Falcon* (1941), both star noir legend Humphrey Bogart, and both were directed by John Huston, but, whereas *The Maltese Falcon* is considered to be a noir film, indeed a classic noir, the other two movies are often not so regarded.

In this essay, I'll give a brief history of the various attempts at defining film noir. I'll then discuss Nietzsche and the problem of definition, and I'll conclude by making a modest proposal for a new way of looking at film noir and the problem of its definition.

## Socratic Definition

Before examining the various proposed definitions of film noir, I want to look at one approach to the question of definition generally, namely, Socrates'. As a philosopher, Socrates took as his central concern ethics: he wanted to know how to live his life, and he believed that the key to living well was knowledge, specifically, knowledge of the virtues. In order to be pious or just, Socrates believes, one must know what piety and justice are. So, in Plato's dialogues,[1] in order to achieve the knowledge he wants, Socrates searches for the *forms* of virtues.

Plato's theory of forms is a theory of universals and essences. A *universal* is the category into which things fall. So, for example, individual, physical chairs or desks are what philosophers call *particulars,* whereas the category *chair* or *desk* is the universal, or the species, under which those physical items are organized. Particulars are concrete, individual things; universals are abstract categories. So, if the form (the universal) is film noir, then the particulars would be the individual films that fall into that category: *Out of the Past* (Jacques Tourneur, 1947), *The Maltese Falcon,* and so on.

But, more than this, the notion of the forms is the cornerstone of Plato's metaphysics, his theory about the nature of reality. For Plato, the continuously changing everyday world of physical objects and events, the particulars, that we see and hear around us is not ultimate reality; it is a pale imitation, like a shadow on a cave wall (to use Plato's famous analogy).[2] Ultimate reality is not what we perceive with our five senses. Rather, it's what we grasp with our minds, the universals. The forms are intelligible rather than sensible, they lie outside space, time, and causality, and they're eternal and unchanging. Further, the forms are the essences of the particulars: they're what make the individual physical objects and events what they are. If someone wants to know what this individual thing made up of plastic, metal, and fabric is, you mention the form: *chair* (or *chairness*, the essence of any physical object of that type). The individual object comes into existence, changes and decays, and ultimately is destroyed. The form, on the other hand, remains the same forever. So, even if every chair in the world were destroyed, what it means to be a chair—that essence and form—would, according to Socrates, still be the same.[3]

So, when Socrates asks for a definition, he is not asking for a dictionary definition, which tells us the way to use a word. Rather, he wants a description of the form. He wants in his case to know what real, essential properties the virtues have. In our case, if we can follow Socrates' lead and articulate the form of film noir, then we'll know exactly what we're talking about, and we'll be able to identify anything of that type.

So is there, in fact, a way of identifying the form of film noir? Can we pick out its essential properties and articulate them in a definition?[4]

## Defining Film Noir

### IT'S A GENRE

There is now a relatively long history of discussion about film noir and, as I mentioned above, a continuing debate about what noir really is.[5] One of the central issues involved in defining film noir is whether it constitutes a genre. So what's a genre?[6] Foster Hirsch says: "A genre . . . is determined by conventions of narrative structure, characterization, theme, and visual design." And, as one of those who argues that film noir is indeed a genre, he finds that film noir has these elements "in abundance":

[*Noir* deals with criminal activity, from a variety of perspectives, in a general mood of dislocation and bleakness which earned the style its name. Unified by a dominant tone and sensibility, the *noir* canon constitutes a distinct style of film-making; but it also conforms to genre requirements since it operates within a set of narrative and visual conventions. . . . *Noir* tells its stories in a particular way, and in a particular visual style. The repeated use of narrative and visual structures . . . certainly qualifies *noir* as a genre, one that is in fact as heavily coded as the western.[7]

So film noir is a genre, according to Hirsch, because of the consistent tone and the storytelling and visual conventions running through the films of the classic noir period. We see all these features, for example, in *The Postman Always Rings Twice,* as I mentioned above: the tone of dark cynicism and alienation, the narrative conventions like the femme fatale and the flashback voice-overs, and the shadowy black-and-white look of the movie.

James Damico likewise believes that noir is a film genre—and precisely because of a certain narrative pattern. He describes this pattern as the typical noir plot, in which the main character is lured into violence, and usually to his own destruction, by the femme fatale. Again, this is exactly the pattern of *Postman:* Frank is coaxed into killing Cora's husband and is ultimately destroyed by his choices and actions. Damico, unlike Hirsch, however, denies that there is a consistent visual style to the films: "I can see no conclusive evidence that anything as cohesive and determined as a visual style exists in [film noir]."[8]

*IT'S NOT A GENRE*

Those who deny that film noir is a genre define it in a number of different ways. In the earliest work on film noir (1955), for example, Raymond Borde and Étienne Chaumeton define noir as a series or cycle of films whose aim is to create alienation in the viewer: "All the films of this cycle create a similar emotional effect: *that state of tension instilled in the spectator when the psychological reference points are removed.* The aim of *film noir* was to create *a specific alienation.*"[9]

Andrew Spicer also identifies noir as a cycle of films that "share a similar iconography, visual style, narrative strategies, subject matter and characterisation." This sounds a good deal like Hirsch's characterization, but Spicer denies that noir can be defined as a genre (or in most other ways, for that matter) since the expression *film noir* is "a discursive critical construction that has evolved over time."[10] In other words, far from being a fixed and unchanging universal category, like one of Plato's forms, *film noir* is a concept that evolved as critics and theorists wrote and talked about these movies and was applied retroactively.[11]

Further, in arguing against Damico's version of noir's essential narrative, Spicer points out that "there are many other, quite dissimilar, noir plots" than the one Damico describes.[12] Classic examples might include those of *High Sierra* (Raoul Walsh, 1941) and *Pickup on South Street* (Samuel Fuller, 1953), neither of which includes a femme fatale who coaxes the protagonist to commit a violent act against a third man.[13] In *Pickup,* for example, the pickpocket Skip McCoy (Richard Widmark) steals classified microfilm from a woman, Candy (Jean Peters), on the subway. She's carrying it for her boyfriend, who is—unbeknownst to her—passing government secrets along to the Communists. The story, then, concerns the efforts of the police to get McCoy to turn the film over to them, which would mean admitting that he's still picking pockets, thereby putting him in danger of becoming a three-time loser; and it concerns the efforts of the conspirators to retrieve the film from McCoy by any means necessary, including killing his friend and information dealer Moe (Thelma Ritter). This is a classic example of a film noir, but it doesn't follow Damico's narrative pattern.

Spicer goes on to say: "Any attempt at defining film noir solely through its 'essential' formal components proves to be reductive and unsatisfactory because film noir, as the French critics asserted from the beginning, also involves a sensibility, a particular way of looking at the world."[14] So noir is not simply a certain plot line or a visual style achieved by camera angles and unusual lighting. It also involves a "way of looking at the world," an outlook on life and human existence.

In addition to its character as a series or cycle of movies, film noir is often identified by, or defined as, the particular visual style, mood, tone, or set of motifs characteristic of the form. Raymond Durgnat, for example, says: "The *film noir* is not a genre, as the western and gangster film, and takes us into the realm of classification by motif and tone."[15] The tone is one of bleak cynicism, according to Durgnat, and the dominant motifs include crime as social criticism, gangsters, private eyes and adventurers, middle-class murder, portraits and doubles, sexual pathology, and psychopaths.

Paul Schrader likewise denies that noir is a genre. He says: "[Film noir] is not defined, as are the western and gangster genres, by conventions of setting and conflict, but rather by the more subtle qualities of tone and mood." He thus rejects Durgnat's classification by motif and focuses his definition on the important element of mood, specifically that of "cynicism, pessimism and darkness."[He continues: "*Film noir*'s techniques emphasize loss, nostalgia, lack of clear priorities, insecurity; then submerge these self-doubts in mannerism and style. In such a world style becomes paramount; it is all that separates one from meaninglessness."[16]

In a classic essay, Robert Porfirio says that "Schrader was right in insisting upon both visual style and mood as criteria." The mood at the heart of noir, according to Porfirio, is pessimism, "which makes the black film black for us." The "black vision" of film noir is one of "despair, loneliness and dread," he claims, and "is nothing less than an existential attitude towards life." This existentialist outlook on life infusing noir didn't come from the European existentialists (like Sartre and Camus), who were roughly contemporaneous with the classic American noir period. Rather: "It is more likely that this existential bias was drawn from a source much nearer at hand—the hard-boiled school of fiction without which quite possibly there would have been no *film noir*."[17] The mood of pessimism, loneliness, dread, and despair is to be found in the works of, for example, Raymond Chandler, Dashiell Hammett, James M. Cain, and David Goodis, whose writings were a resource for and had a direct influence on those who created noir films in the classic period, as I mentioned above. I'll have more to say about Porfirio and the existentialist outlook of noir films below.

Finally, R. Barton Palmer likewise rejects the definition of noir as a genre, calling it instead a "transgeneric phenomenon," since it existed "through a number of related genres whose most important common threads were a concern with criminality . . . and with social breakdown." The genres associated with noir include "the crime melodrama, the detective film, the thriller, and the woman's picture."[18] In other words, whatever the noir element in a film noir is, it can be expressed through a number of genres—melodrama, thriller, etc.—and so film noir is not itself a genre. It's "transgeneric."

*IT CAN'T BE DEFINED*

Another writer, J. P. Telotte, focuses his discussion of film noir's definition on the issue of genre, sidestepping, perhaps prudently, the issue of whether any of these characterizations of film noir do in fact establish it as a genre. The element of noir films that Telotte claims unites them—without necessarily providing a basis for calling noir a genre[19]—is their rejection of traditional narrative (storytelling) patterns. More than any other type of popular film, Telotte says, "film noir pushes at the boundaries of classical narrative." This classical narrative would be a straightforward story told from a third-person-omniscient point of view, which assumes the objective truth of a situation, involves characters who are goal oriented and whose motivations make sense, and has a neat closure at the end (boy gets girl etc.). Telotte goes on to say: "[Noir] films are fundamentally about the problems of seeing and speaking truth, about perceiving and conveying a sense of our culture's and our own reality."[20] So what's common to noir films, according to Telotte, is unconventional or nonclassical narrative patterns, and these patterns point to problems of truth and objectivity and of our ability to know and understand reality. One technique underpinning or establishing these nontraditional patterns is the nonchronological ordering of events, often achieved through flashback. As we saw, this is the technique used in *Postman,* but the best example of it is perhaps *The Killers* (Robert Siodmak, 1946), which brilliantly weaves together Jim Reardon's (Edmond O'Brien) investigation of Ole Andersen's (Burt Lancaster) death with flashbacks that tell the story leading up to the murder. Other techniques are the use of sometimes incoherent plotlines, as in *The Big Sleep* (Howard Hawks, 1946), and characters whose actions aren't motivated or understandable in any rational way. For example, why does Frank agree to go ahead with the second (and successful) attempt on Nick's life in *Postman* when it's such a poor plan and sure to get them caught?

Whereas Telotte sidesteps the issue of definition, James Naremore puts his foot down and concludes that film noir can't be defined. "I contend that film noir has no essential characteristics," he says. "The fact is, every movie is transgeneric. . . . Thus, no matter what modifier we attach to a category, we can never establish clear boundaries and uniform traits. Nor can we have a 'right' definition—only a series of more or less interesting uses." One reason film noir can't be defined, according to Naremore, is that, as mentioned above, the term is a kind of "discursive construction," employed by critics (each of whom has his or her own agenda), and is used retroactively. The other reason has to do with the nature of concepts and definitions generally. Most contemporary philosophers believe that we don't form concepts by grouping similar things together according to their essential properties—the technique employed by Socrates and seemingly by most film theorists who study noir. Rather, says Naremore, we "create networks of relationship, using metaphor, metonymy, and forms of imaginative association that develop over time." In other words, our concepts are not discrete categories but rather networks of ideas in complex relations and associations, networks that we form with experience. Consequently: "Categories form complex radial structures with vague boundaries and a core of influential members at the center."[21] This certainly seems to describe film noir. We all agree that there is a core set of films—such as *Double Indemnity* (Billy Wilder, 1944) and *The Maltese Falcon*—in the noir canon. But the boundary is so fuzzy that we disagree about whether a great many others— for example, *Casablanca* (Michael Curtiz, 1942), *Citizen Kane,* and *King Kong* (Merian C. Cooper and Ernest B. Schoedsack, 1933)—belong there as well.

So Naremore argues that film noir can't be defined, that it has no essential characteristics. On the other hand, there are those, like Nietzsche, who would argue that this doesn't just apply to these movies, that there's something problematic about truth and definition generally, even beyond the issues that Naremore points out about Socratic definition. Before I go on to say something about what noir is, however, I want to examine briefly Nietzsche's position on these issues.

## Nietzsche and the Problem of Truth and Definition

Nietzsche holds a version of what we might call a *flux metaphysics,* the idea that the world, everything, is continually changing, that nothing is stable and enduring. Consequently, he argues, any concept of *being*—something that remains the same throughout change, like Plato's forms, God, or even the self or the ego—is a fiction. Interestingly, he argues that language is one of the primary sources of this fiction. That is, it's impossible to grasp and articulate a world that's continually in motion, one in which nothing ever stays the same. Thus, "understanding" the world, and articulating that understanding, becomes a matter of "seeing" parts of the flux as somehow enduring and stable; that is, it means falsifying what our senses tell us.

One of these falsifications is the subject/predicate distinction that's built into language. For example, we say *lightning flashes* as if there is some thing or subject *lightning* that somehow performs the action of flashing. Similarly, we say *I walk,* or *I talk,* or *I read,* as if there is some stable ego, self, or subject that is somehow separate from these actions. According to Nietzsche, however: "There is no such substratum; there is no 'being' behind doing, effecting, becoming; 'the doer' is merely a fiction added to the deed—the deed is everything."[22] In other words, in a world in flux, you are what you do. Further, the "doer" or subject created by language is, Nietzsche argues, the source of the concept of being, a stable, unchanging, permanent reality behind the ever-flowing flux of the world:

> We enter a realm of crude fetishism when we summon before con-sciousness the basic presuppositions of the metaphysics of language, in plain talk, the presuppositions of reason. Everywhere it sees a doer and doing; it believes in will as *the* cause; it believes in the ego, in the ego as being, in the ego as substance, and it projects this faith in the ego-substance upon all things—only thereby does it first *create* the concept of "thing." Everywhere "being" is projected by thought, pushed underneath, as the cause; the concept of being follows and is a derivative of, the concept of ego.

The fiction begins as merely a stable self, the idea that the ego is something enduring and unchanging and separate from its actions (as opposed to being constituted by those actions), but soon is translated into being, that is, for example, into Plato's forms and a divinity. Nietzsche says: "I am afraid we are not rid of God because we still have faith in grammar."[23]

This falsification introduced by reason and language certainly makes truth, objectivity, and indeed definition problematic, to say the least. In an early and influential essay, Nietzsche says: "Truths are illusions which we have forgotten are illusions."[24] Elsewhere: "All concepts in which an entire process is semiotically concentrated elude definition; only that which has no history is definable."[25] Nietzsche here seems to be agreeing with Socrates: a definition must capture the essence of the thing, that which doesn't change and thus has no history. The catch here is that, as we've seen, Nietzsche denies that there is any such thing, so he's denying that anything at all can really be defined. This is a radical position and seems not to bode well for the project of defining film noir. However, and perhaps ironically, I think that it's Nietzsche who will help us better understand what noir is.

## What Is Noir?

To discover what makes a film a film noir, that is, what the noir element in the film is, it might be instructive to look briefly at noir literature—and especially so if it's through the hard-boiled literature that noir films get their existential, pessimistic outlook, as Porfirio says. I'll take as an example of this literature the 1961 novel *Night Squad* by David Goodis, the author of *Dark Passage* (1946), on which the 1947 Bogart and Bacall/Delmer Daves film was based.[26] The first paragraph of *Night Squad* reads: "At 11:20 a fairly well-dressed boozehound came staggering out of a bootleg-whiskey joint on Fourth Street. It was a Friday night in mid-July and the humid heat was like a wave of steaming black syrup confronting the boozehound. He walked into it and bounced off and braced himself to make another try. A moment later something hit him on the head and he sagged slowly and arrived on the pavement flat on his face." We instantly recognize here the clipped, gritty phrasing of the hard-boiled school, the dirty gutter setting, and the down-on-his-luck character. The boozehound is being mugged by three men while a fourth, Corey Bradford—who turns out to be the protagonist—watches from the other side of the street. Bradford is a former dirty cop and forces the muggers to give him the boozehound's money. He keeps most of it for himself but returns a dollar to the boozehound for cab fare home. Instead of going home, however, the boozehound takes the dollar—his only money—and goes back into the bootleg-whiskey joint for another drink. Before he does, he mutters: "The trouble is, we just can't get together, that's all." Bradford interprets this to mean: "We just can't get together on what's right and what's wrong."[27]

The story largely takes place in a Philadelphia neighborhood known as "the Swamp," where Bradford grew up. The area is just as run-down, dirty, and crime infested as its name implies. In an interior monologue about the neighborhood, Bradford reflects on how tough the place is, and he has nothing but good things to say about the prostitutes. They're "performing a necessary function," like the sewer workers and the trash collectors: "If it wasn't for the professionals, there'd be more suicides, more homicides. And more of them certain cases you read about, like some four-year-old girl getting dragged into an alley, some sixty-year-old landlady getting hacked to pieces with an axe."[28] If the denizens of the swamp couldn't vent their violent and sexual impulses with the prostitutes, they'd take them out on little girls and old ladies. So it's a good thing we have the pros.

Finally, I'll mention in passing that the femme fatale of this story, Lita, is married to the gangster who runs the Swamp. When Bradford first meets her, Goodis describes her thus: "She was of medium height, very slender. Her hair was platinum blonde. Contrasting with her deep, dark green eyes." And she's holding a book: "Corey could see the title on the cover. He didn't know much about philosophy but he sensed that the book was strictly for deep thinkers. It was Nietzsche, it was *Thus Spake Zarathustra*."[29]

[What we see here, and what makes this story noir, is the tone and mood, and the sensibility, the outlook on life, that the critics and writers mentioned above discuss.] We see bleak cynicism (Durgnat), for example, in the protagonist's saving the boozehound from getting mugged, only to keep his money for himself. We witness the loss and lack of clear priorities (Schrader) in the same scene and in Bradford's appraisal of the prostitutes. [Alienation is clearly present (Borde and Chaumeton); the whole story is one of a man adrift, a man who has lost balance and the meaning and value of his life. And we see existential pessimism (Porfirio).] This is clearly evident both in the image of the boozehound going back into the bar to spend his last dollar on another drink and in the dark picture of human nature that Goodis paints when he discusses the need to vent our violent urges with prostitutes.

One other thing, something related to all these other elements, that some writers discuss, but that [I want to emphasize, is what we might call the *inversion of traditional values* and the *loss of the meaning of things*. That is, at the heart of the noir mood or tone of alienation, pessimism, and cynicism we find, on the one hand, the rejection or loss of clearly defined ethical values (we can't "get together on what's right and what's wrong")[30] and, on the other, the rejection or loss of the meaning or sense of human existence.] In essence, Porfirio is, I think, on the right track in talking about the noir sensibility as a kind of "existential outlook" on life.

( Further, I'm agreeing with those who say that what makes a film a film noir is a particular mood, tone, or sensibility, a particular outlook on life. This is clear because it's that tone or sensibility that, as I said, links the literature and the films. Thus, the narrative elements (storytelling conventions) and the filmmaking techniques (oblique camera angles, deep focus, low-key lighting, etc.) are, I think, secondary to the mood or sensibility. They are used to communicate that mood or sensibility,[31] but it's the latter that makes the film a noir. ] )

## The Death of God and the Meaning of Noir

As I mentioned, Nietzsche can help throw light on what film noir is, despite his skepticism about truth, essences, and definition. One of Nietzsche's most infamous and provocative statements is that "God is dead."[32] What he means by this is that not only Western religions but also Western metaphysical systems have become untenable. Both Platonism and Christianity, for example, claim that there is some permanent and unchanging otherworldly realm or substance: the forms in the case of the former and God and heaven in the case of the latter. This unchanging otherworldly something is set in opposition to the here and now, the changing world around us (forms vs. particulars; heaven vs. earth, etc.), and it's the source of, or foundation for, our understanding of human existence, our morality, our hope for the future, among other things.

Again, Nietzsche says that the fiction of being is generated originally through the falsifications involved in reason and language. This concept of being is exposed as a fiction, Nietzsche argues, in the modern period, when natural empirical science begins to replace traditional metaphysical explanations of the world. We cease to believe in the myth of creation, for example, and modern philosophers tend to reject Plato's idea of otherworldly forms. Thus, throughout the modern and into the contemporary period, religion and philosophy—as metaphysical explanations of the world—are supplanted by natural science. At the same time, we try to hold onto our old understanding of human existence, our ethics, an ever-more-feeble belief in an afterlife, etc. What finally, and gradually, dawns on us, says Nietzsche, is that, once the latter is lost, there's no longer any foundation or justification for these adjuncts of metaphysics. We realize more and more the hollowness and untenability of our old outlook, our old values.

The result of this is devastating. We no longer have any sense of who and what we are as human beings. There's seemingly no foundation any longer for the meaning and value of things, including ethical values, good and evil. There's no longer any hope for an afterlife—this life must be taken and endured on its own terms. Before the death of God, we knew as good Platonists or Christians (or Jews or Muslims) who and what we were, the value and meaning our lives had, what we had to do to live a righteous life. Now we're set adrift. We're alienated, disoriented, off balance. The world is senseless and chaotic. There's no transcendent meaning or value to human existence.

This death of God, then—the loss of permanence, of a transcendent source of value and meaning, and the resulting disorientation and nihilism—leads to existentialism and its worldview. Porfirio characterizes existentialism as "an outlook which begins with a disoriented individual facing a confused world that he cannot accept. It places its emphasis on man's contingency in a world where there are no transcendental values or moral absolutes, a world devoid of any meaning but the one man himself creates."[33] As a literary/philosophical phenomenon, set in its particular place in history, existentialism is continental Europe's reaction to the death of God.

My proposal, then, is that noir can also be seen as a sensibility or worldview that results from the death of God and, thus, that film noir is a type of American artistic response to, or recognition of, this seismic shift in our understanding of the world. This is why Porfirio is right in pointing out the similarities between the noir sensibility and the existentialist view of life and human existence. Although they are not exactly the same thing, they are both reactions, however explicit and conscious, to the same realization of the loss of value and meaning in our lives.

## A (Slightly) Different Approach

Seeing noir as a response or reaction to the death of God helps explain the commonality of the elements that critics have noted in noir films. For example, it explains the inherent pessimism, alienation, and disorientation in noir. It affirms that noir is a sensibility or an outlook, as some hold. It explains the moral ambiguity in noir as well as the threat of nihilism and meaninglessness that some note.

As I said, the death of God doesn't just (or even necessarily) mean the rejection of religion. For Americans, our belief in what Nietzsche is calling *God*, the sense, order, and meaning of our lives and the world, is encapsulated in our idealism: our faith in God, progress, and the indomitable American spirit. Consequently, as Palmer notes: "Film noir . . . offers the obverse of the American dream."[34] Most argue that the sources of this obversion or reversal are (or include) anxiety over the war and the postwar period, the Communist scare, the atomic age, the influx of German émigrés in Hollywood, and the hard-boiled school of pulp fiction. Indeed, it's via these influences that an awareness or a feeling came over us, seeped into the American consciousness, that our old ways of understanding ourselves and the world, and the values that went along with these, were gone or untenable. We lost our orientation in the world, the meaning and sense that our lives had, and clear-cut moral values and boundaries.

The similarities between European existentialism and film noir are, as Porfirio points out, apparent. In the classic existentialist work *The Stranger* (1942), for example, Camus depicts the alienation and disorientation of a post-Nietzschean world, one without transcendent meaning or value. The book's main character reacts little to his mother's death, shoots and kills a man for no good reason, and seems indifferent to his own trial and impending execution. Similarly, when, in *The Maltese Falcon,* Sam Spade (Humphrey Bogart) shrugs off his partner's murder or turns his lover, Brigid (Mary Astor), over to the police, or when, in *The Killers,* Ole Andersen passively awaits his assassins, even after being warned that they're coming, we get a sense of the same alienation, the same lack of sense and meaning. And, since film is a visual medium, these noirish elements are also conveyed through lighting and camera techniques. So, for example, extreme close-ups of Hank Quinlan's (Orson Welles) bloated face in *Touch of Evil* (Orson Welles, 1958) and the tilted camera shot of Mike Hammer (Ralph Meeker) in a hospital bed in *Kiss Me Deadly* (Robert Aldrich, 1955) further serve to express alienation and disorientation.

Finally, considering noir to be a response to the death of God also verifies J. P. Telotte's claim that noir films are "fundamentally about the problems of seeing and speaking truth," since it's in a post-Nietzschean world, in the wake of the death of God, that seeing and speaking the truth become problematic. Consequently, and ironically, what makes truth problematic, and what makes definition impossible, according to Nietzsche—the abandonment of essences, the resulting flux metaphysics, the rejection of anything permanent and unchanging in the universe, that is, the death of God—is the same thing that makes noir what it is. That is, the death of God is both the meaning of noir and—if we're to believe Nietzsche—what makes noir impossible to define.

## Notes

Many thanks to Jason Holt, Bill Irwin, Steven Sanders, and Aeon Skoble, who gave me assistance and excellent comments on earlier drafts of this essay.

1. The relationship between Plato and Socrates is somewhat complex. Socrates never wrote anything. He much preferred to engage people in conversation. Plato was one of Socrates' friends and pupils. Most of Plato's writings are in the form of dialogues; they're narratives, and Socrates is very often the main character. Consequently, when we talk about Socrates saying something, most of the time we're referring to what Plato represents him as saying.

2. For the allegory of the cave, see bk. 7, lines 514a–517d, of the *Republic.*

3. For the theory of forms, see line 65d of the *Phaedo* or lines 475e–476a of the *Republic.*

4. There are many other ways of thinking about definition, both ancient and con-

temporary. I mention Socrates because his is a classic approach to the issue and because he makes a nice foil for Nietzsche.

5. I'm not pretending that the history I'm giving is complete or that it mentions every important work or statement on the topic. I merely want to provide the reader with the flavor of the discussion and point out some of the definitions provided in some of the canonical works on noir.

6. According to Wes D. Gehring, a genre in film studies "represents the division of movies into groups which have similar subjects and/or themes" (introduction to *Handbook of American Film Genres*, ed. Wes D. Gehring [New York: Greenwood, 1988], 1).

7. Foster Hirsch, *The Dark Side of the Screen: Film Noir* (New York: Da Capo, 1981), 72.

8. James Damico, "*Film Noir:* A Modest Proposal," in *Film Noir Reader*, ed. Alain Silver and James Ursini (New York: Limelight, 1996), 103, 105 (quote). This is in contrast to those who explicitly identify noir as a visual style (see, e.g., Janey Place and Lowell Peterson, "Some Visual Motifs of *Film Noir,*" in Silver and Ursini, *Film Noir Reader*). Nicholas Christopher also argues (although less explicitly than Damico) that film noir is a genre because of a certain narrative pattern (*Somewhere in the Night* [New York: Henry Holt, 1997], 7–8).

9. Raymond Borde and Étienne Chaumeton, "Towards a Definition of *Film Noir,*" trans. Alain Silver, in Silver and Ursini, *Film Noir Reader*, 25.

10. Andrew Spicer, *Film Noir* (Harlow: Longman, 2002), 4, 24.

11. The term *film noir* was coined in the mid-forties by the French film critic Nino Frank (see his "Un nouveau genre 'policier': L'aventure criminelle," *L'ecran français* 61 [1946]: 8–9, 14). It didn't receive a book-length treatment until Raymond Borde and Étienne Chaumeton's *Panorama du film noir américain (1941–1956)* (Paris: Minuit, 1955) and remained unknown to American filmmakers during the period of classic film noir, becoming part of American film vocabulary only in the late sixties.

12. Spicer, *Film Noir*, 25.

13. To be fair, Damico calls his plot description simply the "truest" or "purest" example of film noir and admits that there are other noir plots. However, the sheer number and variety of other plots would seem to undermine his argument.

14. Spicer, *Film Noir*, 25.

15. Raymond Durgnat, "Paint It Black: The Family Tree of the *Film Noir,*" in Silver and Ursini, *Film Noir Reader*, 38.

16. Paul Schrader, "Notes on *Film Noir,*" in Silver and Ursini, *Film Noir Reader*, 53, 58.

17. Robert Porfirio, "No Way Out: Existential Motifs in the *Film Noir*" (1976), in Silver and Ursini, *Film Noir Reader*, 78, 80, 82–83.

18. R. Barton Palmer, *Hollywood's Dark Cinema: The American Film Noir* (New York: Twayne, 1994), 30, x.

19. "This overview of *film noir*'s main narrative techniques should come with a

warning: like the films themselves, this taxonomy provides but a partial, although valuable, view of their workings, while it points toward, if it never quite satisfactorily resolves, the question of *noir*'s generic status" ( J. P. Telotte, *Voices in the Dark: The Narrative Patterns of Film Noir* [Urbana: University of Illinois Press, 1989], 31).

20. Ibid., 12, 31.

21. James Naremore, *More Than Night: Film Noir in Its Contexts* (Berkeley and Los Angeles: University of California Press, 1998), 5–6. Naremore has Ludwig Wittgenstein in mind here, among others. In his *Philosophical Investigations,* Wittgenstein argues that there isn't a set of essential properties or necessary and sufficient conditions linking, e.g., games (how are football and tic-tac-toe related?); rather, there is only a loose network in which each game is connected to at least one other by a "family resemblance." This would seem to be the case, too, with noir.

22. Friedrich Nietzsche, *On the Genealogy of Morals,* trans. Walter Kaufmann and R. J. Hollingdale (New York: Vintage, 1989), 45.

23. Friedrich Nietzsche, *Twilight of the Idols,* in *The Portable Nietzsche,* ed. Walter Kaufmann (New York: Penguin, 1976), 483 (in the section "Reason in Philosophy").

24. Friedrich Nietzsche, "On Truth and Lies in a Nonmoral Sense," in *Philosophy and Truth: Selections from Nietzsche's Notebooks of the Early 1870's,* trans. Daniel Breazeale (Atlantic Highlands, NJ: Humanities Paperback Library, 1979), 84.

25. Nietzsche, *On the Genealogy of Morals,* 80.

26. I choose Goodis, not only because he's one of my favorite hard-boiled authors, but also because he's much less well-known than, e.g., Chandler or Thompson, and undeservedly so, I think. Admittedly, *Night Squad* is a later work, appearing after the classic film noir period. However, it is still representative of Goodis's work in particular and of hard-boiled pulp literature generally.

27. David Goodis, *Night Squad* (1961; reprint, New York: First Vintage Crime/ Black Lizard, 1992), 3, 8.

28. Ibid., 11.

29. Ibid., 44–45.

30. "Good and evil go hand in hand [in film noir] to the point of being indistinguishable" (Borde and Chaumeton, "Towards a Definition of *Film Noir*," 25).

31. As Porfirio says: "This sense of meaninglessness is ... not the result of any sort of discursive reasoning. Rather it is an attitude which is worked out through the *mise en scène* and plotting" ("No Way Out," 89).

32. This is first expressed in a passage called "The Madman" (see Friedrich Nietzsche, *The Gay Science,* trans. Walter Kaufmann [New York: Vintage, 1974], 181).

33. Porfirio, "No Way Out," 81.

34. Palmer, *Hollywood's Dark Cinema,* 6.

# A Darker Shade

## Realism in Neo-Noir

*Jason Holt*

> Somewhere in between the soft lies of cinema and the harsh truths of
> reality, there exists an element of realism in film noir.
>
> —*Carl Richardson*

Classic film noir ran from the early forties to the late fifties, beginning with
John Huston's *The Maltese Falcon* (1941) and ending with Orson Welles's
*Touch of Evil* (1958). We might widen the scope a bit, citing the little-known
*Stranger on the Third Floor* (Boris Ingster, 1940) as the inception of the
classic period and *Odds against Tomorrow* (Robert Wise, 1959) as the ter-
minus, but, even without settling the disputes about which should count
as the first film noir and which as the last, the historical limits of the period, spanning at most twenty years, are pretty well defined.

Some purists would have it that film noir is essentially circumscribed
by these historical limits, that there can be no noir *in any sense* after the late
fifties. This view is unnecessarily extreme. Many films made since the end
of the classic period exhibit such strong resemblance to classic noir that
they clearly deserve to be called *noir* in *some* sense. Nowadays, the term is
often used generically, applied as much to contemporary films as (retrospectively) to those of the classic period. But, even if noir constitutes a
cycle of films (now closed) or a filmmaking movement (now defunct), this
is perfectly compatible with certain films made after the classic period being dubbed *neo-noir* (also known as *contemporary, postclassic,* or *modern
film noir*). Irrespective of whether film noir constitutes a genre, such modified use obviously does not flout but rather *respects* the historical limits of
the classic period.

The question of how to define *film noir,* or even whether it can be defined, is certainly a vexed one.[1] Nonetheless, it is worthwhile developing a working definition. Noir is often characterized in terms of its bleakly existential tone, cynically pessimistic mood, stylistic elements inherited from German expressionism (low-key lighting, deep focus, subjective camera shots, canted angles, and so on), and stories and narrative patterns adapted from American hard-boiled fiction. These facets of film noir, I would argue, fall roughly under the rubric *stylization,* broadly construed. Tone and mood emerge from style, and the story lines of film noir, for all their contrivances, tend to be highly stylized.

Some other important features of noir are less frequently mentioned and tend to be underemphasized, underappreciated, or outright ignored. It is surprising, for instance, that many accounts of noir either fail to mention or pass quickly over the fact that it is essentially (among other things) a type of *crime film.*[2] After all, it was precisely the desire to label and describe what they saw as a new type of crime film that prompted French critics to introduce the term *film noir* in the first place.[3] Another insight from French critics that is often marginalized is the idea that the characters in films noirs are, from a commonsense point of view, morally ambiguous.[4] This is almost a platitude, since what most clearly distinguishes noir from, say, the more conventional thriller or gangster film is the lack of clarity with which moral distinctions are drawn. While some noir characters are unquestionably evil, many have their evil somehow attenuated (e.g., by a sympathetic motive or by being fully revealed as such only at the end). More important, without a hero or heroine of ambiguous moral standing, noir simply evaporates.

While it has been recognized as somehow involved, *realism* is undoubtedly one of the more consistently underappreciated elements of noir. Realism in noir extends far beyond the verisimilitude of studio production and location shooting. Not only the settings but also the scenes, the action, the depiction of violent crime, and the characters involved are all quite realistic by and large. (*Realism* here is meant in the ordinary sense of being true to life, facing things as they are, and should not be confused with various more technical philosophical senses of the term.)[5] What prevents a spaghetti western like *The Good, the Bad, and the Ugly* (Sergio Leone, 1966) from being neo-noir, despite its undeniable noirishness in other respects, is that the prowess of the main characters (in particular Clint Eastwood's "Man with No Name") is elaborated well beyond plausibility, mythologized, in fact. Like the spaghetti western, however, one of the most distinctively realistic features of noir is the role (or lack thereof) that values play in the characters' lives. In providing a spectrum of characters that shade from the morally ambiguous through the completely amoral, noir behavior—in terms of motive, action, and outcome—mirrors an often unacknowledged and significantly unpleasant chunk of human existence. The downbeat endings typical of noir are generally far more lifelike than those usually found in alternative fare.

The reason that realism has been underrated, I think, is that it enters into a sort of dynamic tension with the more obvious element of nightmarish, surreal stylization, much of which, however, can be subsumed under realism, especially the sort of realism I focus on here. As Carl Richardson puts it: "The real world *is* shadowy, crime-ridden, web-like, amoral, illogical."[6] The tone and mood of film noir are apropos of how things really are, a sense of reality, not distorted, but *conveyed* by expressionist techniques and convoluted plotlines. These capture a psychological realism, if nothing else, a sense of the world as it can be and often seems. The moral ambiguity of characters is no less realistic. But, while the scope and importance of realism in film noir are greater than is usually thought, it is unlikely that all its stylistic elements can be brought comfortably under the heading *realism*. To hedge my bets, my working definition of *noir* will be "stylized crime realism," where each term in the formula is understood as explained above.[7]

In this essay, I explore realism in neo-noir by examining a cross section of films, paying particular attention to the moral ambiguity of characters and the outcome of their actions in the neo-noir world. Not only will this help distinguish noir from neo-noir in a nontrivial way, but it will also reveal a philosophically germane and crucial part of what, all along, has been the essence of noir. While most of the films selected hold a certain charm for me, almost all are uncontested members of the neo-noir class. Collectively, they serve as a representative sample. Where there is some doubt, I speak to it. If there is any glaring omission here, it is the work of Martin Scorsese.[8] However, just as some noir commentators are loath to discuss Alfred Hitchcock, seeing him as sui generis, so too do I demure from engaging Scorsese here.

## No More Spades: *Harper* and *Chinatown*

In the early phase of classic noir, the figure of the private detective was most highly visible.[9] So too with neo-noir, which was more or less sporadically produced in the sixties and seventies before being fully revived in the eighties. Leaving aside such interim films as *Shock Corridor* (Samuel Fuller, 1963), neo-noir began with *Harper* (Jack Smight, 1966). One of the most obvious and, in many ways, best noirs of the seventies was *Chinatown* (Roman Polanski, 1974). Both *Harper* and *Chinatown* are important early neonoirs. Each is about a mystery-entangled private eye, and each has an ending that is paramount to establishing the significance of the whole.

*Harper* begins with the private detective Lew Harper (Paul Newman) making a face at the stale coffee he has made from recycled grounds, which leads us to expect a radical departure from the classic noir detective. Even so, and despite the sixties setting, most of the film proceeds like any classic noir. Elaine Sampson (Lauren Bacall) hires Harper to investigate the disappearance of her husband, who turns out to have been kidnapped and is being held for ransom. Sampson's daughter Miranda (Pamela Tiffin) seems to have no interest in the matter, while the houseguest and pilot Allan Taggert (Robert Wagner) seems too eager to help. The real villain, however, is Albert Graves (Arthur Hill), the Sampsons' lawyer and Harper's friend. Graves, having finally killed his employer, is found out by Harper and taken back to the Sampsons' home along with the ransom money.

While Harper encounters the usual cavalcade of noir characters, and although his attitude is more nonchalant than that of the classic noir detective, what sets *Harper* apart, and finally rewards our expectation from the first scene, is the denouement. In a moment of great drama, Harper walks up the Sampsons' driveway, intending to return the money and incriminate Graves, all the while knowing that Graves is aiming a loaded gun at him. Unable to shoot his friend in the back, Graves uncocks the gun, and Harper, hearing this, essentially relents, dropping the money and raising his hands in a half-shrugging gesture of self-mockery, which severely undercuts the drama of the moment, ending the film on an ambiguous, almost absurd note.

In *Chinatown*, which is set in Los Angeles in the late thirties, the private eye Jake Gittes (Jack Nicholson) is hired to investigate the civic engineer Hollis Mulwray (Darrell Zwerling) by a woman (Diane Ladd) posing as his wife, Evelyn. On flimsy evidence, Gittes leaks a story of Mulwray's infidelity to the press, causing the real Evelyn (Faye Dunaway) to confront him. Mulwray turns up drowned in a reservoir, and Evelyn hires Gittes to find the killer. Gittes's investigation leads to Noah Cross (John Huston), Evelyn's father, who is responsible for the ongoing drought in the area and is fraudulently buying up depreciated land. Once romantically involved with

Evelyn, Gittes learns that the young woman he saw Mulwray with is Evelyn's sister/daughter and Cross's daughter/granddaughter, Katherine (Belinda Palmer). In attempting to help Evelyn and Katherine flee to Mexico, Gittes fails. Evelyn is shot and killed by police, and Cross, having orchestrated Mulwray's murder, is free to reclaim Katherine, escaping justice entirely.

Harper and Gittes, each in different ways, exhibit the departure of the neo-noir detective from such classic noir counterparts as Sam Spade and Philip Marlowe. While both neo-noir detectives are nominally competent in narrowly defined domains, Harper lacks the sort of integrity that allowed Sam Spade to triumph (although Spade would, no doubt, be more intrigued by Miranda), and Gittes lacks the wherewithal to negotiate the increasingly dark vicissitudes of the neo-noir world. While less capable, less admirable than their classic-era prototypes, they are, for that very reason, more realistic. Efforts to correct injustice often enough fail, and, in the face of this unpleasant fact, sometimes the best that one can hope for is stoic resignation. As Gittes is finally told: "There's nothing you can do, Jake. It's Chinatown."

### La Nouvelle Femme Fatale: Body Heat and The Last Seduction

While neo-noir began in the sixties, noir's full resurgence had to wait another fifteen years. Noir came back with a vengeance in the eighties with the release of *Body Heat* (Lawrence Kasdan, 1981), at once an homage to and a reclamation of the classic noir aesthetic. One of the mainstays and most salient icons of classic noir was the femme fatale, fatal not only to the sap who falls for her, and whom she manipulates, but also to herself. Neo-noir revamps the femme fatale. She is no less an object of obsession and desire, no less dangerous, than she was in the classic period, only this time around she gets away with it. Where the classic femme fatale suffers for her crimes, her revamped counterpart prospers.

"You're not too smart, are you? I like that in a man." So says Matty Walker (Kathleen Turner) to Ned Racine (William Hurt) when they first meet up in *Body Heat*. Ned, an affable but somewhat incompetent lawyer, is utterly beguiled, and, after they become involved, Matty has little trouble convincing him that her loveless marriage to rich husband Edmund (Richard Crenna) would be best resolved by murder. As agreed, Ned breaks into their house at night and bludgeons Edmund to death, disposing of the body in one of Edmund's abandoned buildings, which he rigs to burn down.

Edmund's new will, secretly forged by Matty on Ned's stationery, is found invalid, and, instead of receiving only part of the estate, Matty gets it all. When Matty fakes her own death and absconds with the money to a tropical island, Ned alone takes the fall.

There is a particularly striking scene when the plan to kill Edmund is set and, in reference to an earlier conversation, Matty gives Ned a fedora reminiscent of those worn by classic noir heroes, many of whom are not only virile, as Ned is, but capable, as he is not. One beautiful shot in the scene has Matty framed by an open car window, and, as the window goes up, she is visually replaced by the reflected image of Ned, wearing the hat, smiling a bit awkwardly but more genuinely than at any other time in the film. Despite the sap's greed and lust for the femme fatale, she seduces him less into crime than into the inflated self-deception of seeing himself as more competent, more capable, than he knows he really is.

In *The Last Seduction* (John Dahl, 1994), a fledgling doctor, Clay Gregory (Bill Pullman), in debt to a New York loan shark, makes a major drug deal. His wife, Bridget (Linda Fiorentino), skips town with the money and lays low in the small town Beston under the assumed name Wendy Kroy. Although Harlan (Bill Nunn), a private detective hired by Clay, finds her, she kills him before he can get to the money. Bridget convinces her new lover, Mike Swale (Peter Berg), that she is selling murder on the side and, promising a happy future together, inveigles him into making the next hit on a certain "Cahill," who is really Clay. Inept and confused, Mike leaves it to Bridget to kill Clay and then is goaded into some role-playing where, Bridget having covertly dialed 911, he "confesses" that he is raping her and has killed Clay besides.

Whereas the classic femme fatale never escaped justice, the femme fatale of neo-noir, more realistically, often does. This theme has several interesting variations in other films. In *Basic Instinct* (Paul Verhoeven, 1992), not only does Nick (Michael Douglas) fail to bring Catherine (Sharon Stone) to justice, but the pair actually fall in love, albeit in a psychosexually obsessive, deranged kind of way. In *Bound* (Andy and Larry Wachowski, 1996) too, not only do Violet (Jennifer Tilly) and Corky (Gina Gershon) manage to steal the money from Caesar (Joe Pantoliano), but they also fall in love.[10] For this reason, although they are fatal to certain others, it might be appropriate to consider Catherine and Violet *would-be* femmes fatales and not the genuine article. Even so, they illustrate interesting variations on the getting-away-with-it theme.

## Chance and Will: *To Live and Die in L.A.* and *Manhunter*

The moral ambiguity of film noir is often a matter of blurring moral distinctions between the nominally good hero and the villain, whose evil, even in extreme cases, is somewhat attenuated. A prime example is the neo-noir work of the actor William L. Petersen, specifically *To Live and Die in L.A.* (William Friedkin, 1985) and *Manhunter* (Michael Mann, 1986). While *Manhunter* is often discussed as a neo-noir, *To Live and Die in L.A.* almost never is.[11] This is, I believe, because it tends to be woefully underrated as a film, a likely result of its darker tone, blurrier moral distinctions, and much more downbeat ending, in other words, precisely those features that make it an even better candidate for noir status. If *Manhunter* is a neo-noir, there is no reason to deny that *To Live and Die in L.A.* is one as well.

In *To Live and Die in L.A.*, Secret Service Agent Richard Chance (Petersen) tries to bring down counterfeiter "Rick" Masters (Willem Dafoe). When his partner, Jim Hart (Michael Greene), is killed following a lead, Chance seeks to bring down Masters by any means necessary. Undercover with his new partner, John Vukovich (John Pankow), Chance arranges a phony buy with Masters. To get the front money, triple what the Secret Service will allocate, on a tip from his informant and "girlfriend" Ruth Lanier (Darlanne Fluegel) he bullies Vukovich into helping him kidnap a shady diamond-buyer. The robbery goes bad. The buyer, who is really an FBI agent, is killed, and Chance and Vukovich, pursued by an army of gunmen (later revealed to be FBI as well), only narrowly escape. At the buy, Chance is shot and killed, and Vukovich follows Masters to an old studio, where, after a struggle, the building burning down around them, Masters is shot and killed.

The moral ambiguity of the film is quite clear. Masters is a failed painter whose expressionist canvases belie the cold, exact precision of his counterfeit work. His often brutal actions always remain within the bounds of a savvy professionalism, and, despite the unconventional relationship that he has with his girlfriend (Debra Feuer), he treats her rather well. By contrast, Chance extorts sex from Lanier under threat of having her parole revoked, and, despite the plausible nobility of avenging Hart's death, he is driven well beyond the pale of professional and moral standards. In terms of noirishness, this ambiguity is surpassed only by the film's downbeat ending. Not only is Chance dead, but, by killing Masters, Vukovich is essentially transformed, his seduction into the noir world now complete. He takes Chance's place in the dark scheme of things, metaphorically *becoming* Chance. As he says to Lanier in the last scene: "You work for me now."

At the outset of *Manhunter*, Will Graham (Petersen), a former FBI agent, is asked to return to work and help profile and track down a serial killer, who turns out to be Francis Dollarhyde (Tom Noonan), a.k.a. "The Tooth Fairy." He consults Hannibal Lecter (Brian Cox), another serial killer, whom Graham had caught just before suffering a breakdown and leaving the FBI. Graham comes up with several new leads by working the evidence, but his real insights come from watching home movies of the victimized families, trying to empathize with the killer, and even pretending to be the killer himself. On the brink of another breakdown, Graham at last realizes that the killer has seen the home movies, and Dollarhyde, an employee of the film-processing lab, is quickly identified. Dollarhyde is found at home just as he is about to kill his coworker (Joan Allen), and Graham empties his revolver into Dollarhyde's chest.

*Manhunter* is replete with aesthetic niceties, leaving aside the extended scenes in which Dollarhyde is depicted, for all his evil, somewhat sympathetically and Graham's steady progression from third to second to first person in describing the killer's actions. A case in point is Mann's exquisite use of background details and architecture in framing and composing shots as well as his slight, almost imperceptible excisions and repetitions during certain emotionally charged or action-packed sequences. Also notable are various color motifs. The clinical whiteness of the cell underscores the tone, if not the content, of the conversation between Graham and Lecter, each framed in shots from complementary angles by the same prison bars. In the last scene, Graham's son (David Seaman), framed by the homonymous sun reflected in the ocean, is wearing a shirt that matches Graham's but pants that nearly match those of his mother (Kim Greist). Although this ending is somewhat upbeat, the family having been reunited, it is also somewhat grim, as Graham's face is scarred with what could be read as the film's noir "message"—that what it takes to catch a serial killer is tantamount to being one and that, in the final analysis, what separates the two is largely a matter of luck.

The realism of these films is suggested, not only by their grim endings, but also by the moral status of Petersen's characters, both features serving as excellent illustrations of how neo-noir elaborates on the moral ambiguity of noir generally. Such moral ambiguity does not just feel realistic; in the end it *is* realistic. People we encounter in our day-to-day lives are often of morally indeterminate status, either because we have no relevant information about them, or because we have conflicting evidence. To disambiguate, we often rely on moral tests, observing how people behave when it really counts (i.e., when the chips are down). But, even then, results can be inconclusive. In real life, we seldom find heroes who are morally unambiguous holus-bolus. Chance fails the moral test, although his motive is plausibly noble. Graham passes, but only by a whisker, for, to thwart Dollarhyde, he must indulge at great risk his own sociopathic tendencies.

## Odd Investigations, One More Time: *No Way Out* and *D.O.A.*

Many classic noirs were remade in the eighties.[12] While most fail to measure up, some actually surpass their originals by a less than narrow margin. This is particularly true, I would argue, of *No Way Out* (Roger Donaldson, 1987) and *D.O.A.* (Rocky Morton and Annabel Jankel, 1988), which are less remakes per se and more reinterpretations of the provocative premises of the classic noirs *The Big Clock* (John Farrow, 1948) and *D.O.A.* (Rudolph Maté, 1950), respectively. In the first, the hero investigates a murder in which he, unbeknownst to anyone else, is the prime suspect. In the second, the hero attempts to solve his own murder.

*No Way Out* begins with Navy Captain Tom Farrell (Kevin Costner), in line for a Pentagon position under Senator David Brice (Gene Hackman), romancing Susan Atwill (Sean Young), Brice's mistress. Knowing that she has been with another man, Brice kills Atwill in an obsessively jealous rage, Farrell seeing him at her house just prior to the murder. Brice's aide Scott Pritchard (Will Patton) removes incriminating evidence from the scene, and the murder is blamed on Atwill's other man. To keep the investigation in-house, the suspect is conveniently identified as the subject of an unsubstantiated rumor, "Yuri," a Soviet spy allegedly working in the Defense Department. Under Brice, Farrell is assigned to lead the murder investigation/Yuri spy hunt, but there is no corroborating evidence of Brice's guilt, and all the evidence points to Farrell himself. Although Farrell hinders the investigation surreptitiously, a witness who saw him with Atwill catches a glimpse of him in a corridor of the Pentagon, leading to a massive room-to-room search. Dodging the witnesses, Farrell finally manages to escape from the Pentagon just as he is identified as the suspect. He is taken to a safe house and interrogated by agents who turn out to be KGB. Not only is it now believed by the Americans that he is Yuri, but it also turns out against all odds that he actually *is* Yuri.

There are a number of nice things about the film that bear mention. First, several details foreshadowing the twist are subtle enough not to be noticed as significant. At the bar at the posh president's reception where Farrell first meets Atwill, he orders Stoli, a Russian vodka. His landlord, who is perhaps a bit too friendly, has a detectable Eastern European accent. Also, and more centrally, there is a delightful play on the relation between justification and truth. The Pentagon has good reason to believe that Farrell is the one who killed Atwill, which is false, but no good reason to believe that he is Yuri, which is true. That evidence is no guarantee of truth is a lesson worth learning.

Another odd investigation is the subject of *D.O.A.* Dexter Cornell (Dennis Quaid), an English professor and erstwhile novelist, declines to read the first novel of Nick Lang (Rob Knepper), his talented but pestering student, until Nick falls to his death past Dex's office window. Dex later learns that his estranged wife, Gail (Jane Kaczmarek), had been having an affair with Nick. After a night of binge drinking with admiring student Sydney Fuller (Meg Ryan), Dex feels ill and goes to the hospital, where a blood test reveals that he has been poisoned and has only a day or two to live. He returns to Gail's house just in time to see her killed by an unknown assailant. Eluding the police, who suspect him, and with Sydney's help, Dex embarks on a desperate quest to solve his own murder. After a number of false leads, he confronts his seeming friend and colleague Hal Petersham (Daniel Stern), who turns out to have poisoned Dex and killed Nick and Gail so as to plagiarize Nick's novel and publish it as his own. In the ensuing struggle, Dex shoots and kills Hal before staggering to the police station and recording his statement, before his time is up, of the whole affair on video.

Morton and Jankel's *D.O.A.* is presented as continuous with and, at the same time, a departure from Maté's original version. Continuity is established by the basic premise, of course, but more so by the opening and closing sequences in black-and-white: at the beginning, when Dex stumbles through the rain and into the police station, and, at the end, when, his statement concluded, he walks out into the night. Despite minor errors in depicting how such institutions are run, having the story take place in and around the hallowed halls of academe is truly inspired. In many ways, although often in subtler forms, the ivory tower can be just as petty, dark, and sinister as any mean streets.

Moral ambiguity is a key part of these remakes' noir-style realism. Behind our initial sympathy for Farrell lies a niggling doubt (why did he become involved with his boss's mistress?), and, when he is finally unmasked as having worked for the KGB, not only is it revealed that they coerced him, but he also walks out on them at the end. Our sympathy for Dex is likewise diluted by various personal and professional failings. No less realistic are the downbeat endings of both films. The KGB spy escapes, and the professor solves his own murder only and inevitably to die soon after somewhere in the night.

## David Lynch: *Blue Velvet* and *Lost Highway*

My working definition of *noir*, again, is "stylized crime realism." In this section, I examine two neo-noirs by David Lynch, *Blue Velvet* (1986) and *Lost Highway* (1997), which may seem, the latter especially, to push my definition to the breaking point. Bearing in mind the dynamic tension between stylization and realism, the former would seem to dominate in Lynch's nightmarish world. But, for all their stylization, for all their surreality, what the nightmares are *about* (inadequacy, betrayal, the evil of which human beings are capable) is as realistic as the nuances of psychopathology that Lynch routinely exploits. The world *is* wild at heart and weird on top.

*Blue Velvet* begins with Jeffrey Beaumont (Kyle MacLachlan) finding a severed human ear, which he brings to Detective John Williams (George Dickerson). Williams's daughter Sandy (Laura Dern) informs him that the case concerns the lounge singer Dorothy Valens (Isabella Rossellini). Posing as a fumigator, Jeffrey enters her apartment and steals a set of keys, but, when he returns to do more snooping, Valens surprises him, and he must watch from a closet while Frank Booth (Dennis Hopper) engages her in sadomasochistic sex disturbingly charged with fetishism and Freudian role-playing. Jeffrey, romantically involved with Valens, learns that Frank, the leader of a local crime gang in cahoots with corrupt cops, has kidnapped Valens's husband and son—the ear was her husband's—so as to extort sex from her. After Frank takes Jeffrey for a "joyride," brutally beating him, the police raid Frank's place. Frank escapes and hunts for Jeffrey at Valens's apartment, but Jeffrey shoots and kills Frank, and Valens, although her husband is dead, is reunited with her son.

Although Jeffrey is for the most part a sympathetic character, his motives remain morally ambiguous. As Sandy puts it, we don't know whether

Jeffrey is "a detective or a pervert." His family, always watching classic noir on TV, warns him not to go "down by Lincoln," the bad part of town, but he does. The ending is so saccharine, so artificial, that it subverts itself. Back in the family, and paired now with Sandy, Jeffrey is reensconced in the absurd surface appearances of a Norman Rockwell version of small-town America, leaving the seething, violent noir world beneath untouched.

In *Lost Highway,* the jazz tenor saxophonist Fred Madison (Bill Pullman), unable to satisfy his wife Renee (Patricia Arquette) sexually, receives from an anonymous source increasingly invasive videotapes of their home, the last of which shows Fred, in a fit of madness, having killed Renee. He is imprisoned for the crime. More and more unstable (and looking a lot like David Lynch), Fred metamorphoses into Pete Dayton (Balthazar Getty) and is subsequently released. Pete resumes his job as an auto mechanic, once back at work meeting and becoming involved with Alice Wakefield (Arquette, again), the girlfriend of the crime boss Mr. Eddy (Robert Loggia). Alice convinces Pete to commit a robbery with her, on the promise that they will use the proceeds to run away together. In the desert, ostensibly to meet a fence, Alice abandons Pete, at which point he metamorphoses back into Fred. He finds Renee at a hotel with her lover, Dick Laurent (Loggia, again), whom he kidnaps and murders. The police catch up with Fred outside his house, and Fred takes off, racing down the highway with a long line of police cars in hot pursuit.

There are several surreal, metaphysically peculiar, even supernatural elements of *Lost Highway,* and these may exclude the film from the neo-noir class or make it at most a sort of neo-noir hybrid. First, there is the loop. At the beginning, someone informs Fred via intercom that Dick Laurent is dead. At the end, it is Fred himself who speaks into the intercom and does the informing. Then there is the mystery man in black (Robert Blake), who seems at one point to be in two different places at once: at a cocktail party with Fred and inside Fred's house. The mystery man apparently represents homicidal jealousy, and this, together with the loop, suggests that Fred's house is something of a metaphor for his mind. He informs himself (i.e., becomes aware) that Dick Laurent is dead. The jealousy raging within him (i.e., at home) is so vivid that he imagines seeing it in the flesh, projecting it into a semblance of concrete existence. The element that is most disconcerting, however, is the pair of metamorphoses. But, at one point, Fred relates, tellingly: "I like to remember things my own way . . . not necessarily the way they happened." This suggests yet another nonliteral reading. Pete's story can be seen as the noir-stylized version of Fred's story as Fred *wants* to remember it. Note that, while Fred is sexually inadequate, Pete is capable, virile. When Pete is working as a mechanic, Fred's jazz piece comes on the radio, causing Pete to have a severe headache. This is the real profession intruding on the imagined one. In the same way, despite the fevered pitch of Fred's imagination, his disappointment forces its way into Pete's story (when Alice abandons him), bringing Fred back, once more, to himself.

Such interpretations give *Lost Highway* a less surreal and more realistic flavor, at least beneath the surface. The same can be said of *Blue Velvet*'s artificial happy ending. Add to this the moral ambiguity of Jeffrey and Fred/ Pete, and Lynch's noir-style realism becomes discernible as an element of his oeuvre.

## On the Q.T.: *Reservoir Dogs* and *Pulp Fiction*

On the strength of *Reservoir Dogs* (1992) and *Pulp Fiction* (1994), Quentin Tarantino is the standout neo-noir director of the nineties. *Reservoir Dogs* is, somewhat ironically, the quintessential neo-noir heist film, notable for spending, in direct contrast to typical heist films, hardly any time at all on the details of the planning or execution of the crime itself. *Pulp Fiction* is a tapestry of interwoven noir stories whose common thread becomes clear only toward the end. Despite the obviously stylized elements, both films exhibit a gritty realism about criminal violence and its underlying causes. This is particularly evident in the quick cuts to and lingering shots on the physical aftermath of actions whose extreme brutality is triggered by accident as much and as often as by will.

For the most part I will let these films speak for themselves. Up first is *Reservoir Dogs*. Joe Cabot (Lawrence Tierney), a crime boss, and his son Nice Guy Eddie (Chris Penn) bring together an ad hoc gang to pull a jewel heist. Each gang member is given a color code name, including the principals Mr. Blonde (Michael Madsen), Mr. White (Harvey Keitel), Mr. Pink (Steve Buscemi), and Mr. Orange (Tim Roth), an undercover cop. The gang steals the loot but must shoot their way out, scrambling to reunite at the designated hideout, a warehouse. During a carjacking, Mr. Orange is shot and seriously wounded by the driver, whom he then shoots dead. He and Mr. White repair to the warehouse, where Mr. Pink, having stashed the loot, airs suspicions that they have been set up. Returning with a hostage policeman (Kirk Baltz), whom he tortures while the other gang members are absent, Mr. Blonde is shot and killed by Mr. Orange. When the gang returns, Cabot accuses Mr. Orange of being the rat. But Mr. White defends him, resulting in a Mexican standoff in which everyone gets it but Mr. Pink, who runs off with the diamonds, then is possibly shot by the police. Dying, Mr. Orange finally confesses to the wounded Mr. White, who then shoots him as the police arrive.

In *Pulp Fiction*, Vincent (John Travolta) and Jules (Samuel L. Jackson) do a job for their boss, Marsellus Wallace (Ving Rhames), narrowly escaping with their lives. On the return drive, Vincent accidentally shoots and kills Marvin (Phil Lamarr), their inside man, which forces them to repair to a suburban home, where the Wolf (Harvey Keitel), a consultant sent by Marsellus, oversees the cleanup and disposal of the evidence. Vincent and Jules then have breakfast at a diner, which Ringo (Tim Roth) and Yolanda (Amanda Plummer) attempt to hold up. Though Jules gets the drop on Ringo, he lets the couple go, having already decided to quit "the life" himself. Vincent and Jules return to Marsellus, who has just paid Butch (Bruce Willis) to take a dive in an upcoming fight. Perhaps that night, Vincent takes Marsellus's wife, Mia (Uma Thurman), to dinner at his boss's behest. Presumably mistaking it for cocaine, Mia overdoses on Vincent's heroin, and he rushes her to his dealer's (Eric Stoltz) house for a lifesaving adrenaline shot. On a future night, Butch wins his fight, having bet heavily on himself against the highly inflated odds. He meets up with his girlfriend, Fabienne (Maria de Medeiros), at a motel. The next morning, Butch returns to his apartment to retrieve his father's gold watch. By chance, he gets the drop on Vincent, who is staking out the apartment, and kills him with his own gun. On the way back, he runs, again by chance, into Marsellus, whom he tries to run over, smashing up his car. Both are injured, and Marsellus chases Butch, shooting at him, into a shop, where both are knocked unconscious. They wake up bound and gagged. Butch frees himself and returns to save Marsellus, and, in recompense, Marsellus lets Butch go on the condition that he never return to Los Angeles.

Despite Tarantino's bravado in presenting both narratives nonsequentially, their endings are far more traditional than cutting-edge, making his style of neo-noir more the exception than the rule. In *Reservoir Dogs,* no one gets away with his misdeeds, except possibly Mr. Pink, whose levelheaded "professionalism" almost justifies it. Those who survive in *Pulp Fiction* do so on the strength of having somehow redeemed themselves, effectively elevating them *into* a state of moral ambiguity. However, while the ending of *Reservoir Dogs* is appropriately downbeat, the last scene in *Pulp Fiction* is of Jules and Vincent strutting out of the diner, their guns stuck in their shorts, to the accompaniment of an ultra-hip instrumental sound track. Because of this lighthearted, upbeat ending, one might be loath to include *Pulp Fiction* in the neo-noir class. Still, while the "sequential" ending is not downbeat, the "narratival" endings are. Plus, the sequential ending could be seen as making one or both of the following, much darker points: (1) redemption doesn't really matter; (2) the fact that nothing matters doesn't really matter either.[13]

## The Darker Shade

There are a number of obvious differences between classic noir and neo-noir. First off, the former films are predominantly black-and-white, while the latter are predominantly color productions. Certain devices, such as voice-over narration by the protagonist, have been largely phased out, except on rare occasions, when the point is to evoke the classic era. The sporadic use of black-and-white in neo-noir, whether throughout the film or in select scenes, also serves this purpose. The sex is more explicit, the violence more graphic, more extreme, and the forces at work behind both are of a decidedly darker hue. The Production Code, under which classic films noirs were produced, severely limited what could be depicted, how it could be depicted, and, perhaps most important, how it all came out in the end. Once the Production Code was superseded by the ratings system, under which neo-noirs were and are produced, the darker shade could be painted in broad brushstrokes. What once had to be suggested could now be shown.

It might seem a trivial matter that the ratings system allows much more explicit and extreme sex and violence than the Production Code did. And perhaps it is. It might also seem trivial that filmmakers now have much greater freedom in deciding how plots will be resolved and whether they even will be. But this is not so. Not only can a film be much more realistic generally, but it can also *end* much more realistically. As I said, part of what holds film noir together is the realistic appraisal of people's motives, actions, and outcomes. Often enough, people really do have dark, indeterminate motives, committing shadily suspicious, evil, and excessively violent acts. But, while the outcomes of noir in general are realistically downbeat, the Production Code required classic noir to exhibit poetic justice, "morally permissible" endings where the victims are irretrievably lost or definitively reclaimed and the guilty get what's coming to them. Under the auspices of the ratings system, neo-noirs exploit the much more realistic possibility that, often, the guilty fail to get their comeuppance.

The reason that such endings are more realistic is clear enough. While neo-noir by no means has an exclusive right to such endings, it does serve to reinforce a valuable lesson, especially in light of most mainstream and many alternative films, which are replete with poetic justice. In philosophy, it is common to speak of the naturalistic fallacy, the mistake of inferring what ought to be the case (a value) from what merely is the case (a fact), the illicit attempt to derive *ought* from *is*. The inverse, inferring fact from value rather than value from fact, is hardly ever discussed, although it is equally fallacious. I call this the *normativistic fallacy*. That something should be does not mean that it is or that it will be. Of course, it is also fallacious to infer that, because something ought to be the case, it *won't* be—we might call these varieties the *optimist's fallacy* and the *pessimist's fallacy*, respectively—and so, despite being a corrective to the unwarranted optimism implied by the vast majority of films, neo-noir might be seen as equally erroneous. But neo-noir has the advantage. The foundation of mainstream optimism is patently escapist, whereas that of neo-noir is transparently realist. Neo-noir enjoins us to face facts in a way that purely escapist cinema necessarily denies us. Pessimism is irrational only when the world fails to warrant it.

While neo-noir distinguishes itself from classic noir by showing the normativistic fallacy for what it is, writ large, the prodigal departure seems worthy of its lineage, even somehow a vindication of it. In fact, it could be argued that this most important element of realism was at the very heart of film noir all the way along, its final form, its telos, its ultimate purpose. The fact that it was latent in classic noir and only fully realized in neo-noir is of no particular consequence. Classic noir did scene by scene what neo-noir does throughout, only, because of poetic justice, less consistently. People ought not to have bad motives or commit bad acts, but often enough they do. By contrast, the endings of classic noirs, an artifice of the Production Code and compliant creative intentions, almost always ring a little off, false, not only to life, but, much worse, to themselves. A most unfortunate illustration is *The Postman Always Rings Twice* (Tay Garnett, 1946), an otherwise fine noir that ends with Frank (John Garfield) *explaining*, for the audience, the poetic justice that he has received! The better classic noirs downplay poetic justice within allowable limits, making it seem less a matter of moral necessity or accidental rectitude and more a matter of pure chance, with no significance besides. Notice how poetic justice fades, displaced, almost to the point of irrelevance, at the end of *The Maltese Falcon*, a grimly perfect fit, or *Double Indemnity* (Billy Wilder, 1944), a note so delicate, so poignant, that justice is really beside the point. Realism, about values in particular, has always been an essential part of the essence of noir. Values alone have nothing to do with what really happens.

## Notes

My views in this essay owe much to Raymond Borde and Étienne Chaumeton, "Towards a Definition of *Film Noir*," trans. R. Barton Palmer, in *Perspectives on Film Noir*, ed. R. Barton Palmer (New York: G. K. Hall, 1996); Carl Richardson, *Autopsy: An Element of Realism in Film Noir* (Metuchen, NJ: Scarecrow, 1992); and Foster Hirsch, *Detours and Lost Highways: A Map of Neo-Noir* (New York: Limelight, 1999). I thank Mark Conard and Elana Geller for helpful comments. I also thank Elana Geller for seemingly endless hours of viewing and invaluable discussion of classic and neo-noir.

The epigraph to this essay is taken from Richardson, *Autopsy*, 209.

1. See, e.g., Mark Conard, "Nietzsche and the Meaning and Definition of Noir" (in this volume).

2. This is disputed by Paul Schrader, "Notes on *Film Noir*," in Palmer, *Perspectives on Film Noir*, 100; and R. Barton Palmer, *Hollywood's Dark Cinema: The American Film Noir* (New York: Twayne, 1994). Schrader gives no examples. Palmer does (e.g., the woman's picture), although these seem to be either crime films or beyond the bounds of film noir proper. If Schrader and Palmer are right, however, the weakened formulation would be that film noir consists *predominantly* of crime films.

3. See Nino Frank, "The Crime Adventure Story: A New Kind of Detective Film," trans. R. Barton Palmer, in Palmer, *Perspectives on Film Noir*, 21–24.

4. Borde and Chaumeton, "Towards a Definition of *Film Noir*," in Palmer, *Perspectives on Film Noir*, 60–62.

5. More technically, being a realist can mean holding that facts are mind independent and (relatedly) that truth does not depend on what we can know. It can also mean, more specifically, being committed to the existence of certain kinds of entities (e.g., subatomic particles) or properties (e.g., being morally good).

6. Richardson, *Autopsy*, 19.

7. I thank Elana Geller for suggesting this formulation to me.

8. For a detailed discussion of Scorsese as a neo-noir director, see Richard Martin, *Mean Streets and Raging Bulls: The Legacy of Film Noir in Contemporary American Cinema* (Lanham, MD: Scarecrow, 1997).

9. For an interesting discussion of the film noir detective, see Jerold J. Abrams, "From Sherlock Holmes to the Hard-Boiled Detective in Film Noir" (in this volume).

10. In discussing *Bound,* Mark Stephenson, an acquaintance of mine, quipped: "Of *course* the femme fatale is lesbian. She always was."

11. It does, however, make several lists of neo-noirs, including Richard Martin's (*Mean Streets and Raging Bulls,* 170).

12. No less than eleven remakes in the eighties alone, and nineteen in the nineties, are listed in Ronald Schwartz, *Noir, Now and Then: Film Noir Originals and Remakes (1944–1999)* (Westport, CT: Greenwood, 2001).

13. For further discussion of *Pulp Fiction,* see Mark T. Conard, "Symbolism, Meaning, and Nihilism in Quentin Tarantino's *Pulp Fiction*" (in this volume).

# Moral Clarity and Practical Reason in Film Noir

*Aeon J. Skoble*

> Don't be too sure I'm as crooked as I'm supposed to be.
>
> —*Sam Spade,* The Maltese Falcon

Film noir is a genre identified by a variety of stylistic conventions: unsettling or otherwise odd camera angles, the dramatic use of shadow and light, hard-boiled dialogue, settings that emphasize isolation and loneliness. Thematically, film noir is typically said to be characterized by moral ambiguity: murky distinctions between good guys and bad guys, ambivalence about right and wrong, conflicts between law and morality, unsettling inversion of values, and so on.[1] I will argue that there is some pedagogical moral value to the ostensible moral murkiness and that, in fact, films noirs are less morally ambiguous than they are generally said to be. In other words, there are ethical lessons we can derive that belie the superficial appearance of lack of moral clarity.

I have in mind several broad ways in which we see this occur. First, when there is a "right thing to do" but the alternatives are attractive (for whatever reason), the seeming moral ambiguity is in fact an exercise in ethical decision making. Second, when true justice or righteousness is in conflict with prevailing norms of justice or right, we actually have an instance of *refuting* subjectivism (the view that right and wrong are entirely subjective, that whatever I feel is right is right "for me") and affirming moral realism (the idea that moral judgments are in some sense true or false claims about the world or that right and wrong are objectively knowable properties). Third, there can be something morally edifying about *fictional* portrayals of morally flawed characters—if the right sorts of things happen.[2] My examples will, I hope, show that film noir as a genre isn't as morally problematic as it is often assumed to be.

## Ethical Ambiguity and Moral Decision Making

The first way we can derive ethical lessons from film noir can be illustrated by situations in which there is a "right thing to do" but in which the alternatives are attractive. In such situations, the apparent moral ambiguity might be better thought of as an exercise in ethical decision making.

For example, in *The Postman Always Rings Twice* (Tay Garnett, 1946), while it may seem attractive to murder a man in order to take up with his wife, this is, of course, not morally right. The narrative actually dramatizes this, first by showing the process by which the drifter Frank Chambers (John Garfield), enticed by an archetypal femme fatale, the alluring and disgruntled wife (Lana Turner), deliberates about and arrives at the decision to commit the murder of her husband, Nick (Cecil Kellaway). The narrative then goes on to illustrate that this was in fact the wrong decision—Chambers gets sent to the gas chamber. (We see the same narrative in *Double Indemnity* [Billy Wilder, 1944], in which an insurance salesman and a married woman hatch a plan to murder the woman's husband and collect the insurance.)[3]

In contrast, in *The Maltese Falcon* (John Huston, 1941), while Sam Spade (Humphrey Bogart) is perhaps tempted to keep his silence about the crimes of Brigid O'Shaughnessy (Mary Astor) in order to pursue a romance with her, he weighs all the factors and makes a decision about what is the right thing to do. Among Brigid's crimes, of course, is the murder of Spade's own partner, as part of her larger complicity in the pursuit of the Maltese Falcon. Spade offers a variety of reasons for his decision, many of which are plainly prudential—for instance, if he let her get away with it, she'd "have something over" him, and he could never be sure she wouldn't one day turn on him.

It would be a mistake, in other words, to infer from the presence of potentially countervailing reasons that there isn't any basis for decision making. The narrative portrayals of ethical decision making illustrate that there are such things as good reasons, reasons of moral significance, reasons that can be both rationally justified and action guiding—regardless of whether the protagonists come to the right decision. Indeed, both Spade's and Chambers's deliberations (to which the audience is privy, either through dialogue or that other noir staple, the voice-over) are highly instructive examples of what in the *Nicomachean Ethics* Aristotle calls *practical reasoning*— the deliberation from both principles and experience that leads to action. For Aristotle, reason tells us not only how to realize a goal but also which goals are themselves conducive to our overall well-being. Aristotle's concept here, *eudaimonia,* can be partly understood as "happiness," but that translation misses the long-term, ongoing sense that is perhaps better captured by "flourishing." Understood this way, the good life isn't identical with (episodic) happiness or contentment or amusement but instead is a life well lived overall.

For instance, Chambers may be "rationally" deriving an "effective" plan to commit murder (as opposed to simply beating Nick to death in the driveway), but it is a failure of rationality to regard the entire plan as being conducive to, or even compatible with, a flourishing existence. As alluring as Cora is, Chambers is deceiving himself, making a mistake about the nature of his own good (never mind that of his victim) in concluding that murdering Nick and running off with Cora will bring about his own well-being. In contrast, while Sam Spade can partially see the attraction of taking up with Brigid, he is not blinded by this. He understands that to turn a blind eye to Brigid's murderous ways would be literally suicidal, so "not playing the sap" and turning her in for murder is clearly the more prudential move for him. Although most would argue that Sam Spade acts rightly and Frank Chambers wrongly, both characters are deliberating about which action to take, and we the audience see the ethical ramifications of the results of these deliberations.

## Subjectivism and Moral Realism

The second sort of situation is that in which true justice or righteousness is in conflict with prevailing norms of justice or right. In this case, we actually have an instance of affirming moral realism and *rejecting* subjectivism. For instance, consider *Touch of Evil* (Orson Welles, 1958), in which Mike Vargas (Charlton Heston), a Mexican lawman honeymooning in a border town, inadvertently discovers a corrupt American lawman, Hank Quinlan (Orson Welles), collaborating with the very narcotics operation he has been investigating. Here, the fact that Quinlan is a police officer doesn't actually entail any inversion of values. On the contrary, the contrast between good and evil characters in *Touch of Evil* is plain: Vargas, Al Schwartz (Mort Mills), and later Pete Menzies (Joseph Calleia) are good, and Quinlan and Joe Grandi (Akim Tamaroff) are bad. It's entirely coincidental and, moreover, irrelevant that some of the bad guys are police officers; this fact doesn't interfere with the audience's ability to discern the varying morals of the different characters. So for Vargas to seek both to arrest Grandi and to expose Quinlan is not a contradiction or even a conundrum. Although employed as a lawman, Quinlan is, in fact, a criminal, so it's morally correct for Vargas to pursue him.[4] Not only does Quinlan interfere with Vargas's investigation, but he is complicit in Grandi's attempt to intimidate Vargas by means of implicating his new bride (Janet Leigh). Hence, Quinlan becomes the target of Vargas's pursuit, not qua lawman, but qua wrongdoer. So, unless we start from the premise that all actions performed by police officers are by definition rightful, this fails to be an instance of moral ambiguity.

Another example of a deceptively superficial conflict between true and apparent justice is in *The Maltese Falcon*. Consider Spade's admonition to Brigid: "Don't be too sure I'm as crooked as I'm supposed to be." Even if Spade has fashioned a *reputation* for being amoral, he nevertheless does demonstrate a sense of objective right and wrong. He notes that, "when a man's partner is killed, he's supposed to do something about it," and that to do otherwise is dangerous ("bad for every detective everywhere"), suggesting some sort of moral code to which he subscribes, one that he will not violate simply out of physical attraction. When he sums the situation up—"You killed Miles, and you're going over for it"—he also makes it clear that he is making a decision informed by practical reasoning, despite any possible inclination to the contrary. It's not just duty-based reasoning (it's bad for every detective) but also prudential (he can't be sure that she won't eventually kill him).

On the other hand, *actually* amoral noir characters, like Chambers or *Double Indemnity*'s Walter Neff (Fred MacMurray), also do not represent an inversion of values since their decisions and actions are presented to the audience as wrong. Their schemes do not produce the desired results and are thus *poor* examples of practical reasoning. These protagonists may be nihilists, but the films are not thereby nihilistic, inasmuch as the films portray their characters' impulsiveness or narcissism as ultimately fruitless or self-destructive.

## Duty and Virtue

When people do the right thing for wrong reasons or seem morally conflicted, we have occasion to contemplate the distinction between an ethics of duty and other ethical frameworks, such as Aristotle's ethics of virtue. When Spade or Marlowe bends the rules, that isn't a genuine example of moral conflict; it's an example of an ethics of duty being supplanted by an ethics of virtue or of justice.

Our chief philosophical champion of an ethics of duty is the eighteenth-century German philosopher Immanuel Kant. On Kant's moral theory (laid out, e.g., in the *Groundwork of the Metaphysic of Morals* [1785]), once a rule can be shown to be rationally justifiable, violations of that rule can never be justified. Kant sees morality as a *categorical imperative*—a moral duty that all rational creatures have by virtue of its being universally applicable, given a rational standpoint. A paradigmatic case for Kant is the prohibition against lying: a rational creature, the argument goes, could not will that dishonesty be the universal law; hence, we have a duty to be honest in all circumstances. It's hard to reconcile most of what Spade and Marlowe do in the course of their investigations with that! But that doesn't imply that they are immoral—it implies that they are immoral on a Kantian theory.

The larger question is, then, whether we have good reason to accept this theory, and, as I've argued elsewhere,[5] we have good reason not to. Not only does a Kantian insistence on honesty get in the way of sneaky private detective ruses, such as Marlowe's posing as a rare book expert, but it also means that a Belgian ought not lie to the Nazis about Jews hiding in the attic; it means that the Underground Railroad operator ought not lie to the slave catchers looking for runaways.

Nearly two thousand years before Kant, Plato preemptively addressed this sort of fetishism about rules (chiefly in the *Republic*) by showing that, if justice is objective, no rule-based ethic will be satisfactory to realize it. It takes little imagination to envision circumstances in which justice is better served by violating, rather than following, moral rules, even if those rules are generally good guidelines for our deliberations. For Plato, there is an objective and universal reality to justice, which we can discover through philosophical contemplation. We come to acquire a conceptual apprehension of the form of Justice, and then we will know how the concept applies in the particulars, not the other way around. The law may be just or unjust, and so too may an agent of the state be just or unjust.

In other words, even if it's true that *in general* we ought not to lie, the same principles of justice that make that correct also *necessitate* lying in other cases, for instance, in the fugitive slave example. So when films noirs show good protagonists breaking rules in the pursuit of justice (e.g., Spade lying to the police), this represents no inversion of values and is in fact morally instructive—it demonstrates the objective nature of justice. When the noir protagonist is breaking rules in pursuit of unjust goals, of course, such as plotting the murder of a lover's spouse, this is shown to be wrong regardless of which rules are in place.

## Moral and Immoral Role Models

Finally, following Aristotle, and contra Plato, there can be something morally edifying about *fictional* portrayals even of morally *flawed* characters— if the right sorts of things happen. Plato is concerned about the morally corrupting effect of artistic portrayals of vice. Since, on his view, art is supposed to be mimetic, that is, an imitation of reality, negative portrayals of reality can encourage people to emulate the wrong things. We should thus be skeptical about the edifying value of films noirs, on the grounds that amoral antiheroes present bad role models. But, on the Aristotelian view, we can learn moral lessons from flawed characters, provided that they suffer appropriate consequences.

Role models are important for Aristotle, not only in the artistic context, but more fundamentally in the context of moral education and self-development. One contributing factor in my deliberations about the correct course of action is a consideration of how a similar decision might be handled by someone who is flourishing, someone known to be wise and sensible. In real life, I need to consider these role models in the context of my own circumstances, but it's also relevant how artists portray character and deliberation. It would be incorrect on this view to show a thief and murderer prosper as a result of his immoral acts, for example, or to invert values by portraying theft and murder as noble pursuits. But which classic noir does this? As I have been arguing, noirs frequently *do not* present inverted values, moral subjectivism, or antiheroism. They are more often concerned with bringing murderers to justice and so on.

But even in those films noirs in which we are entirely concerned with *immoral* acts (*Double Indemnity, Postman*), the protagonists do *not* prosper or flourish. If bad things happen to bad people, that's as morally edifying as when good things happen to good people. We have no need to fear that impressionable young minds will come away from *The Postman Always Rings Twice* thinking that killing a man so you can take up with his wife is a noble, or even remotely feasible, life choice. No one would think of Frank Chambers as a role model. In those noirs that center around immoral acts, these acts are punished. Typically, killers are killed, cheaters are busted, and thieves go to prison. Sometimes we see vicious types trying to make amends late in life: either they successfully reform themselves (e.g., *Kiss of Death* [Henry Hathaway, 1947]), in which case we are seeing morally correct drama, or they try and fail (e.g., *High Sierra* [Raoul Walsh, 1941]), resulting in tragedy in the classic sense, which is also morally correct from an Aristotelian point of view. Either way, it is not the case that we are presented with morally corrupting role models. The superficial seediness of some noir heroes (e.g., Sam Spade) is ultimately of less consequence than is their integrity. Other noir heroes (e.g., Mike Vargas) aren't even superficially seedy—they're straightforwardly moral, albeit navigating their way through a corrupt world. Viewing that through an Aristotelian lens offers an adequate response to Platonic concerns about role modeling.

Some might argue that noir *is* supposed to be morally ambiguous but that, because of Production Code pressures from the Hays Office, filmmakers were basically forced to tack on endings in which bad characters get what's coming to them, as in the case of *Double Indemnity*. And such an argument might be bolstered by the observation that the so-called neo-noirs, freed from the moral constraints of the Production Code, *do* sometimes show people getting away with theft and murder and, to all appearances, prospering as a result.[6] But, even if there were censorship pressures in some noirs, many others do not hinge on this—*The Maltese Falcon, The Big Sleep* (Howard Hawks, 1946), *Kiss of Death, Touch of Evil* do not—enough to support my contention that noirs should not be thought of as *essentially* characterized by moral ambiguity and inversion of values. Even if it were the case that *Postman* might have been made differently, that wouldn't amount to a genre-defining attribute. It would just mean that *Postman* had a morally ambiguous theme, not that film noir as a genre did. Also, inasmuch as our conception of film noir is essentially the product of a dozen or so landmark films, the counterfactual is irrelevant: we need to consider the *Double Indemnity* that was made, not the one that might have been made.[7]

So where's the moral ambiguity, the inversion of traditional values, that is supposed to pervade film noir? We've got the lonely settings; we've got the strange camera angles; we've got the unsettling use of light and shadow; we've got the hard-boiled dialogue; we've got the femmes fatales.

But we also have, it turns out, a body of films which showcase practical reason and ethical decision making, in settings that affirm moral realism and explicitly reject nihilism. Perhaps surprisingly, films noirs end up being more about moral clarity.

## Notes

I am grateful to Mark T. Conard and Steven M. Sanders for helpful comments and suggestions.

1. See, e.g., the introduction to this volume.

2. To avoid quibbles, I will make my case using only canonical examples, films that everyone would concede are, in fact, noir. If any modern-day neo-noirs bolster my argument, I will mention them in the notes.

3. Compare the neo-noirs *Body Heat* (Lawrence Kasdan, 1981), which has the same plot, and *A Simple Plan* (Sam Raimi, 1998), which has a different plot but the same self-destructive outcome.

4. Likewise, in the neo-noir *L.A. Confidential* (Curtis Hanson, 1997), it's morally correct for Ed Exley (Guy Pearce) and Bud White (Russell Crowe) to pursue the corrupt Captain Smith (James Cromwell).

5. See my "Virtue Ethics and TV's *Seinfeld*," in *Seinfeld and Philosophy,* ed. W. Irwin (Chicago: Open Court, 2000), and "Virtue and Vice in *The Lord of the Rings*," in *The Lord of the Rings and Philosophy,* ed. Gregory Bassham and Eric Bronson (Chicago: Open Court, 2003).

6. See, e.g., *Body Heat,* whose femme fatale, Matty Walker (Kathleen Turner), is shown enjoying the pleasures of a tropical retreat after arranging for the murder of her wealthy husband by the hapless Ned Racine (William Hurt).

7. And there are plenty of neo-noirs in which, in contrast to *Body Heat,* wickedness is, indeed, punished, with no Hays Office pressure, e.g., *Blue Velvet* (David Lynch, 1986), *A Simple Plan,* and *L.A. Confidential.*

# Cherchez La Femme Fatale

## The Mother of Film Noir

*Read Mercer Schuchardt*

> It was during the summer of 1946 that French moviegoers discovered a new type of American film.
>
> *—Raymond Borde and Étienne Chaumeton*

> In 1946 French critics having missed Hollywood films for five years saw suddenly, sharply, a darkening tone, darkest around the crime film.
>
> *—Raymond Durgnat*

> In 1946 French critics, seeing the American films they had missed during the war, noticed the new mood of cynicism, pessimism and darkness which had crept into the American cinema.
>
> *—Paul Schrader*

In 1927, nineteen years before French critics were to notice a change in American cinema, a film was released that gave birth to what would—a generation later—be recognized in its maturity as a new genre. The hallmark characteristics of this new type of "dark film"—retroactively dubbed *film noir* by the French critics—were, nevertheless, present in primordial form in the structure, plot, and fabric of a film that was the first of its kind: a film that displayed to the world the very metaphysical crisis under which the film industry itself would operate for the next one hundred years.

In fact, on opening night, October 6, 1927, three of the most significant events in film history occurred simultaneously. First was the birth of the talking motion picture. This technological triumph has until now eclipsed all subsequent realizations.[1] Second was the establishment of New York over Los Angeles as the archetypal American cinematic city, with the result that the location would ever after receive more miles of film footage than any other.[2] Third was the symbolic triumph of the image over the word by the assimilation of the word into the image and by the representation of reality to such a degree of verisimilitude that reality no longer held primacy among audiences. This had two subsequent effects that are still with us today: (a) the metaphysical replacement of the transcendent narratives of Western religion with the quotidian narratives of filmed entertainment; and (b) the physical replacement of church, synagogue, and theater by the movie palace as the weekly destination of choice for the mass audience.

## The Essence of Noir

Consider these themes: a spiritual medium that moves and talks; the discovery of a murder without the discovery of a corpse; power and dominance; a bleak, melancholic atmosphere; anxiety; dark lighting; action taking place in the city at night; foul play; and moral ambivalence. Are these not the essential ingredients for the genre of film noir? And are these not the essential elements in the first feature credited with spoken dialogue? Are these not the elements that constitute the essence of the classic film *The Jazz Singer,* directed by Alan Crosland and starring Al Jolson?

The spiritual medium is, of course, the medium of film itself, the most technologically perfected form of Plato's ancient cave that modern man has ever devised. Unlike Plato's chained inhabitants, we are willful prisoners, seated facing forward to watch the shadows thrown onto the wall by the technological fire behind and above us, the projector. We return to this cave regularly for the willful suspension of our disbelief because, in fact, the illusion of reality that the silver screen presents to us is so much more satisfying and, thereby, persuasive than the reality outside the theater.

The murder that is discovered is the death of God,[3] whose body is never found but is metaphorically represented in the film by the corpse of Papa Rabinowitz, who has died on his birthday. Papa's birthday presents are four redundant and, now that he's dead, doubly useless prayer shawls, which also symbolically serve as the burial cloth for orthodoxy itself since his death and birthday also occur in the film on Yom Kippur, the highest of Jewish holy days. In this way, not only does Papa Rabinowitz symbolize Judaism, but his birthday death becomes a symbol of the *ouroboros,* the snake eating its tail in constant death and constant regeneration. In the film, the regeneration is symbolized by Jakie Rabinowitz, and Jakie's career choice serves as a redefinition of religiosity—a Judaism that accommodates secularism. The dominance of spiritual leadership shifts from a patriarchal, language-based power to a matriarchal, image- and emotion-based power.

The bleak, melancholic atmosphere and the anxiety are themselves wrought by the very process through which this deicide occurs. The dark lighting is, perhaps, a function of black-and-white film, although the action taking place at night is a function of both most action occurring indoors (where it is timeless or else "always night") and the action itself being almost exclusively devoted to either the evening prayers in the synagogue or the opening curtain of the theater show. The foul play is intellectual and theological, a deliberate and controlled shifting of the moral center of the universe from an external God to the internal voice residing within the protagonist. In psychological terms, this may seem like progress. In theological terms, however, it is a question of the *descriptive* versus the *prescriptive* view of worship: Do we as humans take our sacred scriptures as merely descriptive of how the ancients did it and feel free to add to it with our own contemporary cultural innovations? Or do we take them to mean that God has given us a prescriptive definition of how it should be done and, therefore, that we should not add to it anything that is not already prescribed in the book? Historically, the orthodox (of any faith) have always leaned toward the prescriptive view, which progressives see as being too literal or narrow-minded. Jakie Rabinowitz uses many of his lines of dialogue in the film to recast the terms of religion in order to make the descriptive mode more acceptable.

Finally, the moral ambivalence is retroactive. It is only now, after living with the effects of this primordial murder for four generations, that we can begin to sense the unease with which those first bold sons, like Abraham before them, smashed their fathers' idols and went west, not to Canaan, but to Hollywood to found their own new religion. Moviegoers today are the great-great-grandsons and great-great-granddaughters of *The Jazz Singer,* and, since we know that Mama is still with us (at the end of the film and as a metaphor for sound film itself), we may benefit by reflecting once more on how God the father (represented by Papa Rabinowitz) died.

## The Story

Here is how Neal Gabler summarizes the story:

The plot of *The Jazz Singer* is simplicity itself. Cantor Rabinowitz, the seventh[4] Rabinowitz to become a cantor and the patriarch of his Lower East Side congregation, assumes that his only son, Jakie, will follow the tradition. But Jakie would rather sneak off to the local saloon to entertain, and when his father catches him there and forbids him from ever setting foot there again, the boy runs away.

Years pass. Jakie Rabinowitz has become Jack Robin, a night-club singer. But Jack is barely scraping by until a pretty chorus girl named Mary catches his act and later convinces a producer to sign him up for a new musical revue. Though Jack now returns home and is welcomed back by his mother, his father is unforgiving. The dilemma is set when Cantor Rabinowitz, apparently sagging under the weight of his broken heart, cannot sing the Kol Nidre, the Jewish plea for forgiveness, on Yom Kippur, the Jewish day of atonement and the holiest of Jewish holidays. The congregation pressures Jack to stand in, but Jack's Broadway revue, its producers obviously insensitive to the Jewish audience, happens to be open-ing the same night. As the screenplay puts it, "Jack is besieged by the old life and the new, filial duty against life's ambition, the past against the future."[5]

*The Jazz Singer* was originally a stage play that opened on Broadway on September 14, 1925. The movie version, which came out two years and one month later, is nearly identical. There are just two key differences: (1) George Jessel, the Broadway star, was replaced by Al Jolson in the film version; and (2) the film adaptation changed the ending of the play significantly, giving it a meaning diametrically opposed to that of the original script. Seen at the time as a function of changing times, the new ending was, in fact, more the result of the new medium of sound film itself, about which more later.

The film's plot follows a single character and, as such, revolves almost exclusively around the question of authentic Jewish identity and whether it can be modified successfully to include the modern world yet still please God. By extension, the film takes on questions of race, culture, gender, and history to consider whether religious identity is a fulfiller or a constrainer of destiny. What the film clearly shows, as Gabler points out, is that Ortho-dox Judaism and the culture of the Roaring Twenties do not mix well; there is no compromise that will satisfy either party. Yet, by virtue of the film's publicity as the first "talkie," the real meaning of *The Jazz Singer* has been overlooked: it represents the first time that the death of God is announced to the world through a mass medium. Nietzsche's announcement through the voice of "the madman" in 1882 was contained in a small and not widely read print publication.[6] *The Jazz Singer*, on the other hand, employed the medium of film, ensuring that the message got out to more people than were currently attending either synagogue or cathedral or church in America of the day. And this death—from which all moral ambivalence over subsequent cinematic death flows—is why *The Jazz Singer* should be considered the first film noir text.

## What Nietzsche Predicted

God's death, whether literally or figuratively understood, has profound consequences for the future. Here is how Tom Wolfe described it a hundred years after Nietzsche's death:

> Nietzsche said that mankind would limp on through the twentieth century "on the mere pittance" of the old decaying God-based moral codes. But then, in the twenty-first, would come a period more dreadful than the great wars, a time of "the total eclipse of all values" (in *The Will to Power*). This would be a frantic period of "revaluation," in which people would try to find new systems of values to replace the osteoporotic skeletons of the old. But you will fail, he warned, because you cannot believe in moral codes without simultaneously believing in a god who points at you with his fearsome forefinger and says "Thou shalt" or "Thou shalt not."[7]

*The Jazz Singer* reveals both the death of God and the attempt to get by "on the mere pittance" of the old codes. Let us consider the key moments of the film to see the means by which this deicide is achieved.

The film opens with the conventional title card of an old silent film:

In every living soul,
a spirit cries for
expression—perhaps
this plaintive, wailing
song of Jazz is, after

all, the misunderstood
utterance of a prayer.

The establishing shot shows us a busy street on Manhattan's Lower East Side. The Jewish ghetto is thriving with pedestrian traffic and happy children on a merry-go-round. The title card tells us:

The New York Ghetto—
throbbing to that rhythm of music
which is older than
Civilization.

We are then introduced to the mother and father of Jakie Rabinowitz, the film's protagonist. Jakie, whom we first meet as a twelve-year-old boy, enjoys singing all those "raggy-time songs" in the local saloon. His father is introduced to us in the negative: "Cantor Rabinowitz, chanter of hymns in the synagogue, stubbornly held to the ancient traditions of his race." The key word, *stubbornly*, becomes a foreshadowing of the fate that both his faith and his fatherhood will undergo. Jakie's mother, on the other hand, is introduced in the positive: "Sara Rabinowitz. God made her a woman, and Love made her a Mother." It only barely needs mentioning that, in Jewish tradition, household authority goes to the father but Jewishness is passed on through the mother. By the film's conclusion, both the authority and the inheritance of a new definition of Jewishness will derive from the mother.

## Mom versus Dad

Immediately, the yin of the female and the yang of the male are set in opposition, and the word-biased religion of the judgmental father (a devoutly religious man of the book, the word, and the chant) is set in opposition to the holistic, image-biased love of the all-forgiving mother. The father's "word nature" and the mother's "image nature" are confirmed from their very first dialogue, concerning Jakie's whereabouts while he is off singing in a saloon:

FATHER: Tonight, Jakie is to sing Kol Nidre—he should be here!
MAMA: Maybe our boy doesn't want to be a cantor, papa.

FATHER: What has *he* to say? For five generations a Rabinowitz has been a cantor—he *must* be one!

Shortly afterward, we see Mama glance at a picture of Jakie on the wall. Later, Papa, who won't have it, says to the boy: "I never want to see you around here again!" Mama venerates Jakie's image, while Papa cannot even stand the original from which the facsimile has been made. Mama will figuratively hold him in her heart; Papa will literally obliterate him from his mind.

The meddlesome middleman Moishe Yudleson is introduced to us as "rigidly orthodox, and a power in the affairs of the ghetto." From the very beginning, he is portrayed as slightly hypocritical, as a little too righteous, a religious man who nevertheless enjoys both his beer and the "raggy-time songs" of the saloon until, alas, he discovers that it is one of the cantor's own sons singing.

Jakie, at age twelve (i.e., just before he becomes a man in Jewish tradition), is presented to us as a mama's boy from start to finish. All his songs—from his opening "My Gal Sal" to his famous closing number—are overtly feminine in subject matter. Through the course of his life that the film portrays, it is only through the undying and devoted love of his (somewhat smothering) mother and the stern encouragement of his love interest that he is able to rid himself (and, by extension, we the audience are able to rid ourselves) of the shackles of his father's religiosity. By the time Jack Robin sings "Mammy" at the film's conclusion, we know that he is a case of permanently arrested development, a pre–bar mitzvah boy in a postreligious age. Sustained by show business externally and his mother's love internally, he is helped along by the implied love of the "shiksa" (Mama's term) dancer Mary Dale, whose desire to see him succeed *in show business* is so determined that it exceeds even her desire for Jack's love.

In order for God to die a slow and acceptable death (this is entertainment, after all, not interment), the narrative takes us through three distinct progressions. The first is to reveal God as, in fact, God, the power in the universe that gives meaning and sustenance to all creation. Papa declares this most directly when he threatens physical punishment for Jakie's saloon singing: "I'll teach him better than to debase the voice God gave him!" It is clear, in this scene, that God really is God in the film's narrative. The Hebrew God claims to be the one true and all-powerful God of the universe, and this is clearly the intended view of Papa's character.[8] Mother chimes right in: "But Papa, our boy does not think like we do." As previously suggested, and as the key word *think* here in Mama's sentence confirms, the film consistently represents the father as the left-brain, controlling, dominant intellect and the mother as the simultaneous, emotional, holistic, and artistic side. What Mama really means is that the boy does not think at all; rather, he *feels*. He *feels* the music, *feels* the gestalt, intuitively *feels* the perception of abstract patterns, which he reveals to his parents later, in the film's dialectic-swapping conclusion. These are among our first clues that the real battle being waged is that of, not the past versus the future, but anima versus animus, or the psychic energies associated with the female versus the psychic energies associated with the male. As Erich Neumann explains:

> It is in this sense that we use the terms "masculine" and "feminine" . . . not as personal sex-linked characteristics, but as symbolic expressions. . . . The symbolism of "masculine" and "feminine" is archetypal and therefore transpersonal; in the various cultures concerned, it is erroneously projected upon persons as though they carried its qualities. In reality every individual is a psychological hybrid. . . . It is one of the complications of individual psychology that in all cultures the integrity of the personality is violated when it is identified with either the masculine or the feminine side of the symbolic principle of opposites.[9]

Papa, of course, has no interest in psychology; he merely wants obedience. Jakie does, indeed, receive a whipping—while his mother cries—and he then makes good on his promise to run away from home. He leaves New York and heads to Los Angeles, where he becomes one among many trying to make it big. The title card tells us:

> Jakie Rabinowitz had become Jack Robin,
> the Cantor's son—a Jazz Singer,
> but fame was still an uncaptured bubble.

It is in Los Angeles that Jack Robin meets Mary Dale ("I caught your show in Salt Lake City"), who is, if not Mormon, then presumably not Jewish. When Moishe reads Jack's letter about her aloud to Mama, it is her line, "Maybe he's fallen in love with a shiksa?" that tips us off to her Yiddish. Yet the fact that he is reading the letter to her implies that she is illiterate. This is a strange scene because a later one—when Yudleson enters the backstage area of the theater, looks at the NO ADMITTANCE sign, and says, "Who's smoking?"—indicates that he himself is illiterate. Retrospectively, we realize that, while Yudleson cannot read English, Mama cannot read either English or Yiddish. The strangeness is that Mama's illiteracy is seen as a positive sign of her simple and pure-minded affection for her son while Yudleson's is a sign that he (and, by extension, the cantor) is not merely simpleminded but provincial, quaint, and "of the past." Here again the film offers an ever-so-subtle suggestion that a woman's illiteracy is her strength whereas a man's is his weakness, a view that contributes to the undermining of the logocentric tradition of patriarchal orthodoxy.

## Metaphysical Geography

In his move from New York to Los Angeles, Jakie sheds his Jewishness and takes on a gentile moniker in order to adapt. The film posits this move as the moment that the "new" Jewishness becomes defined. Subsequent dialogue reveals to us how normal this was at the time, another ghetto girl named Rosie Levy having become Rosemary Lee in the process of capturing fame's bubble. By the time the film concludes, Jakie is not just a goy but a goy in blackface, taking on two additional racial layers in order to conceal his racial/religious roots.

Neal Gabler confirms this habit in the culture of the day, describing how the play's star, George Jessel, described Warner Brothers' acquisition of the film rights: "Both signings—those of Jessel and *The Jazz Singer*—indicated something about Harry Warner's objectives. Jack claimed his brother 'desperately' wanted the rights to *The Jazz Singer*. Jessel said he wasn't sure how desperate Harry was, only that Harry had told him 'it would be a good picture to make for the sake of racial tolerance, if nothing else.' But Jessel apparently didn't know that racial tolerance was one of the few causes that could really animate Harry. Other Jewish moguls shied away from their Judaism and hid it. Harry paraded it."[10]

But, if Jakie's conversion to the new Jewishness occurs in Los Angeles, his return to rebaptize the old Jewishness with his new definition of it starts in Chicago, midway between New York and Los Angeles. It is there that he gets the news that he is going to open his first Broadway show. It is also there, we later learn, that Mary Dale, the only other woman in his life besides Mama, pulled the strings for him to get that Broadway show.

In Chicago, Jakie goes to the "Last Chicago Performance" of Cantor Rosenblatt singing sacred songs. Watching him sing, Jakie feels nostalgic and, in a special-effects shot, sees his father's face in the synagogue singing and smiling down at him, proud of him. This is not simply the last performance of this particular cantor. It is the film's way of telling us that this is the end of an era of orthodox Judaism—when Jakie returns to New York, his father dies, and his father's orthodoxy dies with him.

To the viewer, the film creates an intensely depressing tension: we want the protagonist to achieve his dream, but we also see in stark terms just what price he (and his religion) will have to pay for it. As Robert Porfirio writes: "It is the underlying mood of pessimism which undercuts any attempted happy endings and prevents the films from being the typical Hollywood escapist fare many were originally intended to be. More than lighting or photography, it is this sensibility which makes the black film black for us."[11] The purported happy ending of *The Jazz Singer* is, I contend, a screenwriter's whitewash of the film's underlying core, the philosophical embodiment of that mood of pessimism that will undercut "any attempted happy endings" or escapism that films were meant to be. From here on out, as the subsequent history of film noir shows, there really is no such thing as a happy ending because a happy ending cannot result from an insoluble dilemma.

Porfirio goes on to quote William Barrett in explaining the restraint of geography on the spread of existentialism in America, an insight that lends itself directly to *The Jazz Singer*'s plotline: "The American has not yet assimilated psychologically the disappearance of his own geographical frontier, his spiritual horizon is still the limitless play of human possibilities, and as yet he has not lived through the crucial experience of human finitude."[12] Significantly, it is his (and, by extension, Hollywood's) existentialist consumption of the West Coast that is itself the motivating force turning Jakie back toward New York: there is nowhere else to go. Having existentially defined himself as "no longer Jewish," he commits the same sin that proves to be the salvation of the Hebrew race—like Abraham, he smashes his fathers' idols and goes west, not to Canaan, but to Hollywood to redefine what it means to be Jewish. But, having achieved that through film, as Gabler shows (see below), Jakie has now used up his spiritual horizon. The only possible journey left is a return to New York, where, in a bold act of authentication, he converts the old Jews to his new religion. It is, thus, doubly interesting that both Jakie and Hollywood do make (in this film in particular and in film history overall) this return to New York as the new home of both the new Jewishness and the front lot.[13]

Porfirio is succinct in his explanation of existentialism: "Existentialism is an outlook which begins with a disoriented individual facing a confused world that he cannot accept. It places its emphasis on man's contingency in a world where there are no transcendental values or moral absolutes, a world devoid of any meaning but the one man himself creates."[14] It is into this world that Jakie, leaving behind the orthodoxy he can no longer accept, must create a new life for himself in the wider world of the theater. But, further, he must come back to New York and redeem the meaning of religion he has made for himself in the eyes of his father, in order that he may be, if not absolved, then at least at peace. His freedom, authenticity, and responsibility give him the chutzpah to recast the call of the cantor into the song of the jazz singer. Abraham, the father of the world's three monotheisms, is said to have left Mesopotamia in the east and traveled west to start a new religion in Canaan: the worship of one God.[15] In becoming Jack Robin, Jakie Rabinowitz has done the reverse: he has redefined Judaism so that it now includes, if not multiple gods, then at least multiple ways of defining, interpreting, and responding to God. In orthodox terms, however, this is not something that man should have power to do: only God can define how man should worship God. In terms of existentialism, after the damage is done, Jakie is left with the obverse of his freedom and authenticity: the comfort of his mother; the support of his girlfriend; and the sickness, loneliness, and nausea that accompany any new faith with a congregation of one.

## Prescriptive versus Descriptive

Jakie's return to New York triggers the final climactic showdown between the old definition of Judaism (prescriptive) and the new one (descriptive)—and Jakie's victory is hard-won and bittersweet. Unlike the play, in which, according to Gabler, "the Jewish entertainer forsakes show business and takes his father's place in the synagogue," the film tries to have it both ways, offering a solution that pleases both the orthodox and the nonorthodox. Gabler describes the dissolution of the film's final dramatic tension as follows:

> Jack's quandary is that he can bring Judaism to show business, but he cannot bring show business to Judaism—which is to say

that Judaism cannot be reinvigorated or revitalized in America or by America. It is alien to it. . . .

How does Jack's (and the Jews') intractable problem suddenly get resolved? It is certainly not because Jack has found some way to navigate between these competing claims or because one has capitulated to the other, as Zukor and Mayer had surrendered their Judaism. The answer is that the movie, swiftly and painlessly, dissolves the problem altogether. Within the bounds of theatrical realism this could never happen, but the movies, after all, are a world of possibility where anything can happen, and of all the themes of *The Jazz Singer,* this might have been the most important and the most telling for the Hollywood Jews. *The movies can redefine us. The movies can make us new. The movies can make us whole.*

And that is precisely how the Hollywood Jews would use them.[16]

But Gabler's analysis glosses over several key moments and misses entirely the significance of the mother in undermining (or overriding) the authority of the father in the question of Jewish identity. For what the film's progression shows us is a specific semantic trick by which the denial of God (i.e., his death in the mind of the believer) is accomplished.

During the first confrontation between Jakie and his estranged father, the cantor yells at his son: "A singer in a theater—you from five generations of cantors!" Jakie fires right back with his brand of self-righteous religious philosophy: "You taught me that music is the voice of God! It is as honorable to sing in the theater as in the synagogue! My songs *mean* as much to *my* audience as yours to *your* congregation!"

## The Snake Eats Its Tail

Thus attempting philosophical parity between the two practices, Jakie's dialogue in the film's last twenty minutes reveals the last two steps in the three-stage progression of God's death. The second step reduces God from being the God of the universe to simply being one god among many in the pantheon of cultural gods to choose from. What we worship is, etymologically, simply that which we "ascribe worth to," and Jakie's insistence that the theater is just as legitimate as the synagogue makes this point clearly. This is revealed in the scene where Moishe Yudleson comes with Mama to the theater to urge Jakie back to the synagogue to sing the Kol Nidre in his dying father's place. Yudleson uses manipulation and guilt in his attempt to persuade Jakie: "Would you be the *first* Rabinowitz in five generations to fail your God?" Here, the "your God" is significant, and we hear it again subsequently. Jakie, for his part, fires back with his newly minted theology: "We in the show business have our religion too—on every day—the show must go on!"

As he lies dying, Papa Rabinowitz suddenly sits up and says: "My son came to me in my dream. He sang Kol Nidre so beautifully. If he would only sing like that tonight, surely he would be forgiven." Here, the film has the voice of orthodoxy capitulate, equating the loveliness of the singing (the form) with the moral and metaphysical significance of the song (the content).

In the dressing room, as Jakie puts on blackface—perhaps in mourning, as the timing of this scene's dialogue and action seems to suggest—the internal tension mounts to a fever pitch and is revealed in the dialogue between Jakie and Mary Dale:

> MARY: I'm afraid you're worrying about your father.
> JAKIE: I'd love to sing for my father, but I belong here—but there's something after all in my heart, maybe it's the call of the ages—the cry of my race.
> MARY: I understand, Jack, but no matter how strong the call—*this* is your life.

Jakie goes to the mirror and sees himself in blackface; then his image dissolves to the synagogue's cantor scene, and then back:

> JAKIE: The Day of Atonement is the most solemn of our holy days—and the songs of Israel are tearing at my heart.
> MARY: Your career is the place God has put you. Don't forget that, Jack.
> JAKIE: You're right. My career means more to me than anything else in the world.
> MARY: More than me?

When Jakie mouths the words, "Yes, even more than you," Mary's face becomes happy as ever, and her title card exclaims: "Then don't let anything stand in your way! Not even your parents—not me, not anything!"

Up until this point, the viewer is under the illusion that the curtain is about to go up on Jakie's musical debut on Broadway. After Jakie receives a further dose of Jewish guilt from his mother and Moishe Yudleson, the manager comes out and lets the other shoe drop: "Hurry Jack! This dress rehearsal's just as important as the show tonight!" With this, the film breaks the tension and offers the first suggestion that we might be able to have it both ways: Jakie can miss the dress rehearsal, sing the Kol Nidre in the synagogue, and return in time for the eight o'clock curtain. Instead, he chooses the opposite. He goes onstage for the rehearsal, and his mother exclaims as she looks up to the heavens: "Here he belongs. If God wanted him in His house, He would have kept him there." God's powerlessness is hinted at here by the mother, and it is significant that Jakie's song opens with the lines: "When things go wrong and they don't want me, Mother, I still have you."

Jakie then goes home instead of debuting on Broadway, but not to sing in the synagogue. As he says: "I came to see Papa." After being reassured by Jakie that he is healthy, Cantor Rabinowitz opens his eyes and says: "My son, I love you." Then Mama adds: "Maybe if you sing [at synagogue], your Papa will get well." Another progression of dramatic tension ensues between Jakie, Mama, Moishe, Mary, and the manager until, finally exasperated, Mama says: "Do what is in your heart Jakie—if you sing and God is not in your voice, your father will know." Dethroned, and effectively dead, God is now eliminated in this third stage of the process. He has now been reduced to a stage prop to accessorize Jakie's voice, like some primitive synthesizer.

Yet the Broadway crowd has gathered, awaiting, as we see in a close-up shot of the theater program, the opening curtain of a show called *April Follies*. Is this an Easter celebration? Is this the film's suggestion that Jakie has given up his Jewishness simply to serve the trivial religiosity of a Christianity that has baptized former pagan holidays? Or is it a reference to April Fool's Day, and is Jakie the fool? Either way, it is significant to remember that these events transpire on the night of Yom Kippur, the Day of Atonement (which occurs between the end of September and the beginning of October), so the April Follies show is suggestively out of season.

## The Kol Nidre

Jakie finally relents and decides to sing the Kol Nidre in his father's place in the synagogue. The Kol Nidre is itself the source of some interesting subtext in the film. As the opening prayer of Yom Kippur, it sets the tone for much that follows. The literal translation of the prayer, which is sung in Hebrew in the film, is as follows: "All vows, obligations, oaths, anathemas, whether called 'konam,' 'konas,' or by any other name, which we may vow, or swear, or pledge, or whereby we may be bound, from this Day of Atonement unto the next (whose happy coming we await), we do repent. May they be deemed absolved, forgiven, annulled, and void and made of no effect; they shall not bind us nor have power over us. The vows shall not be reckoned vows; the obligations shall not be obligatory; nor the oaths be oaths."[17]

This translation, however, has competing interpretations. According to Tracey Rich:

> This prayer has often been held up by anti-Semites as proof that Jews are untrustworthy (we do not keep our vows), and for this reason the Reform movement removed it from the liturgy for a while. In fact, the reverse is true: we make this prayer because we take vows so seriously that we consider ourselves bound even if we make the vows under duress or in times of stress when we are not thinking straight. This prayer gave comfort to those who were converted to Christianity by torture in various inquisitions, yet felt unable to break their vow to follow Christianity. In recognition of this history, the Reform movement restored this prayer to its liturgy.[18]

Yet no translation of the Kol Nidre appears in *The Encyclopedia of Jewish Symbols* (which mentions it only in passing in the entry on Yom Kippur), nor is there a discussion of it in Douglas Rushkoff's critical perspective on his own religion, *Nothing Sacred*.[19] Tracey Rich says only this of the Kol Nidre: "The evening service that begins Yom Kippur is commonly known as Kol Nidre, named for the prayer that begins the service. 'Kol nidre' means 'all vows,' and in this prayer, we ask G-d to annul all personal vows we may make in the next year. It refers only to vows between the person making them and G-d, such as 'If I pass this test, I'll pray every day for the next 6 months!'"[20] Historically, there is some speculation that the prayer referred to vows *made in the past year* until the eleventh century, when it was changed to refer to vows *made in the coming year*. In either case, modern translations always refer to the coming year.

Gabler does address the Kol Nidre, however problematically, when he claims (in a note on his discussion of *The Jazz Singer*): "Pointedly, the 'Kol

Nidre' is a song of renunciation. Its first lines are 'All the vows that we made that were false to our faith and all the promises and oaths which once we swore shall be void now and forever more.' In short, Jack sings his renunciation of the secular world."[21] There are two potential problems with this interpretation. The first is that Gabler seems to have added the words "that were false to our faith" to the opening line. The second is that, in the context of the film, the prayer of the Kol Nidre can legitimately be read negatively, as a renunciation of the religious life itself. Indeed, this reading *could be the film's key theological moment* if the sympathetic viewer wishes to see Jakie both leave the synagogue to enter the theater and at the same time remain a Jew whose name is written in the book of life. Jakie's conscience is cleaner under this reading than under Gabler's, for renouncing one's father's faith is precisely what the film is about.

In either case, at the conclusion of the Kol Nidre, Papa opens his eyes for one last time before dying and says: "Mama, we have our son again." A special-effects shot (which George Lucas clearly borrowed for the final scene of *Return of the Jedi* [1983] years later) shows the ghost of Papa Rabinowitz smiling in good health and gently touching Jakie's right shoulder approvingly. God is dead, Papa is dead, but at least I didn't kill them, Jakie's conscience tells him. In classic film noir style, the rule of *cherchez la femme* is borne out: Mama Rabinowitz provides the psychological motivation to dethrone Papa's old religion, and Mary Dale provides the final dagger to the heart. This is why it is so significant that Mary Dale gets the last line of the scene, reminding the viewer that all is not well in the state of orthodox religion. She looks on Jakie singing and says: "A Jazz singer—singing to his God." This repetition of "his God" reconfirms for the viewer the idea that the Hebrew God is now simply one among many, a lesser god among a newly ecumenical pantheon that now includes theater and cinema among its houses of worship. And, as the film's conclusion shows us, this is the last time Jakie will sing to this particular god: for ever after, he sings to his goddess.

As Neuman suggests (see above), and as Leonard Shlain repeatedly points out, men are like words and women like images.[22] While both males and females have left- and right-brain hemispheres, Shlain, a neurosurgeon, contends that the balance of power goes to the right brain in women and to the left brain in men. What *The Jazz Singer's* progression really reveals is the feminine image of the film medium as victorious over the masculine word of both synagogue and theater, explaining why the changed ending could work only in the movie version, not in the stage play. Only by assimilating the words into a talkie can Jakie Rabinowitz, now Jack Robin, truly declare: "You ain't heard nuthin' yet!" Jakie commands the film's final scene as the new religious leader at the temple of Broadway. It is a temple, just as the movie house is a temple, that is ecumenical in religious, racial, and economic terms. The show must and, indeed, does go on, and everyone (who can afford a ticket) gets a vision of paradise. Jakie is singing to his mother, the love that sustained his rebellion, and his song is one of devotion to that archetypal force that he and subsequent cinema right down to the Wachowski brothers' 1999 *The Matrix* (Latin for "mother") will worship. He sings "Mammy" as Mama, sitting in the front row, swoons in religious ecstasy to the voice with a tear and a (small-*g*) god in it.

In their classic essay, the first that attempted to define film noir, Borde and Chaumeton claim: "All the films of this cycle create a similar emotional effect: *that state of tension instilled in the spectator when the psychological reference points are removed.* The aim of *film noir* was to create a specific alienation."[23] *The Jazz Singer,* then, is *the film* in which the psychological reference points are *first* removed. *The Jazz Singer* is nothing less than *the story of their removal.* As a film, it is a family drama; as a metaphysical noir, it is a documentary. As film is now on a par with sacred scripture in contemporary culture, *The Jazz Singer* is film history's Book of Genesis—it tells not the fall of man but the fall of God. The films retroactively labeled *film noir* by French critics that occur from 1941 to 1958 are explorations and details of the existing fact. In them, we are not thrown into the abyss; rather, we are already in it, along with the protagonist, from the moment the projector's light passes through the first frame.

## The Future of Film Noir History

If Jack Robin and Mary Dale do eventually get married and have children, then much of subsequent noir history is metaphorically explained. As nineteen-year-old college dropouts, these children begin roaming the streets of New York and San Francisco. I imagine them all grown up with nowhere to go, eventually becoming self-employed private detectives, investigating the death of a God they never knew, and feeling ambivalent, nauseous, and moody as a result. They, in turn, produce some very interesting grandchildren.

Among the grandchildren is one Kaiser Lupowitz, the detective put on the case to find God in Woody Allen's brilliantly hard-boiled short story

"Mr. Big."[24] While not a film, this short story could serve as the origin of the idea of the "existential detective"—the basis for David O. Russel's existential comedy *I Heart Huckabees* (2004), in which the young idealist Albert Markovski (Jason Schwartzman) hires a team of existential detectives, not to find God per se, but to find *meaning*. Another pair of existential detectives can be found in Jake Schram (Ben Stiller) and Brian Finn (Edward Norton), a "God squad" duo of rabbi and priest who believe in the love of the same girl in *Keeping the Faith* (Edward Norton, 2000). These films use love or absurdity to deal with the existential crisis.

Among *The Jazz Singer*'s other descendants are the spiritual devotees of Tyler Durden's (Brad Pitt) neo-noir *Fight Club* (David Fincher, 1996). Tyler's mantra, which he imparts to his cult members, is a perfect embodiment of that which Jack Robin fought so hard to achieve; free of their psychological reference points, they engage in self-inflicted violence for their existential authentication, becoming in the process "*the all-singing, all-dancing crap of the world.*" That most of these films are comedies (even granting that *Fight Club* is a black comedy, *une comedie noir?*) reveals how uncomfortable we still are as a culture in considering religion seriously as a metaphysic tonic.

But, if the show must go on, then we should not be surprised at all if the future of film history—especially the further evolution of film noir—eventually leads our protagonists back to the synagogue.

## Notes

The epigraphs to this essay are taken from Raymond Borde and Étienne Chaumeton, "Towards a Definition of *Film Noir*" (1955), Raymond Durgnat, "Paint It Black: The Family Tree of the *Film Noir*" (1970), and Paul Schrader, "Notes on *Film Noir*" (1972), all in *Film Noir Reader*, ed. Alain Silver and James Ursini (New York: Limelight, 1996), 17, 37, 53, respectively.

1. This eclipsing of significant events by the simultaneous occurrence of a momentous event happens, albeit rarely, in history. Perhaps the most well-known example in the twentieth century is the November 22, 1963, assassination of John F. Kennedy in the United States, an event that eclipsed the deaths on the same day of the British writers Aldous Huxley and C. S. Lewis.

2. These first two events were reconfirmed (and interrelated) a year later by the 1928 release of the first "all-talkie" film, Bryan Foy's *Lights of New York*.

3. For an in-depth discussion of God's death as being essential to film noir, see Mark T. Conard, "Nietzsche and the Meaning and Definition of Noir" (in this volume).

4. The film claims that "five generations" of Rabinowitzes have been cantors. I can only assume that Gabler's "seventh Rabinowitz" is referencing the stage-play version, with which I am not familiar. Otherwise, it is simply erroneous.

5. Neal Gabler, *An Empire of Their Own: How the Jews Invented Hollywood* (New York: Crown, 1988), 144.

6. The passage in question is sec. 125 of Nietzsche's *Fröhliche Wissenschaft* (1882). The first English translation of the *Fröhliche Wissenschaft,* by Oscar Levy, appeared in 1924 as *Joyful Wisdom.* The work is better known to contemporary American readers as *The Gay Science.*

7. Tom Wolfe, "Sorry, but Your Soul Just Died," in *Hooking Up* (New York: Farrar, Straus & Giroux, 2000), 99.

8. It is interesting to note, however, that, despite Papa's orthodoxy, his title cards do not have him use the traditional device of *G-d* when referring to God. This subtlety may have been the filmmaker's further proof that times were now so changed that this custom was no longer worth observing, even for Jewish audiences (with whom the play/film was the biggest hit).

9. Erich Neumann, *The Origins and History of Consciousness* (Princeton, NJ: Princeton University Press, 1954), xxii n. 7.

10. Gabler, *An Empire of Their Own,* 140.

11. Robert Porfirio, "No Way Out: Existential Motifs in the *Film Noir*" (1976), in *Film Noir Reader,* ed. Alain Silver and James Ursini (New York: Limelight, 1996), 80.

12. Ibid.

13. For just how dominant New York City is in Hollywood history, see Chuck Katz, *Manhattan on Film: Walking Tours of Hollywood's Fabled Front Lot* (New York: Limelight, 1999), and James Sanders, *Celluloid Skyline: New York and the Movies* (New York: Knopf, 2001).

14. Porfirio, "No Way Out," 81.

15. Ellen Frankel and Betsy Platkin Teutsch, *The Encyclopedia of Jewish Symbols* (Northvale, NJ: Aaronson, 1992), 1.

16. Gabler, *An Empire of Their Own,* 141, 145 (emphasis added).

17. This transliteration is from Isidore Singer, ed., *The Jewish Encyclopedia: A Descriptive Record of the History, Religion, Literature, and Customs of the Jewish People* (New York: Funk & Wagnall, 1916), 359. For a more complete discussion, including the history of this dispute, as well as the explanation of the origin of the anti-Semitic interpretation, see *The Encyclopedia Judaica* (New York: Macmillan, 1971), 10:1166–69, or http://en.wikipedia.org/wiki/Kol_Nidre (accessed June 8, 2005). Comparing the various entries on the Kol Nidre in different Jewish texts is itself a useful illustration of the complexity of such sensitive ideas as well as of the delicacy with which those issues have been handled at different points in history.

18. Tracey Rich, *Judaism 101,* http://www.jewfaq.org/holiday4.htm (accessed May 17, 2004).

19. See Frankel and Teutsch, *The Encyclopedia of Jewish Symbols*, 197, and Douglas Rushkoff, *Nothing Sacred: The Truth about Judaism* (New York: Crown, 2003).

20. Rich, *Judaism 101*, http://www.jewfaq.org/holiday4.htm#YKL.

21. Gabler, *An Empire of Their Own*, 145.

22. Leonard Shlain, *The Alphabet versus the Goddess: The Conflict between Word and Image* (New York: Viking, 1998).

23. Borde and Chaumeton, "Towards a Definition of *Film Noir*," 25.

24. Woody Allen, "Mr. Big," in *Getting Even* (New York: Vintage, 1978), 139.

# From Sherlock Holmes to the Hard-Boiled Detective in Film Noir

*Jerold J. Abrams*

> A maze is a house built purposely to confuse men; its architecture, prodigal in symmetries, is made to serve that purpose.
>
> —*Jorge Luis Borges*

The time of film noir is Hemingway time—dark and cold, moody and mean, existentially void and grossly atomistic. Here is a "house built to confuse men" and lead them all about in a synthetic prison of their own design. This dark maze of the night is everywhere and nowhere, and the only one who knows it clean is the hard-boiled detective, who navigates its thousand hidden passageways. Sam Spade, Philip Marlowe, and Mike Hammer—these are the classic noir detectives, each one stoic and detached, a cold Cartesian spectator with no hope for redemption and no reason to care. The individuals he meets are entirely self-contained, wrapped in their own fear and self-interest—all terribly malevolent. Of course, true to form, the criminal is always exposed by film's end—but that ending only ever marks a worse beginning. For, beyond the mere simplicity of whodunit, what is really uncovered in all great film noir is a world in which far more questions about the darkness of human nature remain fundamentally unanswered. Indeed, within this unlimited labyrinth of being, there is no safe place to hide, no final hidden doorway, and, ultimately, no possibility of escape.

## Mazes, Clues, and Detectives

Now, at first glance, the detective model and the labyrinth might not appear to have too much in common—but, in fact, they are two of a kind. Consider the ancient myth of the maze. King Minos of Crete had Daedalus build a labyrinth with a Minotaur inside ("a monster with a bull's body and human head,"[1] although the opposite works too) who was fed on a steady diet of young Athenians. Quite reasonably outraged, Prince Theseus of Athens plotted to enter Minos's maze. On his arrival in Crete, however, something unexpected happened to Theseus—he met the young and beautiful Ariadne (none other than Minos's daughter), and the two fell in love. Ariadne, not wanting to lose Theseus inside the terrible maze, equipped him with a sword and a "clue of thread" for safety. Theseus then trailed the thread behind him as he entered the maze, killed the Minotaur with his sword, and was able to escape by following the thread back to the entrance.

This has always been a popular story. But it really seeped into the fabric of modern literature when writers like Sir Arthur Conan Doyle drew directly from it in order to form what we today know as the classic detective story. And, while they aren't always *obvious,* the influences of the myth of the maze are certainly *evident.* For, in the hands of Conan Doyle, the Minotaur is now the criminal, trapped in an underworld "labyrinth of crime"; the "clue of thread" is now the "thread of clues" (clues as signs to be detected); and, of course, the noble Theseus becomes the formidable detective Sherlock Holmes. Take, for example, the story of *The Sign of Four,* in which Dr. John Watson (the narrator and friend of Holmes) tells us that his and Holmes's present crime case is "a labyrinth in which a man less singularly endowed than my fellow-lodger might well despair of ever finding the clue."[2] Clearly, the ancient myth is evident here. And this is hardly an isolated instance: in fact, Watson is constantly describing the world of crime as a "labyrinth" (or sometimes a "maze") and continually noting the need to find the "string of clues."[3] Indeed, the same template is perfectly evident in so many contemporary detective stories.[4] Think, for example, of Borges's stories "The Garden of Forking Paths," "Death and the Compass," "Ibn Hakkan al-Bokhari, Dead in His Labyrinth"—all these involve detectives navigating labyrinths. Or take Umberto Eco's novel *The Name of The Rose* (1980), a murder mystery about labyrinths set in the Middle Ages.[5]

It's the same with film noir too. In fact, it's fair to say that American film noir is simply the most recent natural heir of the classical myth of the maze. That quintessential American detective genre is filled with hard-boiled shamuses navigating labyrinths in the night. And I am hardly the first one to notice. Much of the credit for noticing the labyrinthine character of film noir must be given to Foster Hirsch and his remarkable analysis in *The Dark Side of the Screen*. According to Hirsch, it's the same in virtually every major hard-boiled film noir: "The original request for finding the missing person leads the private eye into a maze."[6] Similarly, and more recently, Nicholas Christopher takes up this point, rightly demarcating in his *Somewhere in the Night* three levels of the maze in classic film noir: the city, the human condition, and "the labyrinth of the hero's inner workings."[7] Hirsch and Christopher are right on target in their respective analyses. However, their points can, I think, be pushed further still. For it is in film noir—and in some contrast to the adventures of Sherlock Holmes—that we find a new and unique form of labyrinth to have emerged, one that is quite specific to the hard-boiled detective of American cinema.

## Umberto Eco on the Philosophy of Labyrinths

In fact, according to Eco, there are "three kinds of labyrinth" (or "maze").[8] The first one is the "classical Greek maze," with all the old star characters— Theseus, Ariadne (with her string), and, of course, the Minotaur. In this maze, according to Eco, you can enter and leave without difficulty; and, while the string may help a little, the only *real* problem is the Minotaur.[9] Certainly, this is the most popular version of the maze, probably because for a long time (from ancient Greece to the Middle Ages) it was thought to capture something very real about the nature of the universe[10]—think, for example, of *The Divine Comedy*, of Dante and Virgil navigating the labyrinth of hell with the Minotaur/devil at the center.

To be sure, it was a pretty good model (for a while anyway)—it explained a lot about reality. The classical Greek maze hit all the right medieval buttons. The world is terribly deceptive, hard to know, and frankly downright dangerous—but not to worry, for, with the "string of faith," you can avoid the devil and escape the deceptive maze of this earthly life, arriving safely at the pearly gates of heaven. But then things changed, as they have a tendency to do in history. The Renaissance happened—and suddenly a new maze came with it. This new maze, according to Eco, was the "mannerist maze," named after the sixteenth-century movement in art marked by a characteristically mazy distortion of perception. Now the maze becomes multistoried and more distorted, with upside-down staircases, each leading into another—an hour inside, and you don't know where are you are. Which room is which? Trapdoors and mirrors watching mirrors—nothing is what it seems in the mannerist maze. No need for a Minotaur either—the mannerist maze of modernity "is its *own* Minotaur."[11] Social fragmentation, moral skepticism, cultural pluralism—the mind splinters forth in a million different directions. Just getting out (with your sanity intact) is really all the challenge requires. But *that* will never happen unless you have the all-important modern version of the Ariadne's string—and *this* (à la Descartes and Kant) is nothing other than "pure reason."

Of course, as I said, things have a tendency to change, and this applies to the mannerist maze too. Its days were numbered. True, it worked for a while, until Nietzsche anyway, and then . . . *whoosh!* Into thin air: pure reason was gone as well, that age-old archaeological dig for the faculty of rationality had uncovered only "will to power." So the Enlightenment willowed, and a *new* dark age descended on humanity and, with it, the *third* form of labyrinth. Pioneered in large part by the American philosopher Charles S. Peirce (1839–1914)[12] and later by the French philosophers Gilles Deleuze and Félix Guattari—*this* is the labyrinth of unlimited clues, or the "rhizomatic labyrinth."[13] The term *rhizome* actually comes from the study of agriculture: it refers to a structure that grows sideways (horizontally), and, in fact, in every direction, rather than vertically (like a tree, from the ground up and out of a singular trunk). Like grass or seaweed, or the Internet, or even language, a rhizome, according to Deleuze, has "neither beginning nor end, but always a middle (*milieu*) from which it grows and which it overspills."[14] As a labyrinth, the rhizome has no center; it has no perimeter; and, worst of all, it has no way out.[15] Here, the Minotaur is *still* the form of the labyrinth itself (as in the mannerist maze), but *now* there is no escaping him with reason (or faith, or any combination of the two). For every Ariadne's string only ever leads further into the labyrinth.

## The Rhizomatic Maze Structure in Noir

It is the rhizomatic maze that, I would like to suggest, is what we really mean by *the maze of film noir*. In order to make this point, I'll begin by giving an analysis of a noir film that is right on the border between mannerist maze and rhizomatic maze—to make the distinction clearly. Consider the film *Lady in the Lake* (Robert Montgomery, 1947). Here, our hard-boiled detective is Philip Marlowe (Robert Montgomery), who is busy filling his pockets with rice. Why? Well, he tells us quite explicitly: "I read a story once, how a detective carried rice in his pocket. He walked along—he distributed it, kernel for kernel." Of course, the story here is none other than "Hansel and Gretel," in which two children are twice forced by their wicked mother to enter a forest maze, to get lost and die. The first time the young Hansel (or would-be Theseus) cleverly fills his pockets with pebbles and uses them as his Ariadne's string; the second time, however, he has only breadcrumbs, which are soon eaten by the forest animals. Lost, Hansel and Gretel discover a house made of candy that belongs to a witch (a female Minotaur), who wants to eat them. But they kill the witch, make off with her riches, and return to their father, their mother (who is *also* really the witch) having died in the meantime.

The relevance of this story to the film *Lady in the Lake* is plainly evident—for Marlowe's string of rice is intended to lead into the labyrinth toward the Minotaur, in this case another evil woman (like the witch), namely, Mildred Havelend (Jayne Meadows). Moreover, Havelend used to be a blonde but is now a brunette because she is masquerading as Chrystal Kingsby, the now-drowned "lady in the lake."[16] So Mildred/Chrystal is the two-faced female witch/Minotaur—the same form found in "Hansel and Gretel." Marlowe, however, is in over his head. His trail of rice has been ruined (just like Hansel's breadcrumbs) by the two-faced cop/criminal Lieutenant DeGarmot (Lloyd Nolan), who has covered for Mildred.[17] So the cops arrive, with little to no string to follow, only after Marlowe has been shot. Now, as I noted, this is a borderline case between a mannerist maze and rhizomatic maze. For, while the string doesn't lead out, and Marlowe has been shot, he does, in fact, recover and lives happily ever after with Adrienne Fromsett (Audrey Trotter)—whereas he should have died on the floor (with no escape from the labyrinth).

As a contrast to this film, consider the much better (and more rhizomatic) noir film *The Third Man* (Carol Reed, 1949). Set in postwar Vienna, during the Occupation, the film takes as its context a labyrinthine weave of four cultures set against a dark Gothic Viennese cityscape. *The Third Man* is essentially a detective story about a pulp fiction writer, Holly Martins (Joseph Cotten), who gathers clues about his missing friend Harry Lime (Orson Welles). Lime—apparently dead and buried even before Martins arrives—is, however, quite alive, although nevertheless "underground," both figuratively, in the sense that he is a criminal, and literally, in the sense that he is in the sewer. The sewer is, moreover, structured distinctly as a labyrinth.[18] Each tunnel leads to other tunnels (some large and others narrow) amid twisting and winding staircases. Passageways reveal dead ends, and darkness makes determining direction nearly impossible. Flash-lights bounce glare off timeworn, shiny stones on curving walls, and flow-ing water creates that classic "house of mirrors" effect found in all great labyrinths.

But, most important, Lime is unable to escape. At the end of the film, he finds his way to the top of the sewer system, after being shot. He barely gets his fingers up through the sewer grate, just cresting the seal between lower and upper Vienna—but to no avail. He collapses, dead. Yet, not only does he not escape the labyrinth of the sewer, but it is also simply impos-sible for him to escape the wider and more rhizomatic labyrinth of Viennese crime. For the labyrinth of the sewer is simply a maze within a maze and the former merely a *representation* of the latter. It is a mannerist maze con-tained within the rhizomatic maze of occupied Vienna. There was no es-cape either way. Lime is trapped in a world of crime, always hunted, never safe—and he can't even trust his friends.

This remarkable theme of the maze within a maze (like Shakespeare's play within a play, "The Mousetrap" within *Hamlet*) is also discussed by Eco in the postscript to *The Name of the Rose*. Indeed, Eco does exactly the same thing in his story: the acting detective William (a medieval Sherlock Holmes) and his apprentice monk Adso (his Watson) must solve a murder mystery by navigating a library that is structured like a maze, in order to slay the Minotaur/librarian at the center. Commenting on this story, Eco writes: "The labyrinth of my library is still a mannerist labyrinth, but the world in which William realizes he is living already has a rhizome struc-ture: that is, it can be structured but is never structured definitively."[19] It is precisely this realization that Lime comes to as well: he acquiesces to Holly and acknowledges that he must be shot. There can never be any escape for him from the wider rhizomatic maze of crime.[20]

## From Holmes to Hard-Boiled: The Anti-Theseus

In fact, it's fair to say that the rise of the rhizomatic maze marks the most significant evolution in the modern detective story from Sherlock Holmes to film noir. For, whereas the maze of the classic detective form represents a mannerist maze (*with* an escape), the maze of the noir detective form is a rhizomatic maze (*without* an escape). And, on this point, the title of Rob-ert Porfirio's 1976 "No Way Out" says it all. Porfirio explains: "The pre-existential world of the classical detective was ordered and meaningful;

social aberrations were temporary and quickly righted through the detective's superior powers of deductive reasoning. A product of a rather smug Western society, such a world reflected a Victorian sense of order and a belief in the supremacy of science. The hard-boiled writers replaced this with a corrupt, chaotic world where the detective's greatest asset was the sheer ability to survive with a shred of dignity."[21] Otherwise put, there is a "way out" in the Holmes stories, and there is absolutely none in film noir. And, of course, I quite agree. Moreover, with the shift in *maze,* there is also a fundamental shift in the detective *character*—from the New England Gothic page to the Hollywood big screen, the original source for all of them (from Holmes to Marlowe and Spade) being Edgar Allan Poe's detective Monsieur C. Auguste Dupin.

Before making this point in full, however, I should note that, for there to be any significant "differences," so much too has to remain the same. And, among these similarities, perhaps the most important is the "positioning" of the detective character. In all detective fiction, the detective's abilities emerge from his positioning between two worlds—the "world of the cops" and the "world of the criminals."/He's part of both, but he's at home in neither. He can think like a criminal, but he's on the side of the cops/Not that they would ever have him—they are, after all, the detective's natural opponents, whether they're from Scotland Yard or the LAPD (noir typically takes place in Los Angeles). And, when they aren't telling him to stay off their turf, they're chastising his unconventional methods. Ultimately, however, the police are always completely inept and are eating their words by film's end.[22] The detective's lack of place, moreover, contributes to his (criminal-like) isolation. Dupin, for example, lives alone with his friend and prefers it that way: "Our seclusion was perfect. We admitted no visitors. . . . We existed within ourselves alone."[23] Holmes, too, lives with Dr. Watson in isolation from the world. In fact, the Holmes character and the Dupin character are very much alike. So much so that it's fair to say (and, in fact, some *have* said) that the character of Holmes is more or less copied outright from Dupin (and Conan Doyle hints at this as well in *A Study in Scarlet*).[24]

But, in noir, this basic classic detective model begins to change considerably. For the hard-boiled detective is even *more* isolated, even *more* Cartesian: he lives entirely alone and has no friends.[25] And this certainly makes his already asocial nature all the worse./The hard-boiled detective is isolated and angry, hopeless and amoral—he's a dark character in an even darker labyrinth. He's unrefined and in many ways perhaps unlikable. But, then, why should he care? As Marlowe (Bogart) puts it: "I don't mind if you don't like my manners. I don't like them myself. They're pretty bad. I grieve over them long winter evenings" (*The Big Sleep* [Howard Hawks, 1946]). The hard-boiled detective is excessively detached—he moves in the shadows and at night, ducking into corners and alleyways. Always he stays "covered," always cloaked in his massive trenchcoat with the collar up to hide his throat. Nothing's getting in there—and not a lot comes out. Hardly the conversationalist, he's a man of few words—although, when he does speak, he's witty and waxes deadpan innuendo about the evils of the human soul, as if it's everyday (nothing really for inquiry). He wears a fedora with the lid down, just barely revealing his strained brow and penetrating detective eyes. Physically, he's expressionless and pretty stiff. He's strong, but not very large, and certainly not very tall, although as Marlowe puts it in *The Big Sleep* (in his typical wisecracking manner): "Well, I try to be."

Of course, this is completely the opposite of Holmes, who is tall and lean and languid, looking every bit the decadent aesthete. Holmes lounges around a lot and enjoys his contemplative free time, even seeing it as part of his method. But not the hard-boiled detective. He never rests and is wound pretty tight: he rarely smiles and quickly gets to the point. He doesn't have time, unlike Holmes, to lay out the case with adornments, giving so many little curlicue details here and there, all speckled with reflections on the nature of reasons and signs. He just goes about his business, mean as ever, holding his cigarette out the side of his mouth, even when he's working a guy over. He trusts no one and needs no friends, least of all *female* friends: women are trouble in his world, sleek and dangerous, beautiful and deadly. He handles them very carefully.

## First-Person Perspective: Sadism versus Masochism

It is this lonely, isolated perspective on the world that is brought to a head with the first-person voice-over of noir. Of course, it's true: *both* detective forms use a first-person perspective. But there is a key difference: Watson narrates (to us) about the great Sherlock Holmes, while the hard-boiled detective tells the story of his own adventures. And, in hearing these two different styles, we also get different aesthetic *feelings:* for the pleasures of hearing about Holmes are intellectually masochistic, meaning pleasures of being intellectually subordinated (typically for the purpose of learning), while the pleasures of watching the hard-boiled detective are intellectually sadistic, satisfactions derived from imagining ourselves harming others. So, when we read Poe or Conan Doyle, we actually enjoy being shown our own weaknesses in the face of a great master detective (not unlike a student before a great professor).

The technique actually goes back to Plato, who wrote in dialogues. And in most of them the form is the same: Socrates leads his interlocutors through a maze of inquiry, all the while needling them and sort of chastising them for what they don't know about truth, or justice, or beauty, or whatever the matter may be. But, beyond this, Socrates is also telling us, the readers, that we know nothing more than his interlocutors—and seemingly, all at once, we are invited into the intellectually masochistic pleasures of the Platonic dialectic. Similarly, with Watson, his ignorance is ours too: for we follow Watson as he follows Holmes, and we take our intellectual beatings along the way. As Holmes famously, and rather insultingly, puts it: "It's elementary, my dear Watson" (except that Holmes doesn't really say this).[26]

But in noir it is quite different: we identify with the hardened detective because he's just like us, an Everyman, not an "Overman" (in Nietzsche's terms)[27]—as Holmes is sometimes made out to be. And we (similarly) enjoy all his rough sadistic pleasures:[28] telling people off, beating up criminals, and, of course, looking cool doing it. The sadism of the hard-boiled detective is, moreover, fairly explicit. Take, for example, *Murder, My Sweet* (Edward Dmytryk, 1944), in which Ann Grayle (Anne Shirley) tells Marlowe (Dick Powell): "You're vicious. You—you take some horrible sort of satisfaction in seeing people torn apart." Even the *titles* of noir films have a sadistic tone, as Raymond Borde and Étienne Chaumeton write in their *Panorama of American Film Noir:* "[Noir films] sometimes had Sadean titles like *Murder, My Sweet* and *Kiss Me Deadly,* and they tended to be derived from the literature of drugs and alcohol."[29]

Adding to this distinction of perspective, a further contrast arises as to the *motivation* of the detective, classic or hard-boiled. For Holmes and Marlowe do what they do for very different reasons. With regard to the hard-boiled detective, Raymond Chandler sums up his motivation succinctly: Marlowe does it for a fee and nothing else; he's every bit the standard mercenary.[30] Poe's Dupin, however, in strong contrast, does it mainly for the intellectual pleasure. He's more upper class than Marlowe. He comes from a long and aristocratic line, and, even though the wealth is now gone,

## The Detective Model

| CLASSIC: SHERLOCK HOLMES | HARD-BOILED: MARLOWE/SPADE |
| --- | --- |
| Setting: less realistic (can be fantastic) | Setting: always realistic (and urban) |
| Uses drugs (morphine and cocaine) | Uses alcohol (typically bourbon) |
| First-person singular about friend | First-person singular voice-over |
| Mind: two sides (slow-creative vs. fast-precise) | Mind: steady, even |
| Lives with friend (Dr. Watson) | Lives alone, has no friends |
| Femme fatale (anti-Ariadne) nonessential | Femme fatale (anti-Ariadne) essential |
| Method: science of deduction (but is really abduction and musement) | Implicit method: abduction (without musement) |
| Character is intellectual (scholarly) | Character is nonintellectual |
| Natural opponents: Scotland Yard | Natural opponents: city cops |
| Artistic (enjoys music, plays violin) | Nonartistic |
| Well traveled (e.g., knows foreign tattoos) | Not traveled |
| Work is a game ("the game is afoot") | Work is just a job (for fee only) |
| Upper-class tastes and manners | Middle class: an "Everyman" |
| Tall, languid, nonphysical | Shorter, tough, aggressive (fistfights) |
| Link to medicine with Dr. Watson (detective clues like medical symptoms) | Stories are typically nonmedical |
| No regular weapons (save reason) | Carries a gun (and shoots people) |
| Smokes a pipe | Smokes cigarettes |
| Form is masochistic | Form is sadistic |
| Hobbies: beekeeping, violin, drugs (stingers, violin, needles signify precision) | No hobbies (flatter character form) |
| Mannerist maze | Rhizomatic maze |

he never resorts to becoming a mercenary—instead, he lives frugally and focuses on the higher pleasures of the mind.[31] Similarly, with Holmes, detective work is hardly just a job; rather, it's a game, a point made evident in "The Adventure of the Abbey Grange," where Holmes rousts Watson: "'Come, Watson, come!' he cried. 'The game is afoot. Not a word! Into your clothes and come!'"[32]

## Detective Logic: Abduction

This *game* in Holmes is pleasurable specifically because it is *logical*—and *logic,* for Holmes, means traditional "deductive logic," a point that carries over rather well into film noir. Take, for example, *Lady in the Lake,* where

Adrienne Fromsett acknowledges Marlowe's path of reason: "You quickly deduced that I left it [a handkerchief] there. Such great blinding brilliance, Mr. Marlowe." But the question arises, Is it really deduction, or is it just guessing? At least for Holmes, the answer is clear: in chapter 1 of *The Sign of Four,* "The Science of Deduction," Holmes plainly insists: "No, no: I never guess. It is a shocking habit,—destructive to the logical faculty."[33] But, in fact, as many Peirce scholars have pointed out, this is not entirely correct. Marcello Truzzi, for example, writes: "More exactly, Holmes consistently displays what C. S. Peirce has called *abductions*."[34] Abduction is Peirce's term for "the logic of guessing." And *this,* I think, is *also* exactly what we find in the hard-boiled detective. Spade, Marlowe, and Hammer— they all use the method of abduction.[35] And this logic contrasts quite distinctly with deduction (and induction).

Consider the following examples:

*DEDUCTION*
*Rule*      All serious knife wounds result in bleeding.
*Case*      This was a serious knife wound.
∴ *Result*  There was bleeding.

*INDUCTION*
*Case*      This was a serious knife wound.
*Result*    There was bleeding.
∴ *Rule*    All serious knife wounds result in bleeding.

*ABDUCTION*
*Rule*      All serious knife wounds result in bleeding.
*Result*    There was bleeding.
∴ *Case*    This was a serious knife wound.[36]

Induction is basically what we mean when we refer to the *scientific method:* generalizing from a set of cases to a rule about them. Deduction, by contrast, reasons from a given rule to a result and really doesn't tell us anything new. We may, for example, reason from a rule, "All men are mortal," and a case, "Socrates is a man," to the result, "Therefore, Socrates is mortal." But, of course, we already *knew* Socrates was mortal. Here, we're simply demonstrating *why* we know he's mortal—because we know something about *all* men, namely, that they're mortal. But abduction is different. It reasons not to a rule or to a result but to a "case"—and it is *cases* that concern us in detective logic, as in *The Case Book of Sherlock Holmes*. Why do we reason to a case? Well, typically, something is amiss, and we want to know *why*. Nine times out of ten in detective fiction, it's a dead body. And it's the job of the detective to discover whodunit.[37] In doing so, typically he uses abduction, which may also be put like this:

> *ABDUCTION*
> The surprising fact, C, is observed;
> But if A were true, C would be a matter of course;
> Hence, there is reason to suspect that A is true.[38]

Taking Truzzi's example above, the dead body gives us a jolt. And, looking for the cause, we make an abduction. If it were true that this was a knife murder, then C (excessive bleeding, perhaps sliced clothing too) would be a matter of course. Noticing that the corpse does, in fact, have these traits, we guess (perhaps wrongly, but reasonably) that it was, indeed, a knife murder.

Or take another example, this one from *The Third Man*. Martins follows and loses Lime, who disappears into thin air. Martins then consults Major Calloway (Trevor Howard) for help:

> MARTINS: I was on that side. His shadow was on that side. And there are no turnings on either side.
> CALLOWAY: What about the doorways?
> MARTINS: I tell you, I heard him running ahead of me!
> CALLOWAY: Yes, yes, yes. And then he vanished out there, I suppose, with a puff of smoke and like a clap of—

Calloway is thinking now, and *then*, suddenly, *Voilà! He's got it!* The inference looks like this: The surprising fact occurs that Lime disappeared into thin air. But, if it were true that a trapdoor is nearby, then Lime's vanishing would follow. Hence, there is reason to suspect a trapdoor nearby. Halloway then tests his guess and finds that he's right.

### Intoxication in Noir

Of course, sometimes the cases are much more difficult than these. And logic alone may not help us. So, characteristically, the detective will rely on unconventional tools to help in achieving the abduction. Now, I noted earlier that Chaumeton and Borde think that film noir derives from the "literature of drugs and alcohol." This is partly correct, although there's a little more to it than that. In fact, intoxication is essential to the detective's method. Remember Watson's introduction to "The Science of Deduction"—well, oddly enough, instead of logical syllogisms, Watson actually launches into a study of Holmes's drug habit. Watson says: "'Which is it to-day,' I asked, 'morphine or cocaine?'"[39] In mulling over a difficult case, Holmes will sink into a dreamy, lounging state, often for hours at a time, and *then*, of a sudden, he will burst up with the solution. This same method appears in Dupin as well—and Peirce, in his own comments on Poe, calls this method *musement*, which he defines as the "pure play" of the mind.[40] It is this capacity for musement, according to Peirce, that is so essential to abduction. As Peirce puts it, "Those problems that at first blush appear utterly insoluble receive, in that very circumstance,—as Edgar Poe remarked in his 'The Murders in the Rue Morgue,'—their smoothly-fitting keys. This particularly adapts them to the Play of Musement."[41] Effectively, the contemplative musing state *rearranges* the clues in a new, enlightening order so that the abduction may appear in a flash.

We find this vague and dreamy (often intoxicated) state in all good detective fiction—and certainly this includes film noir as well. Of course, typically in noir the drug of choice is alcohol, and noir detectives drink as a rule (although they are often drugged as well). For example, in *Kiss Me Deadly* (Robert Aldrich, 1955), Mike Hammer (Ralph Meeker) enters the bar and says: "Give me a double bourbon, and leave the bottle." Now, the noir detective, when he's hot on the trail, usually remains pretty sober. But, when stumped or at a standstill, he'll want to calm his nerves with a drink. At first blush, this looks quite a bit like the method established in Poe and Conan Doyle. But, on closer analysis, it's not entirely clear *how* integral the intoxicated state is to the hard-boiled detective's method. It seems to be just on the side (just something he happens to do). In fact, there's really *nothing* in classic detective noir that resembles Holmes's approach, in which he first gathers clues, then induces intoxication (to rearrange the clues), only to emerge from La-La Land to say with cold, hard eyes: "*I've got it!*" Nor (as I noted earlier) is there anything languid and "lying around" about the hard-boiled detective, listening to classical music, and allowing the mind to play freely, in order to discover the killer. And *this* (in my opinion) is the greatest weakness in the film noir genre. Of course, to be fair, it's true that some neo-noir films *do* make the right link. For example, in the Hughes brothers' *From Hell* (2001), the detective Fred Abberline (Johnny Depp) solves the mystery of the identity of Jack the Ripper by way of opium and absinthe: once in a hallucinatory state, he sees visions of the murders of prostitutes and gradually solves the case. But, in classic noir, it's a miss.

## The Anti-Ariadne and Her String

Alternatively, however, film noir appears to get the femme fatale of classic detective fiction just right. No longer the loving Ariadne who helps Theseus with the string, she is the anti-Ariadne, and she comes clearly into focus in Conan Doyle's "The Disappearance of Lady Frances Carfax." As Watson relates: "Holmes leaned back in his armchair and took his notebook from his pocket. 'One of the most dangerous classes in the world,' said he, 'is the drifting and friendless woman. She is the most harmless and often the most useful of mortals, but she is the inevitable inciter of crime in others. . . . She is lost, as often as not, in a maze of obscure pensions and boarding houses.'"[42] Once a light at the end of the maze, Ariadne is now just one more flickering flash among unlimited simulacra—and the string that she holds out to the detective is typically just long enough to hang him. Here is the origin of the noir femme fatale and so many of her "class," as Holmes puts it.

In *Kiss Me Deadly,* for example, Velda (Maxine Cooper) warns Hammer about finding the Ariadne's string: "First you find a little thread. The little thread leads you to a string. And the string leads you to a rope. And from the rope you hang by the neck." Velda is right: Hammer does "pick up the thread," as he puts it, and, ultimately, it leads to death at the hands of the two-faced Minotaur, Lily Carver, who is really Gabrielle (Gaby Rodgers). Gabrielle has plotted to possess a special box, a Pandora's box, and she desperately wants to know what's inside. Hammer warns her not to open it. But she simply cannot help herself—slowly, she opens it, and suddenly a screaming white light, which burns her alive, and then *wham!* a nuclear explosion.

Indeed, the once-so-valuable Ariadne's string is always dangerous in film noir. And so many noir films make this point explicitly. In Alfred Hitchcock's *Rope* (1948), for example, the detective/professor (James Stewart) discovers the (Ariadne's) rope used to hang his former student. The point also emerges very nicely in *To Have and Have Not* (Howard Hawks, 1944), where Marie/Slim (Lauren Bacall) walks around Harry Morgan/Steve (Humphrey Bogart) and Harry asks her: "Find anything?"

Slim says: "No. No Steve. There are no strings tied to you. Not yet." And then, soon after, Slim warns him: "Look out for those strings, Steve. You're liable to trip and break your neck."[43]

She knows it—the string of signs is dangerous. And, if he follows the clues, he might hang. Part of the problem is that the clues are never so obvious— they can lead us so easily astray. And this has largely to do with the nature of clues, which are defined by Eco (drawing on Peirce again) as one among three different kinds of detective signs: *imprints, symptoms,* and *clues.* All these detective signs are physically made (or what Peirce calls *indexical* signs). Imprints have a one-to-one connection: the footprint looks exactly like the foot. Symptoms, by contrast, lack this point-to-point relation but are made directly to appear by their cause; as Eco puts it: "Red spots on the face mean measles." And, finally, clues are "objects left by an external agent in the spot where it did something, and are somehow recognized as physically linked to that agent." Here, it is "agents" (persons with motives) who may or may not have "done it"—and *this,* according to Eco, is "why a criminal novel is usually more intriguing than the detection of pneumonia."[44]

With this in mind, let's now consider the matter of who killed Chris Lavery (Dick Simmons) in *Lady in the Lake.* Marlowe has some clues: an empty gun found by Mrs. Fallbrook and a handkerchief from Lavery's apartment with the initials "AF," as in Adrienne Fromsett:

> FROMSETT: You went to see Lavery?
> MARLOWE: And found him dead.
> FROMSETT: I repeatedly told you not to go see Lavery.
> MARLOWE: What brand of perfume do you wear? Do you recognize it? The initials are AF.
> FROMSETT: I don't have to ask the obvious question, do I?
> MARLOWE: I found it on the dresser in Lavery's bedroom.
> FROMSETT: And you quickly deduced that I left it there. Such great, blinding brilliance, Mr. Marlowe. What am I supposed to say now? Did you bring a confession for me to sign?
> MARLOWE: No, I just thought you'd like to have your handkerchief back.

Clearly Marlowe suspects Fromsett—but not for very long. After mulling it over, Marlowe rethinks his original inference about Fromsett: "Maybe a woman didn't do it . . . Maybe it was arranged to look that way." The evidence is simply too damning. So Marlowe makes a new abduction. If it were true that someone framed Fromsett, then a startling amount of evidence might be found against her (more than a rational killer would leave), which there is—so maybe Fromsett didn't kill Lavery. And, in fact, it was Mildred Havelend, masquerading as Mrs. Fallbrook.

## No Way Out of the Noir Maze

Of course, as I said, *Lady in the Lake* ends better than it should have and borders on a mannerist maze. But, for the most part, noir films end badly and typically emphasize a fundamental inescapability indicative of the rhizomatic maze. *The Third Man* does this perfectly. And *The Maltese Falcon* (John Huston, 1941) nails it as well. Spade (Bogart) turns in the woman he wants for killing his partner. And when he finally discovers the statue of the falcon—after so many people have been killed—he realizes it's a fake (and is obviously amused), just one more illusion leading back into the labyrinth. It's the same with *Kiss Me Deadly*—perfectly rhizomatic. Gabrielle simply must open the box, killing herself, and blowing up the cottage. Of course, whether Hammer (now shot by Gabrielle) actually dies is left open. So the original ending of that film is better: just the explosion, everyone still in the beach cottage, dead, and then "THE END." Indeed, in virtually all great noir films, the detective will pick up the Ariadne's thread of clues and solve the case—he may even slay a fleeting representation of the Minotaur. But the case of all cases, the dark maze of being, simply has no secret escape hatch, no solution at all. And the hard-boiled detective knows as much—and self-consciously accepts his own isolated fate in the unlimited rhizomatic labyrinth of evil.

## Notes

I am very grateful to Mark Conard and Elizabeth Cooke for reading and commenting on an earlier draft of this essay. I am also grateful to Richard White and Clarinda Karpov for conversations on the relation between Shakespeare and Sherlock Holmes and to Chris Pliatska for conversations on *The Third Man*.

The epigraph to this essay is taken from Jorge Luis Borges, "The Immortal," in *Collected Fictions*, trans. Andrew Hurley (New York: Penguin, 1999), 189.

1. Thomas Bulfinch, *Bulfinch's Mythology* (New York: Random House/Modern Library, 1934), 125.

2. Sir Arthur Conan Doyle, *The Sign of Four,* in *The Complete Sherlock Holmes* (hereafter *CSH*) (New York: Barnes & Noble, 1992), 116.

3. In *The Sign of Four,* Watson explains that he and Holmes are caught in a "labyrinth of streets" (*CSH,* 99). He also talks in *The Sign of Four* about "a perfect labyrinth of landing-places for miles" and "a labyrinth of passages and corridors"; in "The Red-Headed League" about "an endless labyrinth of gas-lit streets until we emerged into Farrington Street"; in "The Adventure of the Blue Carbuncle" about "the labyrinth of small streets which lie at the back of Tottenham Court Road"; and in "The Adventure of the Engineer's Thumb" about "a labyrinth of an old house, with corridors, passages, narrow winding staircases, and little low doors" (*CSH,* 125, 147, 187, 245, 281).

4. *CSH,* 492. For further analysis of labyrinths and detective stories, see John T. Irwin, *The Mystery to a Solution: Poe, Borges, and the Analytic Detective Story* (Baltimore: Johns Hopkins University Press, 1994), and Dale Keiger, "A Sleuth in the Garden of Forking Paths," *Johns Hopkins Magazine: Electronic Edition,* April 1995, http://www.jhu.edu/~jhumag/495web/sleuth.html (accessed May 11, 2005).

5. See the postscript to Umberto Eco, *The Name of the Rose* (1980), trans. William Weaver (New York: Harcourt Brace, 1984), 524–55.

6. Foster Hirsch, *The Dark Side of the Screen: Film Noir* (1981), with a new introduction by the author (New York: Da Capo, 2001), 169 (see also 122).

7. Nicholas Christopher, *Somewhere in the Night: Film Noir and the American City* (New York: Free Press, 1997), 16, 17 (quotation).

8. Eco, *The Name of the Rose,* 525. Following Eco, I'll use the terms *labyrinth* and *maze* interchangeable, to set up his account. Jeff Saward claims that a labyrinth has only one pathway and a maze many (see Jeff Saward, *Labyrinths and Mazes* [New York: Lark, 2003], and "Introduction to the Typology of Labyrinths and Mazes," http://www.labyrinthos.net/typology.htm [accessed May 11, 2005]).

9. Umberto Eco, *Semiotics and the Philosophy of Language* (Bloomington: Indiana University Press, 1984), 81–82.

10. Penelope Reed Doob, *The Idea of the Labyrinth from Classical Antiquity through the Middle Ages* (Ithaca, NY: Cornell University Press, 1990).

11. Eco, *Semiotics and the Philosophy of Language,* 81 (emphasis added).

12. In fact, Peirce even sketched a picture of this labyrinth of signs, reproduced as "Peirce's Representation of the Labyrinth of Signs" in Joseph Brent, *Peirce: A Life* (1993; Bloomington: Indiana University Press, 1998), 310. Peirce also writes: "We find ourselves in the vestibule of the labyrinth. Yes, The Labyrinth—in the Vestibule only, but yet in that tremendous, only Labyrinth" (*The Collected Papers of Charles Sanders Peirce,* ed. C. Hartshorne, P. Weiss, and A. Burks, 8 vols. [Cambridge, MA: Harvard University Press, 1958], vol. 2, p. 42, par. 79).

13. Eco, postscript to *The Name of the Rose,* 525, and *Semiotics and the Philosophy of Language,* 80–82.

14. See Gilles Deleuze and Félix Guattari, *A Thousand Plateaus: Capitalism and*

*Schizophrenia* (1987), trans. Brian Massumi (Minneapolis: University of Minnesota Press, 2002), 21 (see generally 3–25). As Deleuze and Guattari put it: "A rhizome ceaselessly establishes connections between semiotic chains, organizations of power, and circumstances relative to the arts, sciences, and social struggles" (ibid., 7).

15. Eco also points out that "the universe of semiosis [i.e., the flow of signs through the mind] can be postulated in the format of a labyrinth" (*Semiotics and the Philosophy of Language*, 2).

16. For an excellent analysis of the differences between the film *Lady in the Lake* and the novel—and there are plenty of differences—see Stephen Pendo, *Raymond Chandler on Screen: His Novels into Film* (Metuchen, NJ: Scarecrow, 1976), esp. 63–85.

17. In the science fiction neo-noir film *I, Robot* (Alex Proyas, 2004), the detective (Will Smith) is repeatedly told to think of the story of "Hansel and Gretel" (to pick up the string of clues).

18. Hirsch, too, recognizes in noir "the labyrinthine underground of urban crime and of the criminal mentality" (*Dark Side of the Screen*, 67).

19. Eco, postscript to *The Name of the Rose*, 526.

20. For Christopher's analysis of the maze in *The Third Man*, see *Somewhere in the Night*, 71–75.

21. Robert Porfirio, "No Way Out: Existential Motifs in the *Film Noir*" (1976), in *Film Noir Reader*, ed. Alain Silver and James Ursini (1996; New York: Limelight, 2003), 90.

22. *The Third Man* is an exception here, as I'll soon point out: Calloway is a better detective than Martins.

23. Edgar Allan Poe, "The Murders in the Rue Morgue," in *The Complete Tales and Poems of Edgar Allan Poe* (New York: Vintage/Random House, 1935), 144.

24. Of Conan Doyle's debt to Poe, Nancy Harrowitz says: "Dupin, in solving this his first crime, sets up a distinct methodology and philosophy of crime detection which became famous and is still used today in crime fiction. In fact, most of the principles of Dupin's method were lifted outright by Conan Doyle and immortalized in his creation of Sherlock Holmes" ("The Body of the Detective Model: Charles S. Peirce and Edgar Allan Poe," in *The Sign of Three: Dupin, Holmes, Peirce*, ed. Umberto Eco and Thomas Sebeok [Bloomington: Indiana University Press, 1983], 193). See also *A Study in Scarlet*, where Watson says to Holmes: "You remind me of Edgar Allan Poe's Dupin. I had no idea that such individuals did exist outside of stories" (*CSH*, 24).

25. As Hirsch so aptly puts it: "Usually reflective and commonsensical, the voice-over narrator is our guide through the noir labyrinth" (*Dark Side of the Screen*, 75).

26. Thomas Sebeok and Jean Umiker-Sebeok write that, with regard to the sentence "Simple deduction my dear Watson" (commonly attributed to Holmes), "Holmes never uttered the words cited; nor did Holmes ever say, 'Elementary, my dear Watson'" ("'You Know My Method': A Juxtaposition of Charles S. Peirce and Sherlock Holmes," in Eco and Sebeok, *The Sign of Three*, 49 n. 7).

27. *"I teach you the Overman. Man is something that shall be overcome"* (Friedrich Nietzsche, *Thus Spoke Zarathustra*, in *The Portable Nietzsche*, ed. and trans. Walter Kaufmann [New York: Penguin, 1954], 124).

28. An excellent study of the concepts of sadism and masochism (as well as their use in literary voice) is found in Gilles Deleuze, *Masochism*, trans. Jean McNeil (New York: Zone Books, 1991). Deleuze writes that sadism and masochism can be seen even in "the differences in the literary techniques and in the art of Sade and Masoch" (134).

29. Raymond Borde and Étienne Chaumeton, *A Panorama of American Film Noir (1941–1953)* (1955), trans. Paul Hammond (San Francisco: City Lights, 2002), xii.

30. Raymond Chandler, one of the fathers of the hard-boiled detective, lays bare the character's form in a letter: "His moral intellectual force is that he gets nothing but his fee" (Chandler to James Sandoe, May 12, 1949, in *The Raymond Chandler Papers: Selected Letters and Nonfiction, 1909–1959*, ed. Tom Hiney and Frank MacShane [New York: Atlantic Monthly Press, 2000], 114–15).

31. Poe, "The Murders in the Rue Morgue," 143.

32. *CSH*, 636. It should be noted that the line "The game is afoot" first appears in Shakespeare's *Henry V*, act 3, scene 1. I am grateful to Richard White and Clarinda Karpov for pointing this out to me.

33. *CSH*, 93.

34. Marcello Truzzi, "Sherlock Holmes: Applied Social Psychologist," in Eco and Sebeok, *The Sign of Three*, 69.

35. Peirce credits Aristotle, *Prior Analytics*, bk. 2, chap. 25. Of course, there are problems with abduction, even as a form of logic. In fact, some versions of it commit the logical fallacy of affirming the consequent. Nevertheless, according to Peirce, abduction is the fundamental mode by which the mind works—and works very well, especially when it comes to detective work.

36. I get this excellent example (which describes Peirce's logic) from Truzzi, "Sherlock Holmes," 69. I've made only one small emendation to Truzzi's account: he has deduction proceeding from case to rule (just a minor typographical error in the original text).

37. Peirce, who was (at least once) a practicing detective, used this method of abduction to discover the thief of his watch. But, much more famously, he placed this logic at the center of his great contribution to philosophy—really America's main contribution to philosophy—commonly called pragmatism.

38. Peirce, *Collected Papers*, vol. 5, p. 117, par. 189.

39. *CSH*, 89.

40. As Harrowitz puts it: "The parallels between Peirce's abduction and the play of musement and Poe's ratiocination are clear" ("The Body of the Detective Model," 193). On the musement-abduction relation in Peirce and Holmes, see Sebeok and Umiker-Sebeok, "'You Know My Method,'" esp. 26–27.

41. Charles S. Peirce, *The Essential Peirce: Selected Philosophical Writings*, vol. 2,

*1893–1913*, ed. Peirce Edition Project (Bloomington: Indiana University Press, 1998), 439.

42. *CSH*, 943.

43. I am grateful to Mark Conard for pointing out this example to me in conversation.

44. Umberto Eco, "Horns, Hooves, Insteps," in Eco and Sebeok, *The Sign of Three*, 211–12.

# PART 2

## Existentialism and Nihilism in Film Noir

# Film Noir and the Meaning of Life

*Steven M. Sanders*

Film noir is a fabric woven out of many threads. Its various styles, themes, motifs, and forms make it a complex and contested cultural phenomenon. I suspect that many readers of this volume would agree that they know film noir when they see it even though they cannot define the term *film noir* per se. While doubts persist about definition,[1] we can say with some confidence that film noir raises important questions about life's meaning. My aim here is to examine some of these questions and, thus, to use film noir to motivate philosophical thinking about the meaning of life.

A useful place to begin is with the observation by Robert Porfirio that film noir sensibility is an "underlying mood of pessimism which undercuts any attempted happy endings" and "nothing less than an existential attitude towards life."[2] Porfirio suggests the ease and plausibility with which one might string a large number of film noir pearls on an existentialist thread. But what *is* this existential attitude of which he speaks? If it is a pessimistic way of looking at the world, how is it embodied in film noir, and is such an attitude justified?

My discussion will begin with a pan and scan of noir themes. Then I will create a kind of storyboard of film noir's philosophical presuppositions with sketches of meaningless existence, pessimism, the human condition, and freedom and fatalism. Next, I will provide three models of meaninglessness as bases for understanding claims about life's meaning. Finally, I will raise some questions about the attitude we should take toward life as such.

## Noir Themes

It will be helpful to describe those features that appear widely in film noir even if such a characterization lacks the precision of a set of necessary and sufficient conditions.

Noir themes and moods include despair, paranoia, and nihilism; an atmosphere of claustrophobic entrapment; a nightmarish sense of loneliness and alienation; a purposelessness fostered in part by feelings of estrangement from one's own past even as one seems driven to a compulsive confrontation with that past. Film noir presents us with moral ambiguity, shifting identities, and impending doom. Urban locales give noir films authenticity, adding texture to their psychologically dense and convoluted plots.[3]

To get down to cases, film noir is the corrupt detective Hank Quinlan (Orson Welles) in *Touch of Evil* (Orson Welles, 1958) asking the brothel owner Madame Tanya (Marlene Dietrich) to tell his fortune and being told: "You haven't got any . . . your future is all used up." It is the gangster Johnny Rico (James Darren) in *The Brothers Rico* (Phil Karlson, 1957) telling his brother Eddie (Richard Conte): "Maybe I'm gonna die. You've got even bigger problems—you're gonna live." It is the nightclub piano player Al Roberts (Tom Neal) in *Detour* (Edgar G. Ulmer, 1945) saying: "That's life. Whichever way you turn, fate sticks out a foot to trip you." It is the mob lawyer Joe Morse (John Garfield) in *Force of Evil* (Abraham Polonsky, 1948) admitting: "I wasn't strong enough to resist corruption, but I was strong enough to fight for a piece of it." And we know that we are at the center of the gathering forces of film noir's psychological storm when the private eye Jeff Bailey (Robert Mitchum), reflecting on his obsession with femme fatale Kathie Moffat (Jane Greer) in *Out of the Past* (Jacques Tourneur, 1947), says: "I never saw her in the daytime. We seemed to live by night. What was left of the day went away like a pack of cigarettes you smoked."[4]

There is an "underlying mood of pessimism" in all this, to be sure. When we think of the typical film noir outlook, we may think first of a bewildering admixture of alienation, betrayal, desperation, and fear, underscored by odd angles, chiaroscuro visuals, and voice-over narrations. But it is not merely that these films play out dramas that undercut "any attempted happy endings." Nor is it simply a display of the vulnerable private eye confronting danger, corruption, and murder. The typical film noir protagonist, so often in the grip of desperate emotional needs and sexual desire (as typified by encounters with the femme fatale), must act against a backdrop of human duplicity and the threat of imminent death. There is the hand of the past wrenching his life from its present moorings, which may themselves already be unstable. Noir characters seem ever on the run (sometimes literally, sometimes only from themselves), the most hapless of them caught in frames and webs and structures with no escape. Above all, film noir depicts a world of characters trapped in circumstances that they did not wholly create and from which they cannot break free, characters hopelessly isolated and all but immobilized in moral dilemmas whose implications they must follow out, as it were, to the end of the night.

## Philosophical Presuppositions

Despite the affinity of film noir with existentialist themes, it would be a mistake to suppose that American film noir was directly influenced by the work of existentialist philosophers. Although both Albert Camus and Jean-Paul Sartre explored with great intensity in novels and plays those strains in the human condition that give rise to questions of meaning and purpose and how one should live, there is nothing like a direct connection between these writers and noir filmmakers. But, if explicit connections to philosophers are lacking in film noir, the same need not be said of the philosophical ideas and attitudes that these films *presuppose* and without which much of their cachet would be lost. Perhaps we can identify some philosophically salient element that goes beyond noir's inversion of the American dream and that puts the *noir* in film noir. I want to suggest that film noir presupposes something general that gives it its philosophical interest: a metaphysical and moral atmosphere that is the basis of *all* its protagonists' problems and anxieties rather than a specific anxiety or difficulty. The thread running through the design of film noir is the sense that life is meaningless per se, not that one life just *happens* to be going wrong for the time being and in one particular respect. The philosophically most prominent feature of film noir, then, is its portrayal of the problematic fabric of life as such. In this respect, every noir film thrusts its protagonist into crisis because of the very character of life itself.

### MEANINGLESS EXISTENCE

In situating film noir in a context of anxiety about life's meaning, we should keep in mind that many of film noir's most memorable protagonists are in extremis: Frank Bigelow (Edmond O'Brien), an accountant dying from the irreversible effects of poison, explains his "murder" to the police even as (in flashback) he seeks to confront his killer (*D.O.A.*, Rudolph Maté, 1950); a corpse (William Holden), floating facedown in the swimming pool of a famous former Hollywood silent picture star (Gloria Swanson), narrates the strange turn of events that has brought him to this fate (*Sunset Boulevard*, Billy Wilder, 1950); Jeff Bailey (Robert Mitchum), an ex–private detective, spills his guts to his fiancée about his sordid past, only to wind up recapitulating those very mistakes that bring him to the edge of a personal abyss (*Out of the Past*); a former police detective (James Stewart) falls in love with a woman he has been following at the behest of her husband, loses her to (what he believes is) suicide, and spends his days transforming another woman into the image of his lost love. "Judy, please, it can't matter to you," Scottie Ferguson implores the shopgirl Judy Barton (Kim Novak) as he supervises her complete makeover into the woman of his obsession (*Vertigo*, Alfred Hitchcock, 1958).

It may seem odd to suggest that the preoccupations of the characters portrayed by Edmond O'Brien, William Holden, Robert Mitchum, and James Stewart—no-nonsense guys who give every indication that they know who they are and what they are about—have anything to do with the meaning of life. But this oddness can be traced to the widespread misconception that questions of life's meaning are transcendental concerns, that is, questions exclusively about otherworldly meaning, plans, or purposes, or that they concern how our life plans are to be subsumed by, in the words of Thomas Nagel, "a single controlling life scheme," such as the greater glory of God.[5] Leaving aside the psychological appeal of such a meaning-conferring structure, this orientation to questions of life's meaning is remote from film noir's thematic background, where any conceivable otherworldly answers to questions about how to live and what to do are ruled out.

## PESSIMISTIC ARGUMENTS

Philosophers have raised a variety of considerations to support pessimistic conclusions about the meaning of life. Let us look at a few of the most influential ones.

The notion *meaning* can be understood in more than one way. In fact, philosophers have discussed the meaning of life by concerning themselves less with the "positive" concept of meaning than with those general features of human existence that contribute to *lack* or *loss* of meaning. This approach reaches the peak of its perfection in the pessimistic writings of Arthur Schopenhauer (1788–1860), who mounted a devastating campaign against the Enlightenment ideals of human progress, happiness, and perfectibility. "The vanity of existence," he writes, "is revealed in the whole form existence assumes . . . in the contingency and relativity of all things;

in continual becoming without being; in continual desire without satisfaction; in the continual frustration of striving of which life consists."[6] Here, Schopenhauer cites those very features of the human condition that pessimism takes as its point of departure.

Given the transitory nature of all things, the perishability through death of all our achievements, "nothing at all is worth our striving." As we saw Schopenhauer arguing above, life is by its very nature impermanent and transitory, contingent and relative, consisting of continual desire without satisfaction, striving without fulfillment. Moreover, Schopenhauer presents a "moral" critique, one that fastens on the vanity of human wishes, on the spectacle of human folly and wickedness, on the unceasing struggle against boredom, and, more ominously, on the ill will, malice, and cruelty of other people, whom Schopenhauer likens to a "den of sharks and swindlers."[7]

Insofar as Schopenhauer's pessimism is put forward as being in some sense justified and not merely the expression of a mood or feeling, it is appropriate to seek reasons for such conclusions. Some of his reasons derive from his metaphysical system and are unconvincing without it. Others, such as his claim that "that which in a moment ceases to exist [i.e., the present], which vanishes as completely as in a dream, cannot be worth any serious effort," are value judgments with which reasonable people may disagree.[8] Still others are highly general empirical observations, as with his reflections on the essential aimlessness of life, one random event following another for no apparent purpose and ending in death. Pessimists frequently invoke the fact of death to convey the idea that all life is pointless activity coming to nothing. Our successes and achievements, such as they are, do not remove the meaninglessness from our lives because our successes are transitory and fade, our achievements are themselves impermanent and do not last. Think of the ways in which people put countless years of effort into their loves, friendships, and family lives, their education, jobs, and careers—and for what? All of it is a Sisyphean effort leading nowhere and ending in death. Of course, one may have some good effect on the lives of others one cares about, but that serves only to illustrate the pointlessness of it all, for they too will die.

Several types of reply can be made to arguments such as these. A traditional religious response, with its promise of an afterlife and heavenly reward, may satisfy some, but it does not have universal appeal and raises significant problems of its own. In any event, as I have already indicated, it is not the way of noir. Others, such as Thomas Nagel, have argued that, if nothing we do now will matter in a million years, then by the same token nothing that will be the case in a million years matters now.[9] It simply does not matter *now* that in a million years nothing that we do now will matter: how could not mattering in a million years prevent composing a piece of beautiful music from mattering *now?* Furthermore, it does not appear that one *needs* some additional justification for keeping up one's health, reading a novel one enjoys, or pursuing a satisfying career. No comprehensive plan or purpose that ties up all our everyday activities into a neat package is necessary to give them meaning.

## THE HUMAN CONDITION

The fact, however, that the standard pessimistic arguments fail to establish the meaninglessness of life may not dispel the sense of doom that makes film noir *noir*. To explain this, I must turn first to accounts of the human condition and then to the conflict between freedom and fatalism.

Almost without exception, film noir drama is enacted against a secular backdrop; noir characters are typically depicted as living in a godless world. Belief in God and an afterlife are seldom part of the noir protagonist's backstory, and religion is rarely, if ever, invoked as providing solace for or solutions to the problems he or she must face. Film noir's moral universe is filled with psychologically flawed characters: there is a penchant for shyster lawyers, bought-and-paid-for politicians, cops on the take, down-at-the-heels private detectives, businessmen on the skids, prison escapees, ex-cons, psycho killers, party girls, drifters, opportunists, victims, and any number of ethically compromised antiheroes.

The implicit link between narrative strategies employed in film noir (with its extensive use of voice-over, flashbacks, dream sequences, and other experimental narrative devices) and the human condition that it depicts is no coincidence. A *way of seeing* the world becomes a *feature of* the world: film noir makes the defamiliarization of life the fabric of life itself. Thus, as countless instances have memorably illustrated, what emerges from even a remote acquaintance with film noir is a depiction of the human condition in which scenes may begin realistically but quickly veer into surrealism or the absurd, especially when people are shown at the edge of their own desperation. Characters in film noir have a tendency to be dependent on others (think of the greed that binds Brigid O'Shaughnessy, Kasper Gutman, and Joel Cairo in *The Maltese Falcon* [John Huston, 1941]), to be vulnerable to their whims and irrationalities as well as their charms (as the insurance salesman Walter Neff is to the murderous Phyllis Dietrichson in *Double Indemnity* [Billy Wilder, 1944]), or to be in competition with them (the magazine editor George Stroud vs. the publishing magnate Earl Janoth in *The Big Clock* [John Farrow, 1948], the Mexican narcotics investigator "Mike" Vargas vs. the corrupt police chief Hank Quinlan in *Touch of Evil*)— so much so that they are hostage to the malevolence of those whose ill will, while perhaps not inevitable, is almost certainly forthcoming. ("It's what people want and how hard they try to get it," the Van Heflin character says as he tries to explain the corruption, misery, and suffering he has witnessed, and, by the end of *The Strange Love of Martha Ivers* [Lewis Milestone, 1946], he has witnessed plenty.)

## FREEDOM AND FATALISM

A major challenge to any attempt to interpret film noir along strict existentialist lines can be summarized in one word: fatalism. While existentialism's emphasis is on each person's freedom to create his or her own values, film noir offers us a compelling look at the sources of *constraint* on human choice, with particular emphasis on the fatalistic reach of the past. In this fatalism toward life, film noir makes its most dramatic departure from existentialism. The existentialists sought liberation from the gray determinism of their time through highly individualized styles of thought and action in which existential choice was the ultimate redemptive act. As Jean-Paul Sartre writes in *Being and Nothingness:* "For human reality, to be is to choose oneself."[10]

The idea that one often has to choose what to do, and is able to do so, is uncontroversial. However, the existentialist doctrine that our every act is freedom affirming and a choice of ourselves is, clearly, *not* uncontroversial.[11] It is, rather, a highly debatable assertion, one that some philosophers have taken pains to reject because the role of autonomy within the ambit of a person's motivational structure is far from obvious. "It is by no means clear," writes Frederick A. Olafson in his study of existentialism and ethics, "that we can *choose* to love or to trust another human being," although we can choose to do the things that are the natural expressions of love and trust.[12] Nor is it so very obvious that we can freely choose to prefer pleasure to pain or, in general, to choose to experience the world as having both spatial and temporal structure.[13] These appear to be givens, not matters of choice at all. It seems fair to say that there are greater limitations on the things a person can decide or choose to do than the existentialist view acknowledges.

And now we are in a position to see that existentialist freedom is nothing less than the pulled thread in film noir's Freudian fabric, which treats the far-reaching effects of the past (*The Dark Past,* Rudolph Maté, 1948), psychosexual dislocation (*Vertigo*), and psychopathology in general (*Undercurrent,* Vincente Minnelli, 1946) in ways very different from, if not, indeed, inconsistent with, existentialism's emphasis on free choice. How *can* one's criminality, for instance, be the result of free and conscious choice if, at the same time, one is a product of, in the words of Spencer Selby, "the deterministic tyranny of that past" over which one had no control?[14] It is precisely for this reason that film noir exploits the voice-over, confessional flashback: the technique provides the kind of narrative closure that mirrors film noir's inherent fatalism. The viewer thus knows the ending to come in these films because the future is prefigured in the past.[15]

## Three Models of Meaninglessness

Different conceptions of meaninglessness provide models by which we can enhance our understanding of the concept. Philosophers have elaborated at least three such models: worthlessness, purposelessness, and absurdity.

### WORTHLESSNESS

The first model, worthlessness, is suggested by Kurt Baier, who maintains that, by using the criteria of unhappiness, pain, and suffering, we can compare the life of this person and that and judge which is more or less worthwhile, which has a greater balance of suffering over bliss. The standard for judging lives is "the average of the kind," a comparatively worthless life being one that falls far below the average of its kind with respect to the balance of happiness over unhappiness, pleasure over pain, and bliss over suffering: "When we ask whether a given life was or was not worthwhile, then we must take into consideration the range of worthwhileness which ordinary lives normally cover. Our end poles of the scale must be the best possible and worst possible life that one finds. A good and worthwhile life is one that is well above average. A bad one is one well below."[16]

Baier is obviously thinking of such judgments as falling on a continuum: on the scale of worthwhileness, approximately half of us live lives that are above the average, half below the average. (As a matter of logic, we cannot all be above average, any more than we can all be below average.) On this model, meaninglessness is not all or nothing but, rather, more or less, and meaninglessness might well be mitigated by doing things to increase one's balance of happiness, pleasure, and bliss over unhappiness, pain, and suffering, as characters in film noir often try to do through a variety of (mostly illegal) schemes. "I can see you're a man who likes his pleasures," the cabdriver Franz says in *The Asphalt Jungle* (John Huston, 1950) to the fleeing ex-con Doc Riedenschneider, who has masterminded an elaborate robbery and hopes to escape to Mexico to live the good life. "Well, Franz," Doc replies, "what else is there in life, I ask you?" Of course, noir being noir, everything comes unhinged for Doc and his accomplices, who are either caught or killed in the end.

*PURPOSELESSNESS*

The second model, purposelessness, is also suggested by Baier, who distinguishes between two senses of *purpose*, one that applies normally to persons, one that applies normally to things. On the one hand, we can think of the many things a person can do, "such as buying and selling, hiring labourers, ploughing, felling trees, and the like," that "it is foolish, pointless, silly, perhaps crazy, to do if one has no purpose in doing them": "Lives crammed full with such activities devoid of purpose are pointless. . . . Such lives may indeed be dismissed as meaningless." On the other hand, there is the sense in which having or lacking a purpose is attributed to things, such as a row of trees or a pile of rocks. Such things may have (or not have) a purpose depending on whether they have (or have not) been put to use by those who have purposes of their own, in the first sense of *purpose:* "A row of trees growing near a farm may or may not have a purpose: it may or may not be a windbreak, may or may not have been planted or deliberately left standing there in order to prevent the wind from sweeping across the fields. We do not in any case disparage the trees if we say they have no purpose, but have just grown that way. They are as beautiful, made of as good wood, as valuable, as if they had a purpose."[17]

Lacking a purpose, in the second sense of the term, means (according to both Baier and the existentialists) that no purpose has been *allotted* to us by anyone—and especially not by a supreme being to whom we uniquely owe love, veneration, and obedience. Having no purpose, goal, or destiny in this sense shows only that, if life is to have meaning, that meaning will not be imposed on us by any external agency. If (the) meaninglessness (of life) is a matter of pointlessness or a lack of purpose in the latter sense, that does not imply meaninglessness in the former sense: one's life can have meaning in the sense that one might have a purpose (or many purposes) *in* one's life even if one's life (as a whole or in part) does not *serve* anyone else's purpose. Of course, even *self*-imposed purposes are no guarantee of meaningfulness. Something of the idea of such activity to no apparent point or result is suggested by the quest for the Maltese Falcon, "the stuff dreams are made of." For, while Kasper Gutman and Joel Cairo have *their* purposes in seeking the statuette, their efforts come to nothing in the end.

## ABSURDITY

The third model, absurdity, recalls the reflections of Albert Camus on the failure of the universe to fulfill our expectations and needs and Thomas Nagel's idea of "the collision between the seriousness with which we take our lives and the perpetual possibility of regarding everything about which we are serious as arbitrary, or open to doubt." According to Nagel, the absurdity of the human condition consists in just this incongruity between the seriousness with which we view ourselves and the "longer view" from which we are as nothing, grains of sand on an infinitely vast desert, instants on an incomprehensible cosmic clock: "Reference to our small size and short lifespan and to the fact that all of mankind will eventually perish without a trace are metaphors for the backward step which permits us to regard ourselves from without and to find the particular form of our lives curious and slightly surprising." What, then, does Nagel recommend? Neither anger, nor resentment, nor escape, nor scorn, but an ironic acceptance of the absurdity that "is one of the most human things about us": "If a sense of the absurd is a way of perceiving our true situation . . . then what reason can we have to resent or escape it? . . . We can approach our absurd lives with irony instead of heroism or despair."[18]

According to Joel Feinberg, "irony is on balance an *appreciative* attitude. One appreciates the perceived incongruity much as one does in humor, where the sudden unexpected perception of incongruity produces laughter."[19] Although neither Nagel nor Feinberg discusses film noir, it is easy to see how their accounts might help explain its humor and accessibility to parody.[20] It certainly seems at times that film noir protagonists are supreme ironists—serious and playful simultaneously, each of these elements exerting sufficient influence to sustain the psychological equilibrium needed to carry out the actions they have to take. Both Bogart and Mitchum (in character) wisecrack throughout their noir films. And they are not alone. Consider the fast-paced repartee of Glenn Ford and Gloria Grahame: "What's your problem—you don't like lobster?" "When I take a bite of my dinner, I don't expect my dinner to bite back." Or the spot-on cynicism of Clair Trevor to her philandering husband George Montgomery: "A civilized woman does not merely file for divorce, she gets even." Or the irreverent one-liners of the hit man Richard Widmark, who does "business" by day and reads Dickens at night: "It was the best of crimes, it was the worst of crimes."[21] The phenomenon of intentional humor in noir dialogue suggests the possibility of conceiving the noir protagonist-as-ironist as harboring a nonstandard but noteworthy attitude toward life.

## Attitudes toward the Human Condition

Now it is time to pull together the various points I have made about existentialism and film noir and apply them to the question of the proper attitude to take toward life.

Existentialist philosophers have written as though the absurdity of the human condition provides grounds for various negative attitudes—pessimism, despair, defiance, and so on. Albert Camus writes that "there is no fate that cannot be surmounted by scorn," and Jean-Paul Sartre assures us that a life lived authentically must repudiate the "spirit of seriousness" that takes values to be "transcendent givens independent of human subjectivity."[22] Other philosophers have denied that such negative reactive attitudes are appropriate and recommend irony even as they have accepted the data on which existentialist claims about the absurdity of life are based. One might even recommend *indifference* toward meaningless life on the reasonable grounds that, if nothing matters, the fact that life is meaningless doesn't matter either. The assumption behind all these recommendations seems to be that there is *one* proper attitude to take toward life's meaninglessness. But *is* there a single attitude to take toward all of life? Is irony (or resignation, or defiance, or any of the other candidates) always the attitude one should take toward the human condition? Surely it is possible that there simply *isn't* in general one and only one attitude everyone should take toward all of life.

Film noir's attitudinal vector is much in evidence in the titles of the very films we have been talking about. Life is a *Dark Passage,* a *Detour,* a *Journey into Fear* with *No Escape* and *No Way Out.* Film noir characters *Walk Alone;* they *Walk by Night* through *The Naked City,* through *The Asphalt Jungle,* down *A Street with No Name. They Live by Night,* they *Clash by Night,* they are sometimes *Caught,* sometimes *Possessed,* often *Spellbound,* but they are always *On Dangerous Ground,* always *Where Danger Lives,* their *Desperate Hours* ticking down in a deadly throw of the dice with the *Odds against Tomorrow.* On this view, life constitutes a catastrophe that we must escape, if only we could—but we cannot.

I want to conclude by proposing an alternative way to look at life.

No outlook on life will be adequate without acknowledging that a meaningful life is not an all-or-nothing matter but one of degree. Some lives are more meaningful than others, and some stretches of an individual's life are more meaningful than others. Some lives are meaningful in view of being lived under the guidance of a single, dominant end, and others are meaningful even though they have been plotted out along multifarious lines in accordance with a diversity of ends or goals. On this view, there is no reason to insist that there is only *one* way a life can be meaningful, only one plan or purpose sufficiently enriching to justify the judgment that one is leading (or has led) a meaningful life. But does it follow that a person who declares that his or her life has meaning cannot be mistaken?

Paul Edwards comes very close to defending such a position: "The question 'As long as his life was dedicated to the spread of communism it had meaning to him, but was it really meaningful?' seems to be senseless. We are inclined to say, 'If his life had meaning to him, then it had meaning—that's all there is to it.'"[23] Here, one should perhaps distinguish between two senses of *meaningfulness.* According to the first ("partial") sense, to say that a person's life is meaningful is to say that he or she has certain projects that matter to him or her and that these projects are realizable. According to the second ("full") sense, to say a person's life is meaningful is to say that the projects that matter to him or her are both realizable and have positive value. It is in this full sense, I suggest, that we would not say that a person had found the meaning of his or her life (to say nothing of the meaning of life generally) unless we were prepared in some sense to *endorse* that way of life.

I concede that my reluctance to call a life rich in diabolical designs a fully meaningful one may well reflect a linguistic blind spot, not to mention a failure of moral imagination. Conceding this, however, does not mean conceding that, in our judgments of the meaning of life, anything goes. Judging that life is meaningful (or meaningless) involves an evaluation based on certain criteria. (In order to specify these criteria, I would have to put forward a theory of value, a task impossible to undertake here.) While our criteria for a meaningful life may be context dependent and open to revision, it would be a mistake to hold that a meaningful life just *is* the life that a person has chosen and that he or she insists is meaningful. The problem with such a position is that it has the bizarre consequence that a person necessarily must be living a meaningful life (as long as he says he is) even if it involves nothing more than sitting in a room clasping and unclasping his hands. Here, as elsewhere, with no criterion except that of "I say so" or "it seems to me it is," the possibility of any assessment of our lives in this dimension at all is removed.

"On the far side of despair, life begins," Orestes famously intones at the end of Sartre's *The Flies,* while Camus has Caligula declare: "Men die, and they are not happy."[24] Film noir grasps these partial truths about life and conveys them dramatically, exposing us to paradigms of human experience that are expressly dark and laden with conflict. Of course, filmmakers must portray the world as their artistic visions dictate, and we should not be surprised to find that the characters who inhabit such a one-sided universe are uniformly grim in their attitudes toward it. But, to the extent that film noir makes the fates of the doomed Frank Bigelow, the damaged Jeff Bailey, and the obsessed Scottie Ferguson metaphors for the human condition, it runs the risk of affirming that our projects are *unrealizable,* that our lives *must* be meaningless. A more balanced view seems in order, one that fits better with the fact that we are not in the position of the hapless Frank Bigelows or Jeff Baileys or Scottie Fergusons but rather in the position of those for whom many things matter and who must, somehow, make the best of the conditions in which they find themselves.

## Notes

I am grateful to Christeen Clemens for her acute comments on and assistance in the preparation of this essay and to Mark T. Conard for a number of helpful suggestions for improving the final draft.

1. For a thorough discussion of this issue, see James Naremore, *More Than Night: Film Noir in Its Contexts* (Berkeley and Los Angeles: University of California Press, 1998). See also Mark T. Conard, "Nietzsche and the Meaning and Definition of Noir" (in this volume).

2. Robert Porfirio, "No Way Out: Existential Motifs in the *Film Noir*" (1976), in *Film Noir Reader,* ed. Alain Silver and James Ursini (New York: Limelight, 1996), 80.

3. In 1946, Warner Brothers hired Howard Hawks to direct Raymond Chandler's *The Big Sleep.* Chandler's plotline was notoriously labyrinthine, so, during the shooting, reportedly to settle an argument with Bogart, Hawks cabled Chandler to ask who

was supposed to have killed General Sternwood's chauffeur in the original story. Chandler wired back: "NO IDEA" (see David Thomson, *The Big Sleep* [London: British Film Institute, 1997], 34, and Tom Hiney, *Raymond Chandler: A Biography* [New York: Grove, 1999], 163).

4. A useful collection of film noir quotes can be found in Peggy Thompson and Saeko Usukawa, eds., *Hard-Boiled: Great Lines from Classic Noir Films* (San Francisco: Chronicle, 1995).

5. Thomas Nagel, "The Absurd" (1971), in *The Meaning of Life: Questions, Answers, and Analysis,* ed. Steven Sanders and David R. Cheney (Englewood Cliffs, NJ: Prentice-Hall, 1980), 156.

6. Arthur Schopenhauer, "On the Vanity of Existence," in *Essays and Aphorisms,* trans. R. J. Hollingdale (Baltimore: Penguin, 1970), 51.

7. Arthur Schopenhauer, *On the Basis of Morality,* trans. E. F. J. Payne (Indianapolis: Bobbs-Merrill, 1965), 135.

8. Paul Edwards, "Meaning and Value of Life," in *The Encyclopedia of Philosophy,* ed. Paul Edwards (New York: Macmillan, 1967), 472. The Schopenhauer quote is from "On the Vanity of Existence," 52.

9. Nagel, "The Absurd," 155.

10. Jean-Paul Sartre, *Being and Nothingness: An Essay on Phenomenological Ontology,* trans. Hazel E. Barnes (New York: Washington Square, 1966), 538.

11. For an acerbic account of Sartre's ethics, see Mary Warnock, *Existentialist Ethics* (New York: St. Martin's, 1967).

12. Frederick A. Olafson, *Principles and Persons: An Ethical Interpretation of Existentialism* (Baltimore: Johns Hopkins University Press, 1967), 238.

13. Warnock, *Existentialist Ethics,* 55.

14. Spencer Selby, *Dark City: The Film Noir* (Jefferson, NC: McFarland, 1984), 43.

15. This observation was suggested by Jeremy G. Butler's "*Miami Vice:* The Legacy of *Film Noir,*" in Silver and Ursini, *Film Noir Reader,* 295.

16. Kurt Baier, "The Meaning of Life" (1957), in Sanders and Cheney, *The Meaning of Life,* 60.

17. Ibid., 51.

18. Nagel, "The Absurd," 157, 163, 165.

19. Joel Feinberg, "Absurd Self-Fulfillment," in *Time and Cause,* ed. Peter van Inwagen (Dordrecht: D. Reidel, 1980), 277.

20. For a helpful discussion of noir's humor and accessibility to parody, see Naremore, *More Than Night,* 196–202.

21. No doubt these quotes have analogues in actual film noir, but I made these up, complete with phony attributions. Doesn't that prove the point about film noir's susceptibility to parody?

22. Albert Camus, *The Myth of Sisyphus,* trans. Justin O'Brien (New York: Vintage, 1955), 90; Sartre, *Being and Nothingness,* 766.

23. Edwards, "Meaning and Value of Life," 473. My distinction between *partial* and *full* senses of *meaningful* here corresponds approximately to Edwards's distinction between *subjective* and *objective* senses of *worthwhile*.

24. Jean-Paul Sartre, *The Flies,* trans. Stuart Gilbert (New York: Knopf, 1962); Albert Camus, *Caligula and Three Other Plays,* trans. Stuart Gilbert (New York: Knopf, 1958).

# The Horizon of Disenchantment

Film Noir, Camus, and the Vicissitudes of Descent

*Alan Woolfolk*

> I don't blame myself—you see, Mr. Gittes, most people never have to face the fact [that at] the right time and the right place they are capable of *anything.*
>
> —*Noah Cross to Jake Gittes,* Chinatown

> "Everything is permitted," exclaims Ivan Karamazov. That, too, smacks of the absurd. But on condition that it not be taken in the vulgar sense.... The absurd does not liberate; it binds. It does not authorize all actions. "Everything is permitted" does not mean that nothing is forbidden.
>
> —*Albert Camus*

Film noir may be understood as a cinematic form that, even more than standard film genres (e.g., melodramas, musicals, westerns), defies exact definition, not only because it is transgeneric in origin and to a considerable extent derivative of other genres, but also because it picked up certain subversive cultural motifs of a rapidly changing late industrial society and equivocally reshaped them in a way that, at best, challenged widespread assumptions about material and moral progress and, at worst, merely confirmed the most devastating illusions of a culture vacillating, as Philip Rieff once wrote, "between dead purposes and deadly devices to escape boredom."[1] The desolate urban landscapes of classic film noir complemented a societal backdrop of dead and corrupt purposes, ranging from middle-class conformity and faceless bureaucracies to corruption at the top among social and political elites. Likewise, the "deadly devices" of guns and violence, alcohol and drugs, cars and speed, and especially the erotic machinations of femmes fatales, which were featured in the foreground of such films, were both symptoms of these dead and corrupt purposes and compelling in their sheer immediacy. But the central drama of film noir, even into the postindustrial age, or perhaps in the hindsight of our time, has continued to be the struggle of the protagonist to achieve in some way mastery of an ethically irrational universe, what Max Weber called a *disenchanted world,* rather than to succumb to it.[2] Or, alternatively, the entire history of film noir might be tentatively sketched in terms of the tenuous resistances of protagonists to their fatal attractions, beginning with the superficial but successful dandyism of Sam Spade in John Huston's protonoir *The Maltese Falcon* (1941) and ending with (take your pick) Scottie Ferguson's devastating failure to secure a self-identity in Alfred Hitchcock's *Vertigo* (1958), the defeated dandyism of Jake Gittes in Roman Polanski's neo-noir masterpiece *Chinatown* (1974), or the complete surrender to psychopathology of Nick Curran in Paul Verhoeven's *Basic Instinct* (1992).[3]

The mark of the noir protagonist during the classic period of these films, 1941–58, was neither moral victory nor moral defeat so much as a personal struggle to define and maintain a coherent self-identity in the face of a gnostic world of overwhelming darkness and distant light.[4] Self-mastery within a disenchanted world inevitably required a spiritual descent into the darkness of society and the human soul, with the protagonist, in many instances, simply attempting to control the terms of the descent and, at other times, putting up all manner of resistances. The distinction between control and resistance is important and, perhaps, most starkly illustrated by contrasting Marlow in Joseph Conrad's *Heart of Darkness* (1902) with Captain Willard in Francis Ford Coppola's *Apocalypse Now* (1979), which was, of course, a cinematic adaptation of what James Naremore refers to as "the urtext of British modernism."[5] In Conrad's seminal text, the narrator, Captain Marlow, recollects with exquisite modesty his spiritual journey toward Kurtz's heart of darkness and his character-defining moment of resistance to that darkness; in Coppola's film, the narrator, Captain Willard, is a professional assassin who recounts his murderous journey toward and ritual elimination of Colonel Kurtz in order to become his successor. Where Marlow triumphs by resisting the transgressive possibilities of Kurtz's disenchanted world, a world in which literally anything can be made to happen—mass killings, torture, cannibalism—the appropriately named Willard triumphs by embracing and making them his own, resulting in an undisguised triumph of the will.

The noir worldview denies to the protagonist the realization of either a transformative moment of resistance to its darkness or a triumph of the will to power. Film noir's dark vision does not permit the possibility of an unequivocal character-defining moment of denial because it is set in a world so disenchanted that no ethic of resistance can hold. No compelling symbol system of militant ideals defines the cultural horizon. No vocation or social practice ensures the discipline of character formation. (Obviously, the self-interested efforts of the typical private detective are but a shabby substitute for the work ethic of Conrad's beloved merchant marine.) The most that one may expect is the ambivalent effort of Bart Tare in Joseph Lewis's *Gun Crazy* (1950) *not* to kill or the self-destructive call of Jeff Bailey to the police at the end of Jacques Tourneur's *Out of the Past* (1947) in a last desperate effort to stop the lethal Kathie Moffat.[6]

Yet the noir protagonist also proves incapable of anything approaching a triumph of the will. Unable to make Marlow's ascent, the protagonist is also typically unable to consummate Willard's descent into an indifferent and hostile world because of some residual attachment to a world not yet completely disenchanted. Trapped, or at least severely constrained, by social and personal circumstances, he typically moves more deeply into an ethically unintelligible universe in which accident, caprice, and misjudgment rule and anything is possible, only to discover (again, typically) that a female antagonist has descended more quickly and more adeptly ahead of him—accepting and then betraying his love (e.g., *The Killers* [Robert Siodmak, 1946], *Criss Cross* [Robert Siodmak, 1949]), revealing herself to be ruthless and cold-blooded (e.g., *Detour* [Edgar G. Ulmer, 1945], *Kiss Me Deadly* [Robert Aldrich, 1955]), or simply proving that she is more experienced in the ways of a world in which anything is possible (e.g., *Vertigo, Chinatown*). In the end, the classic noir protagonist can neither escape nor embrace the not-so-benign indifference of the universe.[7]

## The Horizon of Disenchantment

As the philosopher Charles Taylor has explained with considerable insight, our lives unfold and take on meaning against preexisting cultural horizons that are beyond the individual's choice and that can be suppressed or denied only in self-defeating moves, moves that have become all too prevalent in a "subjectivist civilization" that emphasizes individualist conceptions of the self. Such inescapable frameworks normally define a cultural background of human intelligibility that makes "qualitative distinctions" between the high and the low, the good and the bad, the dignified and the undignified: "To think, feel, judge, within such a framework is to function with the sense that some action, or mode of life, or mode of feeling is incomparably 'higher' than others which are more readily available to us." These frameworks have always defined human lives, even when the frameworks have undergone transformations, are challenged, or have grown increasingly unintelligible, as they have in modernity and, especially, the twentieth century. "What Weber called 'disenchantment,' the dissipation of our sense of the cosmos as a meaningful order," Taylor argues, "has allegedly destroyed the horizons in which people previously lived their spiritual lives." But, he maintains, the very lack of a preexisting, unchallengeable framework has created a new and very different type of spiritual agenda, one with its own spiritual obstacles and risks that cannot be denied.[8]

Taylor contends that our cultural horizons, our spiritual frameworks, have become "problematic" in the modern world, that the "existential predicament" on our "spiritual agenda" is no longer one in which "an unchallengeable framework makes imperious demands which we fear being unable to meet." Rather: "The form of danger . . . which threatens the modern seeker . . . is something close to the opposite: the world loses altogether its spiritual contour, nothing is worth doing, the fear is of a terrifying emptiness, a kind of vertigo, or even a fracturing of our world and body-space." However, the very fact that we no longer have an established background of intelligibility has itself been taken up as the basis of a new kind of framework, one in which the model of higher life "consists precisely in facing a disenchanted universe with courage and lucidity." Within this disenchanted horizon, dignity comes from the "ability to stand unconsoled and uncowed in [the] face of the indifferent immensity of the world" and to find purpose in confronting it.[9] Weber himself clearly belonged within this spiritual framework, as did Nietzsche, as did Camus, as have so many of the intellectual and spiritual guides who helped define the inner life of the twentieth century.

Although film noir is clearly set within this horizon of disenchantment, it is much more doubtful that the noir protagonist discovers dignity and purpose in confronting "the indifferent immensity of the world." Aside from the fact that he is not an intellectual but more narrowly focused on immediate problems, what accounts for such discrepant responses? What explains, if anything, the more vulnerable and tenuous stance of the fully developed noir protagonist—ranging from Walter Neff in *Double Indemnity* (Billy Wilder, 1944) through Scottie Ferguson in *Vertigo* during the classic noir period—let alone the extended period of neo-noir? In addition to the fact that the horizon of disenchantment is generally unrelenting and hostile to human purposes in film noir, what sets the noir protagonist apart? Here, the work of the French existentialist Albert Camus offers some insights.[10]

Camus is helpful because he was a leading French literary figure and exemplar of high culture who was directly influenced by the hard-boiled American fiction of the twenties and thirties, which figured so prominently in film noir.[11] This influence is most evident in Camus' early short novel *The Stranger* (*L'Etranger*, 1942), originally titled *The Indifferent*, in which an ordinary, unreflective protagonist, Meursault, who is completely unaware of his existence, inadvertently commits a motiveless killing for which he is, in turn, tried and sentenced to death largely because he refuses to play the socially acceptable role of a repentant criminal. On the one hand, Meursault resembles many noir protagonists in the spareness of his inner and outer life. (He is certainly no self-conscious existential intellectual like Roquentin in Sartre's *Nausea* [1938], who is disgusted with his own existence.) On the other hand, despite the terse, taciturn style of the novel and the fatal entrapment of the protagonist by a series of circumstances and apparent accidents, *The Stranger* lacks the dark gnosticism and grim fatalism of the noir worldview (evident in some of Camus' other early works, such as the plays *Caligula* [1938] and *The Misunderstanding* [1944])—because Camus, in effect, qualified the horizon of disenchantment.

## The Limits of Honesty

In *The Stranger,* Camus attempted to counter the horizon of disenchantment with an ethic of honesty. As he wrote in a 1955 preface, Meursault is "condemned because he does not play the game . . . he refuses to lie."[12] Indeed, Camus even went so far as to incorporate a vignette about *The Misunderstanding* into *The Stranger* from which Meursault draws the simple conclusion that one "should never play games," even though this conclusion elides the dark vision of the original play.[13] But Camus was able to employ his ethic of honesty in criticism of bourgeois society only because that ethic was safely grounded in a neo-Romantic conception of nature as moral source, drawn primarily from Rousseau.[14]

In the closing scene of the novel, Meursault exemplifies a sort of popularized version of Nietzsche's eternal return, in which he consciously affirms his life of self-love (i.e, *amour de soi*) against the vanity and pride (i.e., *amour-propre*) of the conventional bourgeois society with which he has come into conflict. As a consequence, he becomes defiant rather than resigned, his self-identity solidified rather than subverted and defeated. In stark contrast to the noir protagonist, who cannot escape the past, Meursault is spiritually reborn, and time itself is redeemed:

> And I felt ready to live it all again too. As if that blind rage had washed me clean, rid me of hope; for the first time, in that night alive with signs and stars, I opened myself to the benign indifference of the universe. Finding it so much like myself—so like a brother, really—I felt that I had been happy and that I was happy again. For everything to be consummated, for me to feel less alone, I had only to wish that there be a large crowd of spectators the day of my execution and that they greet me with cries of hate.[15]

Whether or not one finds Camus' vision of self-transformation compelling, it is significant that the false and hypocritical vanity of the bourgeois society that sends Meursault to his death is linked with the modern city and the denial of nature. Indeed, time and again in Camus' work, the spiritual defeats of modernity are associated with those who turn their backs on the beauty of nature and the natural world, whether out of middle-class habit and routine or because of the intellectual overlays of civilization.[16] While the natural indifference of the universe is simply "benign," the horizon of disenchantment is darkened by civilization itself. Where Camus suggests that there are safeguards built into human nature, ensuring that human beings possess a limited power of agency and freedom to create their own world, if only they can manage to rebel against the falsehoods of civilization, the noir worldview suggests that deception and falsehood may be built into the aspirations of human existence itself. Both perspectives raise unanswered questions, but it is Camus' that may, in fact, pose the greater difficulties.

In the noir vision, an uncorrupted world of nature is almost completely absent, finding no intersection with society. Or the idyllic becomes associated with a hopeless retreat into childhood memories, as in the cases of Dix Handley in *The Asphalt Jungle* (John Huston, 1950) and Bart Tare in *Gun Crazy.* Nonetheless, in *Out of the Past,* duplicity and falsehood extend into the idyllic natural community itself. In the closing scenes of the film, the deaf-mute Jimmy falsely confirms to Jeff Bailey's love, Ann, that Jeff had decided to leave with the femme fatale Kathie just prior to their deaths so that Ann may, unlike the noir protagonist, leave the past behind. Jimmy's final gestures of loyalty to Jeff may represent, as R. Barton Palmer argues, "the world of melodrama" reasserting "its control."[17] But they are also a repetition of Marlow's "saving lie" of civilization, which he tells to Kurtz's fiancée at the close of *Heart of Darkness*, albeit with an unusual twist: where Marlow falsely confirms Kurtz's devotion to his beloved on his deathbed, Jimmy suppresses the truth about Jeff's love for Ann. In the noir version of the lie of civilization, the higher motives of the protagonist are repressed in the memory of community so that its members can get on with their lives. In both versions of the lie, however, civilization cannot withstand too much honesty, especially when it concerns the contradictions and confusions of the self. Hypocrisy and deception are sometimes necessary. For, without Camus' myth of a Rousseauian natural man or some other limiting fiction,[18] an ethic of honesty too easily leads to disturbing personal revelations of the sort that are barely suppressed in films such as *The Glass Key* (Stuart Heisler, 1942) and *Kiss Me Deadly* and later explode to the surface in films such as *Vertigo* and *Chinatown*.

## Resisting "the Cult of Multiplied Sensation"

As a loosely defined genre, what came to be called *classic* film noir drew on the long-standing conflict between what Matei Calinescu has called "two distinct and bitterly conflicting modernities," a conflict that has been largely resolved with the rise of a postmodern, therapeutic culture. On the one side, modernity was conceived as a moral and political project grounded in a doctrine of progress, scientific and technological advancement, and capitalist economics and centered on the bourgeoisie, especially the morality of the bourgeois family. On the other side, an oppositional aesthetic or cultural modernity arose out of the Romantic movement that was "inclined toward radical antibourgeois attitudes," a modernity that led to the rise, not only of modernism, but also eventually of the political and artistic avant-gardes.[19] Originally, film noir drew on the modernist heritage of aesthetic modernity, exploiting its critique of bourgeois modernity at a time when the tension between conventional modernity and modernism, bourgeois and bohemian, was growing to a close. Indeed, as Naremore has argued, the "blood melodrama" of noir films reveals the affinity between these films and modernism as well as the close ties between this variety of cinematic modernism and commercial culture.[20]

By the term *blood melodrama*, Naremore means the influence of the European art cinema on American directors and genres, specifically the films of those Weimar Germans who specialized in "gothic horror, criminal psychology, and sinister conspiracies"; French films about "working-class crime"; and English films by Hitchcock on international intrigue. "What united the three types of cinematic modernism," according to Naremore, "was an interest in popular stories about violence and sexual love, or in what Graham Greene once called 'blood melodrama.'" However, Naremore also contends that the influence of blood melodrama may be seen in the literature of Anglo-American high culture (e.g., Joseph Conrad, Henry James) as well as in the rise of a "countertradition" to the conventional detective story that built on the rapid rise of American working-class pulp fiction during the twenties and the growth of novels about crime in the late twenties and thirties that appealed to the middle class. This "second-generation modernism," according to Naremore, "interacted" with the mass culture and, eventually, influenced the Hollywood cinema.[21] But the nature of this interaction needs further clarification.

Palmer similarly contends that Hollywood gradually became receptive to producing full-blown film noir because the middle class began to accept male, working-class pulp fiction during the thirties, but he also argues that this shift in American popular culture, however important, was in itself not enough. In addition to the expanding readership, one must also point to the increasing hopelessness and fatality of the noir worldview. "In the 1940s," Palmer observes, "the hard-boiled world became a grimmer place where omnipresent evil and oppressive fatality reduce individual action to insignificance." From being romantic individualists who lived and survived by their own code (e.g., Dashiell Hammett's *The Maltese Falcon* [1930]), the protagonists became rebels "doomed by their own natures and the fatal force of circumstance" (e.g., James M. Cain's *Double Indemnity* [1944], Cornell Woolrich's *The Black Angel* [1943]) who attracted a broader readership. "These two changes together," Palmer concludes, "account for the advent of film noir and determine many of the phenomenon's essential features"—once the popularity of noir fiction had been clearly established among the American middle class by the late forties.[22]

The rise of a bleaker noir vision—one in which self-possessed individuals, usually detectives, living by their own codes, underwent a marked decline—is directly linked with the decline of an important ideal of aesthetic modernity closely associated with perhaps the single most significant figure of aesthetic modernity, Baudelaire. As Stanley Cavell has argued, Baudelaire's ideal of the dandy has been an instructive presence in American film for some time: "Our most brilliant representatives of the type are the Western hero and Bogart; but we include the smaller and more jaded detectives and private eyes of the past generation; and the type is reiterated in the elegant nonprofessional solver of mysteries."[23] Like Baudelaire, Cavell identifies the feature of a "hidden" or "latent" fire as essential to the character of the dandy—what Baudelaire describes as "an air of coldness which comes from an unshakeable determination not to be moved . . . a latent fire which hints at itself, and which could, but chooses not to burst into flame."[24] But what Cavell fails to note is that the jaded protagonists of film noir are distinguished by their failure to keep their fires *banked*.

For Baudelaire, the dandy was an aesthetic model for living that opposed both the corruption of the bourgeoisie and the temptations of a disorderly bohemian life—what Baudelaire called "the cult of multiplied sensation."[25] But, with the decline of the dandy as a model for life, noir protagonists arose who were increasingly defenseless against the cult of multiplied sensation. Where in the proto-noir *The Maltese Falcon* Bogart can maintain a cold self-possession, even when his passions flare or he appears to have lost control of a situation, in classic film noir the protagonist loses control of himself and his circumstances; his fires are no longer banked. Philip Marlowe is literally drugged and at the mercy of the world, including his own confusion and petulant temper (*Murder My Sweet* [Edward Dmytryk, 1944]); Al Robert's "detour" begins when his fiancée leaves him, and he initially loses emotional control while playing Brahms on the piano (*Detour*); the Swede is so resigned to his fate that he proves incapable of resisting his killers because he has been betrayed by Kitty (*The Killers*); and Scottie Ferguson suffers from a spiritual vertigo so severe that his adolescent "wanderings" leave him inwardly at the mercy of Gavin Elster's seductive world of "freedom and power" (*Vertigo*). All lack the dandy's self-possession and determination.

The model of the dandy also appears in the background of Camus' oeuvre and informed his second line of symbolic defense against the horizon of disenchantment, most clearly developed in *The Rebel* (1951) and *The Fall* (1956). Evidence of the influence of Baudelaire's model (and also of the early Nietzsche) is evident in Camus' attempt to justify life as an aesthetic, rather than a moral, phenomenon in *The Myth of Sisyphus* (1942) as well as in later writings in which he developed even further the notion that the artist has important lessons to offer concerning the conduct of life. All these efforts centered on attempts to restrict the possibilities of a disenchanted world in which everything and anything is possible. In *The Myth of Sisyphus*, Camus explicitly invoked aesthetic criteria, writing: "'Everything is permitted' . . . on condition that it not be taken in the vulgar sense."[26] In the 1958 preface to the *Lyrical and Critical Essays*, Camus stated: "I have artistic scruples just as other men have moral and religious ones. If I am struck with the notion 'such things are not done,' with taboos in general rather alien to my free nature, it's because I am a slave, and an admiring one, of a severe artistic tradition."[27]

But, in *The Rebel*, Camus probed the contradictions of his moral universe more systematically and deeply when he based the model of the rebel on his ideal of the artist, which he juxtaposed to both the complacent bourgeois and the committed political revolutionary.[28] His vision of the artist as exemplary rebel had its origins in Sartre's study of Baudelaire's revolt against his middle-class origins, in which Sartre charged that the rebel, as opposed to the revolutionary, "shows signs of a bad conscience and of something resembling a feeling of guilt. He does not want to destroy or transcend the existing order; he simply wants to rise up against it. . . . In the depths of his heart he preserves the rights which he challenges in public."[29] Camus took this image of an ambivalent Baudelaire and fashioned it into his own model of the literary artist as an ascetic cultural guide. In this reformulation, the artist limits the danger of moving in strange perspectives through devotion to vocation. In his 1956 study of Roger Martin du Gard, for instance, Camus singled out du Gard's commitment to an "ascetic vocation" and his "withdrawal from the world" as well as his "obstinate pursuit of psychological truth" as the key to his integrity. But, even so, his pursuit of "psychological truth" was limited by a sense of personal modesty and shame.[30]

Time and again in Camus' work one finds that his exemplary models of conduct are entrapped in prisons of their own inhibitions—modesty (*modestie, pudeur*), honesty (*honnêteté*), shame (*honte*)—and, in some instances, engaged in vocations that apparently give them the inner strength to confront and resist the disturbing possibilities of an indifferent universe. Without such saving inhibitions, one lacks what Camus called *character*. But character alone may not offer a vaccination sufficiently strong to resist plagues and other diseases, whether natural or unnatural. In addition, Camus' "good modern nihilist," Jean-Baptiste Clamence in *The Fall*, learns how to exploit character flaws through his inverted vocation of "judge-penitent."[31] In his case, the pursuit of psychological truth (uncovering "the fundamental duplicity of the human being")[32] leads to the emptying out of his character resistances and an escape into the spiritual flatlands. Unlike Scottie Ferguson, Jean-Baptiste no longer suffers from a serious dread of spiritual ascent and fears no devastating consequences from moral falls because he has moved beyond the noir topography of vertical descents and dark pasts. He stands for nothing. The noir protagonist, in contrast, stubbornly clings to character flaws because, if nothing else, they reflect the flawed nature of the disenchanted universe and, therefore, lend a certain authenticity to the fractured narrative of the self.

## Backward and Downward

As what Palmer has called a filmic *chronotope* (adapting a concept from Bakhtin), film noir defines a narrative structure, a form of cinematic modernism, that emphasizes the "dark pasts" of its protagonists and resists assimilation to standard Hollywood genres and the "consensus" values they normally affirm. For Bakhtin, a chronotope "expresses the inseparability of space and time (time as a fourth dimension of space)." In fact: "It is precisely the chronotope that defines genre and generic distinctions, for in literature the primary category in the chronotope is time."[33] Film noir merges narrative space, time, and events in such a way as to give priority to time past—"someone (or something) is always coming 'out of the past.'" This "backward turning" may be accomplished by "the discursive arrangement of story events, whose forward movement is interrupted by the filling in of some bypassed gap." Or it may figure as a "narrator relating what has gone before and thereby demonstrating the presence of the past" within the narrator's thoughts. Or: "A third possibility is that the present admits the return of characters who were thought to belong to the past who, it seemed, had been bypassed as the protagonist embarked on a 'fresh start.'"[34]

   Or, to take Palmer's formulations one step further: film noir threatens to subvert the very concept of time, to obliterate the distinction between past, present, and future, by placing individuals at the mercy of unknown forces that not only negate simple notions of making a clean break with the past but also deny the very notion of a coherent narrative of character development. Thus, neither Jeff Markham in *Out of the Past* nor Jake Gittes in *Chinatown* achieves a decisive moment of transformation, melodramatic or otherwise, that resolves his crisis and leads toward an integral life within a stable community. Rather, as with many another noir protagonist, the unknown and dark forces that transfix both characters are, paradoxically, deeply personal and frighteningly impersonal, intimate and indifferent, in a way that precludes any unifying personal knowledge of the self, society, and the world. On the one hand, individuals are at the mercy of psychological obsessions and compulsions that threaten and frequently lead to self-destruction; on the other hand, they confront impersonal social and universal forces that preclude any remedy. Film noir tells us that existence is irremediably fractured, that the self can neither be integrated into a community nor find a home in the universe, that self-identity is itself highly contingent and subject to disintegration.

In film noir, there is no integrity of time and space because time is contingent and space is discontinuous and fragmented. The protagonists are always in transit. Once again, taking *Out of the Past* as his exemplary example, Palmer argues: "Lacking a moment of reformative turning, the film noir juxtaposes the false promise of a future with the reality of a present that, instead, turns back to the past, trapping the protagonist 'between times' and in a multiplicity of irreconcilable spaces." Of course, thanks to institutional and cultural pressures for happier endings, many such films too easily resolve the problem of arrested character development by imposing artificial resolutions in which the protagonists escape into a life of singular identity and devotion (e.g., *The Glass Key, Murder My Sweet*). But such artificial, reformative turnings do not gainsay Palmer's analysis of the dominant, disenchanted vision of "cruel stasis" beneath the "illusion of movement" that seems to define the dark inspiration of the film noir chronotope.[35]

Nonetheless, the focus on the dark pasts of film noir protagonists and the backward look of such films need further elaboration, for many of these films appear to be as much *downward* looking as backward looking, in some cases more so. In *Kiss Me Deadly*, for example, which reduces the focus on the past to a minimum, the quest of the narcissistic, ruthless Mike Hammer for the "great whatzit" takes him ever more deeply into a world of amoral indifference and confusion, which even he can't handle. In the end, Hammer is finally forced to utter pathetically that he "didn't know" the gravity of the object of his search, which turns out to be a symbolic container of highly dangerous radioactive material. Likewise, in the protonoir *The Glass Key,* the predominantly amoral Ed Beaumont does not so much look backward as descend into a sadomasochistic nightmare relationship with the henchman Jeff. In both films, the external forces that batter and humiliate the tough, calculating ego of the protagonist evoke inner threats that threaten the security and very identity of the self. As in more obviously backward-looking noir films, it is the ego of the protagonist, and, by implication, the overweening, muscular ego psychology of Americans, that seems to be under attack by unknown forces within the self, society, and an impersonal, indifferent universe.

## "A Cauldron Full of Seething Excitations"

If, for the moment, we give priority to the perspective that it is unknown forces within the self, forces that are merely triggered by external events, that shape and seal the fates of noir protagonists, then the psychology of Nietzsche and Freud, rather than academic faculty psychology, is clearly relevant because the study of unconscious motivations not only influenced noir filmmakers but still offers important insights in its own right. In the parlance of a now largely discredited psychoanalytic theory, these unknown forces are the forces of the unconscious psyche, a return of the repressed, specifically those of the libido or the id, as conceived by Freud (not Jung or Adler). In the most powerful examples of film noir, it is the unknown and unknowable id that is approached—"the dark, inaccessible part of our personality" that is primitive and chaotic. "We approach the id," Freud states, "with analogies: we call it a chaos, a cauldron full of seething excitations."[36] What could better describe the "great whatzit" of *Kiss Me Deadly,* the Pandora's box of radioactive material that burns and kills those who dare to open it and to view its contents directly? Noir films are, of course, populated with male protagonists who encounter and probe their unconscious only to find a disturbing and deadly knowledge that frequently comes via a femme fatale.

The femme fatale may come from out of the past in a variety of ways. She may reenter the protagonist's life after a physical or even a psychic absence, evoking memories of a very personal past that is suddenly near with its baggage of obsessions and compulsions, or she may simply draw to the surface of consciousness fatal weaknesses and vulnerabilities in the protagonist that have been denied and repressed. Regardless, she inevitably drags the male protagonist downward into the nethermost depths of the psyche, in which the "reason and good sense" of the ego, the "reality principle," are left behind. In this nether region, "the id of course knows no judgements of value: no good and evil, no morality." But the primitive unconscious also knows no "law of contradiction," no negations, no "idea of time." Thus: "Contrary impulses can exist side by side." Love can exist alongside hatred, attraction alongside repulsion, respect alongside contempt, pleasure alongside pain, but the unconscious never says no and does not recognize the passage of time. Impulses and impressions are "virtually immortal."[37] Everything becomes possible in the enormity of the present, even Noah Cross's incestuous relationship with his guilty daughter, Evelyn Mulwray.

Everything becomes possible because the femme fatale frequently helps the protagonist identify downward with forbidden impulses and desires until, as Ned Racine says to Matty Walker in *Body Heat* (Lawrence Kasdan, 1981), "It's real, all right." In Ned's case, the "it" that emerges into consciousness (albeit too easily) from "the it" or id of his unconscious is the idea of murdering Matty's husband. In the original Billy Wilder film *Double Indemnity*, of which *Body Heat* is a remake, Walter Neff had already been consciously thinking about "ways to crook the house," which he had learned as an insurance salesman. Here, the manipulative Phyllis Dietrichson provides the opportunity and, perhaps, some additional incentive, but she lacks the erotic power of many another femme fatale, such as Kitty Collins in *The Killers*, to draw the protagonist on her own toward self-destruction. But, even in cases of powerful and dangerous women in classic noir films, such as Kitty Collins, Anna in *Criss Cross*, and Kathie Moffat in *Out of the Past*, their eroticized allure depends to a great extent on the depiction of, and appeal to, a society, however corrupt, in which some semblance of normative controls on transgressive sexuality still remains—or is at least implied. Conventions of dress and language, symbol-laden manners, forms of indirection and concealment, may be the most effective means of conveying the danger of identifying downward with the indifferent, impersonal, hidden god of the unconscious.

By the time *Body Heat* was made in the eighties and *Basic Instinct* in the nineties, the eroticism of the femme fatale could no longer be so effectively depicted without more explicit, and, especially in the case of the latter film, transgressive, expressions of sexuality. But how can the power of the forbidden be depicted in a culture that seems less and less concerned about preserving some idea of forbidden knowledge? The stripping away of civilized veneers and unmasking of instincts can only briefly shock a media-savvy postindustrial society in which forms and rituals of translation between private and public life are seen as superfluous and inauthentic. Under such pressures, inherited limitations become nothing more than barriers to personal happiness that must be overcome, as in John Sayles's *Lone Star* (1996), in which the interdict against incest is reduced to merely another prejudice of the past. Not surprisingly, about the time a full-blown postmodern therapeutic culture broke to the surface of American culture in the sixties, the era of classic film noir had ended. Not only was the Production Code revised (1966) and the claustrophobic urban industrial setting of early film noir dying, but the very notion of leading an experimental life in "transit" was becoming increasingly widespread and acceptable.

## Notes

The second epigraph to this essay is taken from Albert Camus, *The Myth of Sisyphus and Other Essays*, trans. J. O'Brien (New York: Vintage, 1955), 50.

1. Philip Rieff, *The Triumph of the Therapeutic: Uses of Faith after Freud* (1966; Chicago: University of Chicago Press, 1987), 11. As R. Barton Palmer has argued, the term *transgeneric* implies that film noir defined itself through, and in opposition to, a variety of genres, rather than as a self-conscious, well-defined genre during the classic period of the forties and fifties (*Hollywood's Dark Cinema: The American Film Noir* [New York: Twayne, 1994], 27–31).

2. As employed in this study, *disenchantment* refers to both the decline of normative controls grounded in a vision of an ordered and meaningful cosmos and the dissipation of what Charles Taylor calls *strong evaluations* (see his *Sources of the Self: The Making of Modern Identity* [Cambridge, MA: Harvard University Press, 1989], 4). Both readings are consistent with Weber's emphasis on the experience of ethical irrationality as central to the disenchantment of the modern world; however, where Taylor subordinates the moral to the spiritual, what is right to what is good, and, therefore, associates disenchantment with a declining vision of the good life, this study assumes that disenchantment cannot be separated from the dissipation of authoritative moral limitations (see Max Weber, *From Max Weber: Essays in Sociology*, trans. and ed. and with an introduction by H. H. Gerth and C. W. Mills [New York: Oxford University Press, 1946], 129–56, 267–301).

3. The ideal of the dandy received its definitive articulation in *The Painter of Modern Life* (1863), in which Baudelaire suggested, in anticipation of the early Nietzsche and Oscar Wilde, that life should be lived according to aesthetic, rather than moral, criteria. Life should become, in effect, a work of art or beauty. See Charles Baudelaire, "The Dandy," in *The Painter of Modern Life and Other Essays*, trans. and ed. J. Mayne (New York: Da Capo, 1964), 26–29.

4. As one of early Christianity's chief competitors, gnosticism found no saving grace in a created world. According to Hans Jonas: "The cardinal feature of gnostic thought is the radical dualism that governs the relation of God and world, and correspondingly that of man and world. The deity is absolutely transmundane, its nature alien to that of the universe, which it neither created nor governs and to which it is the complete antithesis: to the divine realm of light, self-contained and remote, the cosmos is opposed as the realm of darkness. The world is the work of lowly powers which though they may mediately be descended from Him do not know the true God and obstruct knowledge of Him in the cosmos over which they rule" (*The Gnostic Religion,* 2nd rev. ed. [Boston: Beacon, 1963], 42).

5. James Naremore, *More Than Night: Film Noir in Its Contexts* (Berkeley and Los Angeles: University of California Press, 1998), 43.

6. For an analysis of a film noir subgenre that proves the exception to this thesis, see R. Barton Palmer, "Moral Man in the Dark City: Film Noir, the Postwar Religious Revival, and *The Accused*" (in this volume).

7. The adaptation of Camus' well-known line from the closing passage of *The Stranger* is R. Barton Palmer's (in a personal conversation).

8. Taylor, *Sources of the Self,* 19, 17.

9. Ibid., 18, 94.

10. Existential motifs in film noir have been traced in a number of studies (see, e.g., Robert Porfirio, "No Way Out: Existential Motifs in the *Film Noir*" (1976), in *Film Noir Reader,* ed. Alain Silver and James Ursini [New York: Limelight, 1996], 77–93).

11. See, e.g., Herbert Lottman, *Albert Camus: A Biography* (Garden City, NY: Doubleday, 1979), 207, 243–44; and Albert Camus, *Lyrical and Critical Essays,* ed. P. Thody, trans. E. C. Kennedy (New York: Vintage, 1968), 348.

12. Camus, *Lyrical and Critical Essays,* 335–36.

13. Albert Camus, *The Stranger,* trans. M. Ward (New York: Vintage, 1988), 80.

14. See Taylor, *Sources of the Self,* 355–67.

15. Camus, *The Stranger,* 122–23 (translation altered).

16. See, e.g., Albert Camus, "Helen's Exile," in *Lyrical and Critical Essays,* 148–53.

17. R. Barton Palmer, "'Lounge Time' Reconsidered: Spatial Discontinuity and Temporal Contingency in *Out of the Past,*" in *Film Noir Reader 4,* ed. Alain Silver and James Ursini (New York: Limelight, 2004).

18. Meursault, indeed, exemplifies many of the traits of Rousseau's man in the state of nature—unreflective, uncommunicative, wholly absorbed in the present, motivated by "physical" rather than "moral" love, unaware of death, etc. (see Jean-Jacques Rousseau, "Discourse on the Origin and Foundations of Inequality among Men," in *The Basic Political Writings,* trans. and ed. D. Cross, with an introduction by P. Gay [Indianapolis: Hackett, 1987], esp. 39–60).

19. Matei Calinescu, *Five Faces of Modernity* (Durham, NC: Duke University Press,

1987), 41–42. For a seminal discussion of therapeutic culture, see Rieff, *The Triumph of the Therapeutic,* esp. 1–78.

20. Naremore, *More Than Night,* 45.

21. Ibid., 45–46.

22. Palmer, *Hollywood's Dark Cinema,* 36.

23. Stanley Cavell, *The World Viewed: Reflections on the Ontology of Film,* enlarged ed. (Cambridge, MA: Harvard University Press, 1979), 56.

24. Baudelaire, *The Painter of Modern Life,* 29.

25. Baudelaire quoted in Jerrold Seigel, *Bohemian Paris: Culture, Politics, and the Boundaries of Bourgeois Life, 1830–1930* (New York: Penguin, 1986), 109.

26. Camus, *The Myth of Sisyphus and Other Essays,* 50.

27. Camus, *Lyrical and Critical Essays,* 15.

28. For an elaboration of the analysis of Camus presented here, see Alan Woolfolk, "The Pestilent Intellect: Camus's Post-Christian Vision," in *Poets, Princes, and Private Citizens,* ed. J. Knippenberg and P. A. Lawler (Lanham, MD: Rowman & Littlefield, 1996), 91–117.

29. Jean-Paul Sartre, *Baudelaire,* trans. M. Turnell (Norfolk, CT: New Directions, 1950), 51–52.

30. Camus, *Lyrical and Critical Essays,* 259–62.

31. Ibid., 364.

32. Albert Camus, *The Fall,* trans. J. O'Brien (New York: Vintage, 1956), 84.

33. M. M. Bakhtin, *The Dialogic Imagination: Four Essays by M. M. Bakhtin,* ed. M. Holquist, trans. C. Emerson and M. Holquist (Austin: University of Texas Press, 1981), 84.

34. Palmer, "'Lounge Time' Reconsidered," 58.

35. Ibid., 63, 65.

36. Sigmund Freud, *New Introductory Lectures on Psychoanalysis,* ed. and trans. J. Strachey (New York: Norton, 1965), 73.

37. Ibid., 73–76.

# Symbolism, Meaning, and Nihilism in Quentin Tarantino's *Pulp Fiction*

*Mark T. Conard*

*Nihilism* is a term that describes the loss of value and meaning in people's lives. When Nietzsche proclaimed that "God is dead,"[1] he meant that Judeo-Christianity has been lost as a guiding force in our lives and that there is nothing to replace it. Once we ceased really to believe in the myth at the heart of Judeo-Christian religion, which happened after the Scientific Revolution, Judeo-Christian morality lost its character as a binding code by which to live one's life.[2] Given the centrality of religion in our lives for thousands of years, once this moral code is lost and not replaced, we are faced with the abyss of nihilism. Darkness closes in on us, and nothing is of any real value any more. There is no real meaning in our lives, and one way of conducting oneself and one's life is just as good as another, for there is no overarching criterion by which to make such judgments.

Quentin Tarantino's *Pulp Fiction* (1994) is an odd film. It's a seemingly complete narrative that has been chopped into vignettes and rearranged like a puzzle. It's a gangster film in which not a single policeman is to be found.[3] It's a montage of bizarre characters, from a black mobster with a mysterious bandage on the back of his bald head to hillbilly sexual perverts; from henchmen dressed in black suits whose conversations concern what fast-food items are called in Europe to a mob problem solver who attends dinner parties early in the morning dressed in a full tuxedo. So what is the film *about*? In general, we can say that the film is about American nihilism. First, a quick rundown of the film.

## The Vignettes

# PART 1

Ringo and Honeybunny decide to rob a coffee shop. Jules and Vincent discuss what a Quarter Pounder with Cheese, among other things, is called in France. They collect a briefcase that belongs to Marsellus Wallace from Brett, Marvin, et al. Before Jules kills Brett, he quotes a passage from the Old Testament. Marsellus has asked Vincent to take out Mia (Mrs. Marsellus Wallace), and Vincent is nervous because he heard that Marsellus maimed Tony Rocky Horror in a fit of jealousy. Vincent buys heroin and gets high, then takes Mia out to Jack Rabbit Slim's, a restaurant that is full of old American pop icons (Buddy Holly, Marilyn Monroe, Ed Sullivan, Elvis); they win a dance contest. Mia mistakes heroin for cocaine and overdoses, and Vincent has to give her a cardiac needle full of adrenaline to save her.

Butch agrees to throw a fight for Marsellus Wallace. Butch as a child receives a watch from his father's friend, an army comrade who saved the watch by hiding it in his rectum while he was in a Vietnamese prisoner-of-war camp. Butch double-crosses Marsellus and doesn't throw the fight; his boxing opponent is killed. Butch must return to his apartment, despite the fact that Marsellus's men are looking for him, to get his watch; he kills Vincent. Butch tries to run over and kill Marsellus; they fight and end up in a store with Zed, Maynard, and the Gimp, hillbilly sexual perverts. The perverts have subdued and bound Butch and Marsellus and begin to rape Marsellus. Butch gets free and saves Marsellus by killing a hillbilly and wounding another with a samurai sword.

# PART 3

Returning to the opening sequence, one of the kids Jules and Vincent are collecting from tries to shoot them with a large gun; he fails, and Jules takes this as divine intervention. Jules and Vincent take Marvin and the briefcase; Marvin is shot accidentally, and the car they're riding in becomes unusable. Jules and Vincent stop at Jimmy's, and Marsellus sends Winston Wolf to mop up. Jules and Vincent end up in the coffee shop that Ringo and Honeybunny are robbing. Ringo wants to take the briefcase, but Jules won't let him. Jules quotes the biblical passage again to Ringo and tells him that he would quote this to someone before he killed that person. This time, however, Jules is not going to kill Ringo. Ringo and Honeybunny take the money from the coffee shop; Jules and Vincent retain the briefcase.

## Transient Symbols

As I said, in general, the film is about American nihilism. More specifically, it is about the transformation of two characters, Jules (Samuel L. Jackson) and Butch (Bruce Willis). In the beginning of the film, Vincent (John Travolta) has returned from a stay in Amsterdam, and the content of the conversation between Jules and Vincent concerns what Big Macs, Quarter Pounders with Cheese, and Whoppers are called in France, the Fonz on *Happy Days,* Arnold the Pig on *Green Acres,* the pop band Flock of Seagulls, Caine from *Kung Fu,* TV pilots, etc. These kinds of silly references seem at first glance like a kind of comic relief, set against the violence that we're witnessing on the screen. But this is no mere comic relief. The point is that this is the way these characters make sense of their lives: transient, pop cultural symbols and icons. In another time and/or another place, people would be connected by something they saw as larger than themselves— most particularly religion—that would provide the sense and meaning that their lives had and that would determine the value of things. This is missing in late-twentieth-century (and now early-twenty-first-century) America and is thus completely absent from Jules's and Vincent's lives. This is why pop icons abound in the film: these are the reference points by which we understand ourselves and each other, empty and ephemeral as they are. This pop iconography comes to a real head when Vincent and Mia (Uma Thurman) visit Jack Rabbit Slim's, where the host is Ed Sullivan, the singer is Ricky Nelson, the waiter is Buddy Holly, and among the waitresses are Marilyn Monroe and Jane Mansfield.

The pop cultural symbols are set into stark relief against a certain passage from the Old Testament, Ezekiel 25:17:[4]

> The path of the righteous man is beset on all sides by the iniquities of the selfish and the tyranny of evil men. Blessed is he, who in the name of charity and good will, shepherds the weak through the valley of darkness, for he is truly his brother's keeper and the finder of lost children.
> And I will strike down upon thee with great vengeance and fu-

rious anger those who attempt to poison and destroy my brothers. And you will know my name is the Lord when I lay my vengeance upon thee.

Jules quotes this just before he kills someone. The point is that the passage refers to a system of values and meaning by which one could lead one's life and make moral decisions. However, that system is missing from Jules's life, so, as we will see, the passage is meaningless for him.

## The Hierarchy of Power

The absence of any kind of foundation for making value judgments, the lack of a larger meaning to the characters' lives, creates a kind of vacuum in their existence, a vacuum that is filled with power. With no other criteria available to them by which to order their lives, they fall into a hierarchy of power in which Marsellus Wallace (Ving Rhames) calls the shots. Things come to have value in their lives if Marsellus Wallace declares it to be so. What he wants done they will do. What he wishes becomes valuable for them and thus becomes the guide for their actions at the moment, until the task is completed by whatever means necessary.

This is perfectly epitomized by the mysterious briefcase that Jules and Vincent are charged to return to Marsellus. It is mysterious because we never actually see what's in it, but we do see people's reactions to its obviously valuable contents.[5] The question invariably arises, What's in the briefcase? However, this is a trick question. The answer is really, It doesn't matter. It makes no difference what's in the briefcase. All that matters is that Marsellus wants it back, and thus the thing is endowed with worth. If Jules and Vincent did have an objective framework of value and meaning in their lives, they would be able to determine whether what was in the briefcase was ultimately of value, and they would be able to determine what actions were justified in retrieving it. In the absence of any such framework, the briefcase becomes of ultimate value in and of itself, precisely because Marsellus says so, and any and all actions required to procure it become justified (including, obviously, murder).

In addition to the pop iconography in the film, the discourse on language here concerns naming things. What is a Big Mac called? What is a Quarter Pounder with Cheese called? What is a Whopper called? (Vincent doesn't know; he didn't go to Burger King.) When Ringo (Tim Roth) calls the waitress "garçon," she informs him: "*Garçon* means 'boy.'" Also, when Butch's girlfriend refers to his means of transportation as a *motorcycle,* he insists on correcting her: "It's not a motorcycle, it's a chopper." Yet—and here's the crux—when a lovely Hispanic cabdriver asks Butch what his name means, he replies, "This is America, honey; our names don't mean shit." The point is clear: in the absence of any lasting, transcendent, objective framework of value and meaning, our language no longer points to anything beyond itself. To call something *good* or *evil* renders it so, given that there is no higher authority or criteria by which one might judge actions. Jules quotes the Bible before his executions, but he may as well be quoting the Fonz or Buddy Holly.

## Objective Values

I've been contrasting nihilism with religion as an objective framework for or foundation of values and meaning because that's the comparison that Tarantino himself makes in the film. There are other objective systems of ethics, however. We might compare nihilism to Aristotelian ethics, for example. Aristotle says that things have natures or essences and that what is best for a thing is to "achieve" or realize its essence. And, in fact, whatever helps a thing fulfill its nature in this way is, by definition, good. Ducks are aquatic birds. Having webbed feet helps the duck achieve its essence as a swimmer. Therefore, it's good for the duck to have webbed feet. Human beings likewise have a nature that consists in a set of capacities, our abilities to do things. There are many things that we can do—play the piano, build things, walk and talk, etc. But the essentially human ability is our capacity for reason, since it is reason that separates us from all other living things. The highest good, or best life, for a human being, then, consists in realizing one's capacities, most particularly the capacity for reason. This notion of the highest good and Aristotle's conception of the virtues, which are states of character that enable a person to achieve his essence, add up to an objective ethical framework according to which one can weigh and assess the value and meaning of things as well as weigh and assess the means one might use to procure those things.

To repeat, this sort of framework, whether based on religion or reason, is completely absent from Jules's and Vincent's lives. In its absence, pop culture is the source of the symbols and reference points by which the two communicate and understand one another. And, without reason or a religious moral code to determine the value and meaning that things have in their lives, Marsellus Wallace dictates the value of things. This lack of any kind of higher authority is depicted in the film by the conspicuous absence of any police presence whatever. This is a gangster film—people shoot other people dead, they deal and take drugs, they drive recklessly and get into car accidents—yet there is not a single policeman to be found. Again, this symbolizes Marsellus's absolute power and control in the absence of any higher, objective authority.

## Jules

*Pulp Fiction* is, in part, about Jules's transformation. When one of his targets shoots at him and Vincent from a short distance, empties the revolver, and misses completely, Jules interprets this as divine intervention. The importance of this is not that it really was divine intervention but that the incident spurs Jules on to reflect on what is missing. It compels him to consider the biblical passage that he's been quoting for years without giving much thought to it. Jules begins to understand—however confusedly at first—that it refers to an objective framework of value and meaning that is absent from his life. We see the dawning of this kind of understanding first when he reports to Vincent that he's quitting the mob and then (most significantly) when he repeats the passage to Ringo in the coffee shop and then interprets it. He says:

> I've been saying that shit for years, and if you heard it—that meant your ass. I never gave much thought to what it meant, I just thought it was some cold-blooded shit to say to a motherfucker before I popped a cap in his ass. But I saw some shit this morning that made me think twice. See, now I'm thinking, maybe it means: you're the Evil Man, and I'm the Righteous Man, and Mr. 9mm here—he's the Shepherd protecting my righteous ass in the valley of darkness. Or it could mean: you're the Righteous Man, and I'm the Shepherd; and it's the world that's evil and selfish. Now, I'd like that, but that shit ain't the truth. The truth is: you're the Weak and I'm the Tyranny of Evil Men. But I'm trying, Ringo, I'm trying real hard to be the Shepherd.

Jules offers three possible interpretations of the passage. The first interpretation accords with the way he has been living his life. Whatever he does (as commanded by Marsellus) is justified, and thus he is the Righteous Man, with his pistol protecting him, and whatever stands in his way is bad or evil by definition. The second interpretation is interesting and seems to go along with Jules's pseudoreligious attitude following what he interprets as a divine-mystical experience (he tells Vincent, recall, that he wants to wander the earth like Caine on *Kung Fu*). In this interpretation, the world is evil and selfish and has, apparently, made Jules do all the terrible things he's done up to that point. He's now become the Shepherd, and he's going to protect Ringo (who, after all, is small potatoes in mob terms, robbing coffee shops, etc.) from this evil.

But that's not the truth, he realizes. The truth is that he himself is the evil that he's been preaching about (unwittingly) for years. Ringo is weak, neither good enough to be righteous nor strong enough to be as evil as Jules and Vincent. And Jules is trying to transform himself into the Shepherd, to lead Ringo through the valley of darkness. Of course, interestingly, the darkness is of Jules's own making, meaning that the struggle to be the Shepherd is Jules's struggle with himself not to revert to evil.

In this struggle, he buys Ringo's life. Ringo has collected the wallets of the customers in the coffee shop, including Jules's, and Jules allows him to take fifteen hundred dollars out of it. Jules is paying Ringo the fifteen hundred dollars to take the money from the coffee shop and simply leave so that he, Jules, won't have to kill him. Note that no such transformation has taken place for Vincent, who exclaims: "Jules, you give that fucking nimrod fifteen hundred dollars, and I'll shoot him on general principle." The principle is, of course, that whatever means are necessary to achieve my end are justified, the end (again) most often determined by Marsellus Wallace. This attitude of Vincent's is clearly depicted in his reaction to Mia's overdose. He desperately tries to save her, not because she is a fellow human being of intrinsic worth, but because she is Marsellus's wife and he, Vincent, will be in real trouble if she dies. Mia has value because Marsellus has made it so, not because of any intrinsic or objective features or characteristics she may possess.

## Butch

The other transformation in the film is that of Butch. There is a conspicuous progression in the meaning and relevance of the violence in the story. In the beginning, we see killings that are completely gratuitous: that, for example, of Brett and his cohorts, particularly Marvin, who is shot in the face simply because the car went over a bump and the gun went off. There is also the maiming of Tony Rocky Horror, the reason for which is hidden from all, save Marsellus. Again, this is evidence that it is Marsellus himself who provides the meaning and justification for things, and his reasons—like God's—are hidden from us. (This may, in fact, be what the bandage on Marsellus's head represents: the fact that his motives and reasons are hidden to us. Bandages not only help heal; they also hide or disguise what we don't want others to see.) The meaninglessness of the violence is also epitomized in the boxing match. Butch kills his opponent. When the cabdriver, Esmarelda Villalobos (Angela Jones), informs him of this, his reaction is one of complete indifference. He shrugs it off. Further, when Butch gets into his jam for having double-crossed Marsellus, he initially decides that the way he is going to get out of it is to become like his enemy, that is, to become ruthless. Consequently, he shoots and kills Vincent and then tries to kill Marsellus by running him over with a car.

The situation becomes interesting when Butch and Marsellus, initially willing to kill one another without a second's thought, find themselves in the same unpleasant situation: held hostage by a couple of hillbillies who are about to beat and rape them. I noted earlier the conspicuous absence of policemen in the film. The interesting quasi exception to this is the pervert Zed. Marsellus is taken captive, bound, and gagged. When Zed shows up, he is dressed in a security guard's uniform, giving him the appearance of an authority figure. He is *only* a security guard, not a real policeman, however, and this is our clue to the arbitrariness of authority. In the nihilistic context in which these characters exist, in the absence of an objective framework of value to determine right, justice, and goodness, Marsellus Wallace is the legislator of values, the ultimate authority. In this situation, however, his authority has been usurped. Zed holds the shotgun now, and he takes his usurpation to the extreme by raping Marsellus.

## Butch's Transformation

Just as Jules's transformation has a defining moment, namely, when he is fired on and missed, so too Butch's transformation has a defining moment. This is when he is about to escape, having overpowered the Gimp, but returns to save Marsellus. As I said, initially the violence is gratuitous and without meaning. However, when Butch returns to the cellar to aid Marsellus, the violence for the first time has a justification: as an act of honor and friendship, he is saving Marsellus, once his enemy, from men who are worse than he and Marsellus are. Note that Butch gets out of his jam, not by becoming like his enemy, that is, ruthless, but in fact by saving his enemy.

Butch's transformation is represented by his choice of weapons in the store—a hammer, a baseball bat, a chain saw, and a samurai sword. He overlooks the first three items and chooses the fourth. Why? The sword clearly stands out in the list. First, it's meant to be a weapon, while the others are not (and I'll discuss that in a moment). But it also stands out because the first three items (two of them particularly) are symbols of Americana. They represent the nihilism that Butch is leaving behind, whereas the samurai sword represents a particular culture in which there is (or was) in place a very rigid moral framework, the kind of objective foundation that I've been saying is missing from these characters' lives. The sword represents for Butch what the biblical passage does for Jules: a glimpse beyond transient pop culture, a glimpse beyond the yawning abyss of nihilism, to a way of life, a manner of thinking, in which there are objective moral criteria, in which there is meaning and value, and in which language does transcend itself.

## Butch's Paternal Line

In contrast to the (foreign) samurai sword, the gold watch is a kind of heirloom that's passed down in (American) families. It represents a kind of tradition of honor and manhood. But let's think about how the watch gets passed down in this case. Butch's great-grandfather buys it in Knoxville before he goes off to fight in World War I. Having survived the war, he passes the watch on to his son, Butch's grandfather, who then leaves it to his own son, Butch's father, before he goes into battle during World War II and is killed. Butch's father, interned in a Vietnamese prisoner-of-war camp, hides the watch in his rectum, and, before he dies (significantly) from dysentery, he gives it to his army comrade (Christopher Walken), who then hides it in his own rectum. After returning from the war, the comrade finds Butch as a boy and presents him with the watch. The way in which Butch receives the watch is, of course, highly significant. His father hides it in his *rectum*. The watch is a piece of shit; or, in other words, it is an empty symbol. Why empty? For the same reason that the biblical passage was meaningless: it is a symbol with no referent. That to which it would refer is missing.

The sword is also significant because it, unlike the gold watch (an heirloom sent to Butch by a long-absent father whom he little remembers), connects Butch to the masculine line in his family. The men in his family were warriors, soldiers in the various wars. Choosing the sword transforms Butch from a pugilist, someone disconnected who steps into the ring alone, into a soldier, a warrior, one who is connected to a history and a tradition and whose actions are guided by a strict code of conduct in which honor and courage are the most important of values.

Note also how Butch is always returning. He seems doomed to return, perhaps to repeat things, until he gets it right. He must return to his apartment to get his watch. This return is associated with his decision to become his enemy. There's his return to the cellar to save Marsellus, when he transcends his situation and begins to grasp something beyond the abyss. There's also his return to Knoxville. Recall that the watch was originally purchased by his great-grandfather in Knoxville, and it is to Knoxville that Butch has planned to escape after he doesn't throw the fight. After he chooses the sword and saves Marsellus, Butch can rightfully return to Knoxville, now connected to his paternal line, now rightfully a member of the warrior class.

Note finally that Butch's transformation is signified by the motorcycle—excuse me, *chopper*—that he steals from Zed and on which he and Fabienne (Maria de Medeiros) make their escape to Knoxville. The chopper is named "Grace," indicating that Butch has at last found his redemption.

## Notes

I wish to thank Lou Ascione and Aeon Skoble, who have helped me clarify and refine my ideas about *Pulp Fiction* in discussions we've had. Earlier versions of this essay appeared as "Symbolism, Meaning, and Nihilism in Quentin Tarantino's *Pulp Fiction*," *Philosophy Now*, no. 19 (winter 1997–98): 10–14, and as "Pulp Fiction: The Sign of the Empty Symbol," *Metaphilm*, posted July 20, 2004, at http://metaphilm.com/philm.php?id=178_0_2_0.

1. See Friedrich Nietzsche, "The Madman," in *The Gay Science*, trans. Walter Kaufmann (New York: Vintage, 1974), sec. 125, p. 181.

2. Actually, Nietzsche means something broader than this: by saying that God is dead, he means that any notion of objective, absolute value or truth is lost, not just

those inherent to Judeo-Christianity, but it is the latter that concerns Tarantino in *Pulp Fiction,* so I'm restricting my discussion to it.

3. With one very important exception, to be noted below.

4. The quote is a paraphrase of the biblical passage and comes from the Sonny Chiba movie *Bodigaado Kiba* (The Bodyguard; Tatsuichi Takamori, 1973). Chiba's version ends: "And you will know my name is Chiba the Bodyguard when I lay my vengeance upon thee."

5. Cinematically, the briefcase is a reference to Robert Aldrich's classic noir *Kiss Me Deadly* (1955), in which the characters (notably the protagonist, Mike Hammer) chase after a box that contains some mysterious, glowing contents, believing it to be wildly valuable. Ironically, it turns out to be radioactive material, and, once released, it unleashes an apparent nuclear holocaust.

# PART 3

## Six Classic Films Noirs

# Film Noir and the Frankfurt School

## America as Wasteland in Edgar Ulmer's *Detour*

*Paul A. Cantor*

> It is easier for me to say this, coming from Europe, an area where nature can be seen as friendly and domesticated, unlike the USA, where nature is seen as either to be exploited or to be fled to as a relief from civilization. I am continually shocked by the unhumanized nature in this country, no parks, no formal gardens. Nature never intended human beings to live in the USA—only in just a little bit of Europe and in New Zealand.
>
> *W. H. Auden,* Lectures on Shakespeare

In the history of film noir, Edgar G. Ulmer's *Detour* (1945) occupies an honored place, appearing on just about everybody's short list of classics of the genre, and frequently cited as the director's best work.[1] At the time Ulmer made the movie, he was operating on the fringes of the motion picture industry, virtually as an independent producer. Although *Detour* was famously made in under a week and for less than $20,000, Ulmer delivered a professional piece of work, showing why he came to be known as the "King of the B-Movies." Despite some signs of haste and cheapness in the production, *Detour* offers a textbook illustration of film noir. In terms of technique, Ulmer makes use of many film noir conventions: voice-over narration, unusual camera angles, and an effective use of lighting that harks back to his training in the twenties when he worked in Berlin with F. W. Murnau at the peak of German expressionist cinema. In terms of its subject matter, *Detour* tells a typical noir tale of an ordinary, basically decent man who, through a quirk of fate, is drawn into a web of crime, chiefly as a result of a chance encounter with a femme fatale. The story unfolds quickly, with a strong sense of inevitability, as every step the hero takes to avoid his doom only brings him closer to it.

A film noir encyclopedia conveniently offers a summary of the plot of *Detour:*

> Al Roberts is a pianist in a New York nightclub where his girl friend, Sue, is a singer. The two plan to marry, but Sue is ambitious and leaves for "stardom" in Hollywood. Left alone, Roberts calls her one night and Sue tells him that she works as a waitress. He decides to hitchhike West and join her. Eventually, he is picked up by Haskell, who is carrying a lot of cash and driving all the way to Los Angeles. Haskell talks about a female hitchhiker who scratched him viciously when he made a sexual advance. Later, he goes to sleep while Roberts drives. When it begins to rain, Roberts attempts rousing Haskell to put up the convertible top, but Haskell is mysteriously dead, although his head hits a rock when Roberts accidentally causes the body to fall out of the car. Roberts, believing the police will never accept his innocence, hides the body and drives on alone. The next day Roberts picks up Vera, initially unaware that she is the same woman who scratched Haskell. Questioning him about the man's death, she does not believe Roberts' story but agrees to remain silent if he will follow her plans. Arriving in Los Angeles, they rent a room; and Vera plans that Roberts will sell the car using Haskell's identity. But when she discovers that Haskell was the heir of a dying millionaire and that his family has not seen him for years, she plans to pass Roberts off as Haskell. That night they quarrel about this scheme, and Vera runs into the other room threatening to call the police but collapses drunkenly on the bed with the telephone cord entwined about her neck. Roberts pulls on the cord from the other side of the locked door, inadvertently strangling her. Without even seeing his fiancée, Roberts flees to Reno, where he sits in a diner and reflects on the strange circumstances that have put him in such a hopeless situation.[2]

## Deconstructing the American Dream

Even in such a bare summary, the bitterness and cynicism of *Detour* are clearly evident. The film is a systematic deconstruction of the American dream. The hero's quest for happiness—to find simple contentment with the woman he loves—leads him only to his corruption and, eventually, to his destruction (he is being arrested as the film ends). Like any good American, Roberts wants to make a better life for himself, and his chance encounter with Haskell seems to give him the opportunity, providing him with all the external signs of success in American terms: a luxury automobile, a fancy suit, and a wad of cash in his pocket. Roberts seems able to trade places with the outwardly successful Haskell; he can step right into Haskell's clothes, and they fit him perfectly. But all these newly acquired material goods turn out to be a burden to Roberts and are, in fact, what trap him into committing further crimes.

The full polemical thrust of Ulmer's film becomes evident when one realizes that he is using *Detour* to restage a particular archetype of the American dream. As a hitchhiker headed for California, Roberts is following Horace Greeley's immortal injunction: "Go west, young man." But no pot of gold, real or metaphoric, awaits Roberts at the end of the California rainbow. Indeed, his girlfriend, Sue, has preceded him to Hollywood and already failed to achieve her dream of becoming a star as a singer. Haskell turns out to be a two-bit chiseler and gambler whose dream of a big payoff at a West Coast racetrack ends with his body lying somewhere in the Arizona desert. Vera, who dreams of making a fortune with a con game at the expense of the legitimate heirs in the Haskell family, ends up strangled in a hotel room. Everywhere one looks in *Detour*, the American dream, particularly of striking it rich, turns into a nightmare, and the West—traditionally the land of opportunity in American mythology—is revealed to be, in truth, the land of shattered dreams.[3]

Thus, *Detour* is an anti-Hollywood film in both a general and a specific sense. It serves as a counterweight to the typical product of the Hollywood dream factory. Ulmer inverts a standard pattern of Hollywood romance, one in which a young couple must go their separate ways in order to pursue their independent goals in life but are in the end happily reunited, usually with their goals accomplished and their love intact and even deepened as a result of the obstacles they have encountered and overcome. That Ulmer had the false narrative clichés of Hollywood romance in mind is evident in the script of *Detour*. At one point, Roberts is contemplating how things might work out with Vera and imagines a variety of stock Hollywood happy endings: "If this were fiction, I would fall in love with Vera, marry her, and make a respectable woman out of her. Or else she'd make some supreme class A sacrifice for me and die. Sue and I would bawl a little over her grave and make some crack about there's good in all of us." The implication of these lines is clear: "If this were fiction . . . but it isn't." Ulmer establishes the realism of his film by contrasting it with the fantasy and sentimentality of standard Hollywood melodrama.[4]

But Ulmer goes further—he is debunking not just the generic Hollywood version of the American dream but the dream of Hollywood itself. Early in the story, Sue decides to advance her singing career by leaving New York for the West Coast: "I want to try my luck in Hollywood." Roberts tries to prevent her from pursuing this empty dream: "Don't you know millions of people go out there every year and end up polishing cuspidors?" Aware of the deceptive allure of Hollywood, Roberts later tries to console Sue over the phone when she finds that reality does not measure up to dreams in California: "Those guys out in Hollywood don't know the real thing when it's right in front of them." At the beginning of the film, Roberts thinks that he can distinguish reality from illusion, even if Hollywood talent scouts do not know the real thing when they see it. But, as he journeys west, Roberts gradually loses his grip on reality and allows himself to be drawn into pursuing a dream as false as anything in Hollywood.

By creating an antifantasy film, Ulmer is criticizing Hollywood for serving up illusions to the American public, always telling them that their dreams will come true if they just try hard enough and get a lucky break or two. And he is specifically criticizing Hollywood for offering itself as its most potent fantasy. The greatest myth that Hollywood has ever created is the myth of being discovered in Hollywood (preferably at Schwab's Drugstore) and becoming a star overnight. We know how a movie like *Detour* would have ended in the hands of the average Hollywood studio. Sue would have gotten her big break as a singer, made the most of it, and used her newly acquired wealth to get Roberts out of his predicament. In the last scene, he would have been making his long-delayed debut as a concert pianist at Carnegie Hall, with Sue in the audience cheering him on. But, at every turn, Ulmer thwarts the plot expectations that his audience has inherited from standard Hollywood fare. "This is the way life really is," he seems to be saying, "not the way you see it in the movies."

## Eminent Émigrés

It would be all too easy to give an autobiographical interpretation of *De-*

*tour.* Ulmer had more reason than most to distrust the Hollywood dream—for a time he lived it, and then suddenly he lost it all. Having immigrated to Hollywood in the early thirties after some earlier experience in the film industry, Ulmer got his big break when Universal chose him to direct a feature film called *The Black Cat* (1934), a major assignment considering that it was to be the first project to unite the studio's two most famous horror movie stars, Bela Lugosi and Boris Karloff. *The Black Cat* was a triumph for Ulmer; many consider it one of the most sophisticated and powerful horror movies ever made, and, more to the point, with Lugosi and Karloff giving perhaps their best screen performances, and certainly their best together, the film was a box-office success; it "proved to be Universal's hit of the season, with a profit of $140,000."[5]

Ulmer's future in Hollywood seemed bright. But, in a moment that seems to anticipate the lurid plot twists of his own later movies, he had an affair with the wife of a nephew of Carl Laemmle, the head of Universal. The resulting divorce and Ulmer's marriage to the woman he loved led to his being banished from the Universal lot. Indeed, Laemmle was so powerful in the industry that Ulmer was effectively exiled from Hollywood for over a decade, thus sending him off on his checkered career as a more or less independent filmmaker, or at least one operating largely outside the major studio system. Thus, Ulmer had personal experience of the elusiveness of the Hollywood dream and reason to criticize a system that had at first embraced him and then rejected him. One could justifiably read *Detour* as the work of a man bitterly disillusioned with Hollywood and determined to get his artistic revenge with a film that exposes the illusory character of the typical Hollywood fantasy and presents Hollywood itself as the biggest illusion of them all.

But as much as *Detour* may have grown out of Ulmer's personal experience, to view the film as solely a product of his private vendetta against Hollywood would be to reduce its power in our eyes. To see how *Detour* transcends merely personal issues, we need to place it in the larger cultural and intellectual context of its day. In fact, in retrospect, we can now understand *Detour* as an act of what has come to be known as *culture critique*. In its attitude toward America in general and Hollywood in particular, Ulmer's film displays remarkable affinities with the thinking of the Frankfurt school of philosophy. Discussing *Detour* and the Frankfurt school together will mutually illuminate the two phenomena. The ideas of the Frankfurt school will help clarify what Ulmer is saying about Hollywood in *Detour,* and

Ulmer's film will, in turn, help us understand the impulses behind the Frankfurt school and the whole movement of culture critique.

The Frankfurt school is named after the institution where its members first gathered, the Institute for Social Research (Institut für Sozialforschung), founded in Frankfurt am Main, Germany, in 1923. Broadly speaking Marxist in its orientation, the Frankfurt school nevertheless drew on the whole German intellectual tradition, including Kant, Hegel, Nietzsche, and Heidegger, and it was also heavily influenced by Freud. Among the figures associated with the Frankfurt school over the years were Theodor Adorno, Walter Benjamin, Erich Fromm, Max Horkheimer, Leo Lowenthal, and Herbert Marcuse.[6] Because the Frankfurt school associates were left-wing intellectuals (several of the founders were members of the Communist Party), they were forced to flee Nazi Germany in the thirties, especially since many of them were Jewish or of Jewish ancestry. Those who managed to leave Germany safely generally immigrated to the United States, mostly to New York, but some to Los Angeles.[7] Adorno, for example, ended up living during World War II in the Brentwood area of greater Los Angeles and Horkheimer in Pacific Palisades, thus placing them just west of Hollywood.[8] As refugees from Nazi Germany, the Frankfurt school members were generally welcomed by the Hollywood community and, thus, had something in common with Ulmer in terms of their initial experience of the United States.[9]

## The Culture Industry

The central work of the Frankfurt school is *Dialectic of Enlightenment* by Horkheimer and Adorno, first published in German in 1944 as *Dialektik der Aufklärung*. The best-known chapter of this book, and the one most relevant to *Detour,* deals with Hollywood—"The Culture Industry: Enlightenment as Mass Deception." As the chapter's title indicates, Horkheimer and Adorno set out in it to present Hollywood as a fountain of illusions, just the sort of dream factory that Ulmer has in mind in *Detour:* "The culture industry perpetually cheats its consumers of what it perpetually promises. The promissory note which, with its plots and staging, it draws on pleasure is endlessly prolonged; the promise, which is actually all the spectacle consists of, is illusory: all it actually confirms is that the real point will never be reached, that the diner must be satisfied with the menu. In front of the appetite stimulated by all those brilliant names and images there is finally set no more than a commendation of the depressing every-day world it sought to escape."[10]

In general, the Frankfurt school marks a turn in twentieth-century Marxism from an economic to a cultural critique of capitalism. The Frankfurt school thinkers were smart enough to see that orthodox Marxism was losing the economic argument against capitalism. Traditionally, Marxists had claimed that capitalism would lead to the progressive impoverishment of the masses. By the forties, despite the significant setbacks of the Depression, the standard of living of workers in capitalist countries had risen substantially since the days of Marx—Adorno speaks of "the greater abundance of goods within reach even of the poor."[11] "The poor with a greater abundance of goods" is one of those marvelously paradoxical concepts devised by twentieth-century Marxists, and, indeed, it was especially difficult for someone arriving from Europe in the middle of southern California to conclude that Americans were materially worse off because of capitalism. Adorno and other members of the Frankfurt school had to find a way of showing that the abundance of commodities that capitalism produces is, in fact, bad for the masses—that, although they seem to be materially enriched by capitalism, they are really being spiritually and culturally impoverished.[12] The work of the Frankfurt school came to focus on culture critique, on analyzing the harmful effects of the commercial culture of capitalism, especially insofar as it takes the form of mass culture.

Thus, Hollywood seemed tailor-made for the Frankfurt school thinkers, and, if they had not been atheists, they might have seen the hand of Providence at work when their flight from Hitler dropped them in the midst of a power they came to regard as equally sinister—Hollywood. "The Culture Industry" attempts to show that motion pictures with their links to commercial advertising are the capitalist equivalent of totalitarian propaganda. In an argument that has become familiar and widely accepted, Horkheimer and Adorno claim that the motion picture industry manipulates and even controls the American public. It gives the appearance of merely providing the public with what it wants, but, in fact, it creates the desires that it claims to be satisfying.

In the view of Horkheimer and Adorno, Hollywood is always foisting unwanted products onto a gullible public: "It is claimed that standards were based in the first place on consumers' needs, and for that reason were accepted with so little resistance. The result is the circle of manipulation and retroactive need in which the unity of the system grows ever stronger. . . . The man with leisure has to accept what the culture manufacturers offer him." Horkheimer and Adorno present American audiences as the passive victims of an all-powerful entertainment industry that manipulates them as cleverly (and cynically) as fascist dictators. In a remarkable variant of the moral equivalence argument, they claim that "the bourgeois . . . is already virtually a Nazi." Later, they compare "the spread of popular songs" to the rapid diffusion of Nazi propaganda slogans, and, in a bizarre passage, they equate the radio transmission of a Hitler speech with an NBC broadcast of Toscanini conducting a symphony (this argument is particularly odd in view of the Italian conductor's courageous and unwavering opposition to fascism in his homeland and elsewhere).[13]

## The Big Casino

One might already note parallels in this view of the American public to the vision of life in the United States that Ulmer develops in *Detour*. Critics have often noted the passivity of the characters in film noir and particularly in *Detour*—the way their lives seem to be governed by forces beyond their control. The characters in *Detour* seem incapable of generating authentic desires; they are always setting their goals on the basis of the models that American society offers them, and, as we see quite literally in the case of Roberts, their aim becomes to step into the shoes of the other guy only because he is admired in the community.

As we have seen, Ulmer strongly suggests that Hollywood is the principal source of these images of desire, shaping the dreams that govern the average person's life. But the parallels between Ulmer's *Detour* and the Frankfurt school go deeper than this. Horkheimer and Adorno view the entertainment industry as capitalism at its most exploitative, forcing people to spend their hard-earned money on forms of amusement that they could easily do without and that they never wanted in the first place.[14] But, for the Frankfurt school, the sinister role of capitalism extends beyond merely dumping unwanted goods on a hapless public. Itself the ultimate expression of capitalism, the entertainment industry seeks to provide an ideological justification for capitalism, to help make the system as a whole function and sustain its power over the masses.

To accomplish this purpose, as the Frankfurt school understands it, the entertainment industry must reconcile the masses to the system that exploits them and, thus, prevent them from even thinking about rebelling against it. With this end in view, Hollywood creates a mass cultural myth of hope, tantalizing the American people with the prospect of bettering their lives and escaping from their downtrodden condition. Hollywood manufactures a picture of society as a kind of giant lottery in which anyone can win the big payoff. The vast majority of individuals in the capitalist system may have to live with being exploited and accept their passive roles as losers, but, if they can be bombarded with striking images of winners, of people who have been lucky enough to beat the system, they can live on in hope that they too might someday cash in on good fortune and join the magic circle of the successful.

Horkheimer and Adorno see that the culmination of this image of society as a lottery is the myth of success in Hollywood itself. A key passage in "The Culture Industry" is worth quoting at length:

Not everyone will be lucky one day—but the person who draws the winning ticket, or rather the one who is marked out to do so by a higher power—usually by the pleasure industry itself, which is represented as unceasingly in search of talent. Those discovered by talent scouts and then publicized on a vast scale by the studio are ideal types of the new dependent average. Of course, the starlet is meant to symbolize the typist in such a way that the splendid evening dress seems meant for the actress as distinct from the real girl. The girls in the audience not only feel that they could be on the screen, but realize the great gulf separating them from it. Only one girl can draw the lucky ticket, only one man can win the prize, and if, mathematically, all have the same chance, yet this is so infinitesimal for each one that he or she will do best to write it off and rejoice in the other's success, which might just as well have been his or hers, and somehow never is.... Increasing emphasis is laid not on the path *per aspera ad astra* (which presupposes hardship and effort), but on winning a prize. . . . Movies emphasize chance. . . . [Moviegoers] are assured that they are all right as they are, that they could do just as well and that nothing beyond their powers will be asked of them. But at the same time they are given a hint that any effort would be useless because even bourgeois luck no longer has any connection with the calculable effect of their own work.[15]

The relevance of this passage to understanding *Detour* should be obvious. Just like Horkheimer and Adorno, Ulmer, as we have seen, portrays an America obsessed with the lottery idea, of striking it rich. Haskell is literally a gambler; significantly, the horse he intends to bet on at Santa Anita is named Paradisical, pointing to the American hope for heaven on earth. But all the main characters in *Detour* are in one way or another gamblers, and in the background, in Sue's story, we sense that Hollywood may be the biggest gamble of them all. Ulmer wants to efface the distinction between gambling as an illicit or illegal activity and gambling as a part of everyday life in America—perfectly symbolized by the way the decent citizen Roberts seamlessly steps into the role of the bookie Haskell. Vera and Roberts play cards to pass the time while waiting to sell Haskell's car. And the film is narrated from Reno, Nevada, where Roberts ends up in his effort to escape Los Angeles—Reno, the capital of legal gambling in the United States at the time *Detour* was made (Las Vegas was still only a gleam in Bugsy Siegel's eye in the early forties). When one adds up all the instances in the film, Ulmer seems to be presenting gambling as the American way of life, or, rather, the idea that the American way of life is fundamentally a gamble.

## Mechanical Reproduction

There are more specific parallels between the way Ulmer pictures America in *Detour* and the thinking of the Frankfurt school. The core of the Horkheimer-Adorno critique of American culture is that it is a mass phenomenon and that, in order to reach wide audiences, the entertainment industry has to mechanize and merchandise culture. Here, they were drawing on Benjamin's well-known essay "The Work of Art in the Age of Mechanical Reproduction," in which he argues that, in the modern world, the work of art is losing its unique aura because it is being reproduced ad infinitum by a capitalist economy—packaged, advertised, and, thus, commodified.[16] Adorno, who was a musicologist and a composer, was particularly interested in how this process was playing out in the world of music. He adamantly defended the virtues of live performance; he objected to presenting the musical classics in recorded form. As we have seen in his strange equation of Hitler and Toscanini, he even objected to radio broadcasts of live performances. Adorno believed, with some justification, that only when people are physically present at a live performance can they experience the full impact of the music. He was not impressed by the counterargument that radio and records were making classical music available to multitudes of listeners in a way that was simply impossible in the nineteenth century.[17] For Adorno, great classical music is inevitably compromised by any effort to make it widely accessible. He was struck by the fact that radio stations play both classical and popular music and was obviously disturbed by hearing performances by Toscanini right next to performances by Guy Lombardo (Lombardo was a bandleader who specialized in syrupy arrangements).[18]

Adorno believed that America was corrupting the sublime achievements of European composers by effacing the distinction between classical and popular music: "The jazz musician Benny Goodman appears with the Budapest string quartet, more pedantic rhythmically than any philharmonic clarinetist, while the style of the Budapest players is as uniform and sugary as that of Guy Lombardo."[19] Here, Adorno actually claims that the playing style of the Budapest String Quartet was contaminated by contact with American popular culture. Above all, he inveighed against jazz, America's distinctive contribution to world music.[20] For Adorno, jazz summed up everything that is vulgar and debased in American culture, and he was particularly appalled by jazz arrangements of classical music: "No Palestrina could be more of a purist in eliminating every unprepared and unresolved discord than the jazz arranger in suppressing any development which does not conform to the jargon. When jazzing up Mozart he changes him not only when he is too serious or too difficult but when he harmonizes the melody in a different way, perhaps more simply, than is customary now."[21]

One would not expect to find this kind of sophisticated argument about classical music translated into cinematic terms, especially in a B-movie, yet that is just what Ulmer does in *Detour*. As the film opens in a roadside cafe in Nevada, the first music we hear comes from a jukebox—the Benjaminian technological nightmare par excellence. Roberts reacts violently to the jukebox music and wants it turned off. He is upset because the song reminds him of his lost love, Sue, but, almost as if he were a member of the Frankfurt school himself, he also seems to be reacting against the sheer mechanical reproduction of the music. In the first of the many flashbacks that make up the movie, we see, by contrast, Roberts performing live as a pianist in a small jazz combo with Sue as the vocalist. But, when the set is over and we get to hear Roberts performing for himself, he is playing classical music—Chopin's Waltz in C# Minor, op. 64, no. 2. Sue addresses him: "Mr. Paderewski, I presume. It's beautiful. You're going to make Carnegie Hall yet, Al."

Ulmer sketches in the background quickly, but the basic story is clear. Roberts has aspirations of being a great classical pianist like Paderewski and performing in the high temple of classical music, Carnegie Hall. But, for the moment, his aspirations are thwarted, and he must earn a living playing jazz for the paying customers in a cheap nightclub. Ulmer reinforces the point; the next scene begins with Roberts playing Brahms's Waltz in A, op. 39, no. 15, but, after a few bars, he begins to jazz it up, launching into a full-scale boogie-woogie version of Brahms's original, delicate melody. Roberts earns a ten-dollar tip from a nightclub patron for prostituting his art and Brahms's. It almost seems as if Ulmer has been reading Adorno.

But, evidently, Ulmer did not need Adorno to teach him about classical music. It was his lifelong passion, and he was extremely knowledgeable in the area. His daughter, Arianné Ulmer Cipes, reports that, at one time, he wanted to be a conductor; perhaps as compensation for not becoming one, he sometimes used a baton when directing his actors.[22] He was friends with some of the most famous classical musicians of the twentieth century. For example, the Hungarian conductor Fritz Reiner was godfather to Ulmer's daughter. With Reiner's connections, Ulmer made the film *Carnegie Hall* (1947), which features a remarkable number of major figures in classical music, including Jascha Heifetz, Artur Rubenstein, Gregor Piatigorsky, Leopold Stokowski, Bruno Walter, Ezio Pinza, Lily Pons, and Reiner himself. Although his low budgets constrained him, Ulmer tried to make the most of the musical scores in his movies. *The Black Cat,* for example, contains some of the most effective and inventive use of classical music in any Hollywood score.[23] It draws on some classical warhorses, such as Tchaikovsky's *Romeo and Juliet* and Bach's Toccata and Fugue in D Minor, but it also includes unusual orchestrations of solo piano works, used in Wagnerian fashion as leitmotifs—for example, Liszt's Sonata in B Minor and Brahms's Rhapsody in B Minor, op. 79, no. 2.

## Civilization and Barbarism

It may be hard to believe that the man who created movies with titles like *Girls in Chains, The Man from Planet X, The Daughter of Dr. Jekyll, Naked Venus,* and *The Amazing Transparent Man* was a highly cultivated aficionado of classical music, but Ulmer certainly was. And this point is important because it helps suggest an explanation for the otherwise puzzling affinities between Ulmer and the Frankfurt school. Sometimes the resemblances can be uncanny. Ulmer's daughter describes his background: "He was a European intellectual who had based most of his thinking on the great minds of the German language, only to find that it led to a stupid monster of an Austrian painter named Hitler. For the rest of his life he tried to understand how civilization could end up in barbarism."[24] This formulation seems to echo Benjamin's famous statement in his "Theses on the Philosophy of History": "There is no document of civilization which is not at the same time a document of barbarism."[25] Horkheimer and Adorno offer a similar formulation of their task in *Dialectic of Enlightenment:* "It turned out, in fact, that we had set ourselves nothing less than the discovery of why mankind, instead of entering into a truly human condition, is sinking into a new kind of barbarism."[26] But, despite what appear to be verbal echoes of the Frankfurt school in reports of Ulmer's thinking, I have been unable to uncover evidence of any direct connection between him and Horkheimer and Adorno. I would not, however, rule out the possibility because, through the Hollywood factor, their circle of acquaintances probably overlapped.

But, if we set aside the question of direct or indirect contacts between Ulmer and Horkheimer or Adorno, we do know that they grew out of the same intellectual and cultural milieu and might well have been expected to converge in their thinking, especially about their adopted home, the United States. The similarity between Ulmer and Frankfurt school members went well beyond a common passion for Austro-German classical music. Ulmer also grew out of the same political tradition; his daughter says that "he was part of the socialist revolutionary beliefs of his European era." Ulmer was well educated—in his youth he studied architecture and philosophy in Vienna. His daughter points out that "he loved Thomas Mann, Schiller, and Goethe."[27] Thus, he had the same literary tastes as the Frankfurt school. The mention of Thomas Mann is especially significant since Adorno was closely associated with Mann; for example, he helped with the musicological details of Mann's novel *Doktor Faustus* (1947), which tells the story of a twelve-tone composer loosely modeled on Arnold Schoenberg. In short, even if Ulmer never heard of Horkheimer and Adorno, his intellectual profile was remarkably similar; in the forties, he was known around Hollywood as "the aesthete from the Alps."[28]

Thus, what we are witnessing in the case of Ulmer, as well as that of Horkheimer and Adorno, is the reaction of elite products of European high culture to the vulgarity of American popular culture. All three were well positioned to be critical of culture in the United States, to measure it by the sophisticated standards of European culture and find it wanting. But we should remember that, as outsiders, they were also prone to misunderstand and misinterpret American culture. However intelligent and insightful they may have been, they never had an insider's feel for American culture; it was easy for them to miss its nuances and, hence, whatever complexities it might embody.

Their reaction—one might say their overreaction—to American popular culture was also colored by their status as more or less displaced persons in the United States (this was truer of Horkheimer and Adorno than of Ulmer, who came to America earlier and more voluntarily). Having been plunged into an alien environment—and what could be more alien than the bizarre world of Hollywood?—they inevitably had problems adjusting, and it is no wonder that they found themselves repelled by many American phenomena. Their largely grim vision of America reflected their own alienation. In *Detour*, Ulmer portrays America as a land of lonely drifters, homeless and perpetually on the move. This may have corresponded to the reality of America (particularly during the Depression),[29] but it corresponded even more closely to Ulmer's own situation as a European émigré. Having left his homeland to come to the United States, and then finding himself exiled from Hollywood, he must have experienced a strong sense of displacement, which then translated into his film noir vision of individuals alienated from the landscape and the community.[30]

This dark vision of the rootlessness of America is perhaps the most interesting point of convergence between Ulmer and the Frankfurt school. Europeans have always been struck by the mobility of Americans and have usually reacted negatively to it. What looks like freedom to Americans looks like chaos to Europeans. Coming from more centrally ordered and hierarchical societies, many Europeans have difficulty appreciating the quintessentially American desire to be able to go one's own way. In particular, Europeans are often puzzled by Americans' devotion to—some might say their obsession with—their cars. Europeans prefer trains, with their fixed routes and rigid timetables, whereas Americans long for the freedom of the open road—significantly called the *freeway* in Los Angeles. Europeans frequently sing the praises of public transportation while condemning the extravagance and wastefulness of that most private of vehicles—the automobile. Socialists in particular hate the automobile; for them, it has often served as the ultimate symbol of capitalism.

All this suggests why the Frankfurt school members who ended up in southern California must have felt—despite the climate—that they had been plunged into some kind of hell specially reserved for European socialists. Woody Allen has shown that, for someone who cannot drive, Los Angeles is, indeed, hell, and it is documented that at least Adorno never learned to drive.[31] It is, therefore, revealing that Adorno often reacts negatively to precisely those aspects of American culture that center around the automobile.

## "On the Road Again"

Adorno's *Minima Moralia* (1951)—written during his stay in Los Angeles in the mid-forties and, hence, right at the time of *Detour*—is filled with reflections on the peculiar mobility of Americans and the effect that this has on their culture. When Adorno looks at the United States, what he sees is a country crisscrossed by empty roads: "[The roads] are always inserted directly in the landscape, and the more impressively smooth and broad they are, the more unrelated and violent their gleaming track appears against its wild, overgrown surroundings. They are expressionless. . . . It is as if no-one had ever passed their hand over the landscape's hair. It is uncomforted and comfortless. And it is perceived in a corresponding way. For what the hurrying eye has seen merely from the car it cannot retain, and the vanishing landscape leaves no more traces behind than it bears upon itself." Adorno could see the positive side of this kind of scene: "Beauty of the American landscape: that even the smallest of its segments is inscribed, as its expression, with the immensity of the whole country."[32] Still, as a European used to a densely populated countryside, he was obviously intimidated by exactly what Americans have always cherished—the wide-open spaces from sea to shining sea.

Adorno was also repulsed by what he saw growing up alongside all those endless American roads—the culture of motels and roadside restaurants. He inveighs against the poor service in the United States, contrasting American technical efficiency with the old-fashioned elegance he was used to in Europe:

The division of labour, the system of automatized facilities, has the result that no-one is concerned for the client's comfort. No-one can divine from his expression what might take his fancy, for the waiter no longer knows the menu. . . . No-one hastens to serve the guest, however long he has to wait. . . . Who would not prefer the "Blauer Stern" in Prague or the "Österreichischer Hof" in Salzburg, even if he had to cross the landing to reach the bathroom, and was no longer woken in the small hours by unfailing central heating? The nearer the sphere of immediate physical existence is approached, the more questionable progress becomes, a Pyrrhic victory of fetishized production.[33]

We see in such passages how much Adorno's critique of America grows out of unabashed nostalgia for an aristocratic European past.[34] His ultimate nightmare is a peculiarly American institution, the drugstore lunch counter: "the drugstore, blatantly a shop, behind whose inhospitable counter a juggler with fried-eggs, crispy bacon and ice-cubes proves himself the last solicitous host."[35] As Nico Israel writes: "The word 'snob' flies off of the page in passages like these" (for me, the words *old fogey* were not far behind).[36] Adorno may have a point about the shabbiness of American tourist establishments, but it seems a bit odd for a Marxist to use the standard of European luxury hotels, the exclusive preserve of a wealthy elite, in order to condemn the simple lunch counters of America, which tried to make restaurant food available to all at a price anybody could afford. As in his criticism of the music broadcasting and recording industry, Adorno seems to condemn America principally for making available to the masses what was reserved for a privileged elite in Europe.

## Home on the Range

Ulmer does not seem to share Adorno's snobbishness and elitism,[37] but he does have a very similar vision of America. *Detour* opens with a shot of an empty road stretching out to the horizon in an empty landscape, and that scene becomes typical of the film. *Detour* revolves around the automobile. The plot centrally deals with the efforts of Roberts and Vera to sell a stolen car. That eventually takes them to the most distinctively American of all institutions—the used-car lot. A large percentage of the film consists of characters talking in a moving car, first Roberts and Haskell, then Roberts and Vera. Hitchhiking from the East Coast to the West, Roberts becomes the perfect symbol of American mobility. And, in Ulmer's distinctively European vision of the United States, there is nothing between New York and Los Angeles—just a vast wasteland. Like the Frankfurt school refugees, Ulmer lived a bicoastal existence in America, with New York and Los Angeles essentially constituting the sum total of his experience of the United States. At most in *Detour* one finds Reno between the coasts, "the biggest little city in the world," as its famous advertising sign proclaims (glimpsed in the film)—a sort of reproduction of Los Angeles or New York in the middle of the desert, which is to say in the middle of nowhere.

It is, in fact, extraordinary how empty the American landscape is in *Detour*—miles and miles of bleak and inhospitable terrain. All Roberts encounters on his journey west are gas stations, motels, roadside cafés, and, finally, the one locale that sums up everything Adorno despised about America—a drive-in restaurant, where he and Vera can eat without ever leaving their car. And, above all, Roberts must always keep moving. For him, life in America has turned into an endless journey, and, as the film concludes, he is being picked up by a passing police car.

As Ulmer presents Roberts, he epitomizes the rootlessness of America. When Roberts tries to settle down in an apartment with his "wife," Vera, it is, of course, a complete sham; Vera can only sarcastically refer to it as "home sweet home." Roberts spends most of the film separated from his real fiancée, Sue, and they are forced to communicate—or not communicate—by phone. When Roberts finally manages to get to the West Coast, he finds that he is still separated from Sue: "Far from being at the end of the trip, there was a greater distance between Sue and me than when I started out." There are no families anywhere in *Detour*—in Ulmer's vision, America is a land of atomistic individuals. The truck driver looking for companionship who approaches Roberts at the beginning of the film stands for all Americans: "I ain't got nobody at all." In the eyes of a European socialist, this is the ultimate result of American capitalism—it destroys community, and it isolates the individual.

Of course it would be wrong to dismiss Ulmer's vision in *Detour* simply as a European misperception of America. The United States *is* a land of highways, motels, and roadside restaurants, and the mobility of Americans is genuinely one of their distinguishing characteristics. The vision of America as perpetually on the move is by no means restricted to European observers. An episode of the television series *The X-Files* entitled "Drive" is very similar to *Detour* in the way it allegorizes the American landscape. Owing to a government experiment gone awry, the main character of the story must keep moving in a speeding car, and, just as in *Detour*, he must specifically keep heading west until he reaches California (with even more disastrous results—in his case, his head explodes when he "runs out of west," as the episode puts it).[38]

*The X-Files* is an American television show, but it is just as capable as any European source of identifying rootlessness as the fundamental condition of the United States. Still, in evaluating the truthfulness of Ulmer's vision of America in *Detour*, it is worth bearing his European origins in mind. Even for a noir film, *Detour* presents an extraordinarily bleak view of the United States, and one might with some justification question whether the American landscape is quite as empty as Ulmer pictures it or as devoid of positive human interaction. What is quite literally absent from Ulmer's view is the American heartland—just the portion of the landscape with which a bicoastal European émigré is least likely to be familiar.

## Under European Eyes

Thus, while granting a degree of genuine insight into the American condition to both Ulmer and the Frankfurt school—a perceptiveness enabled precisely by their position as outsiders—one must also wonder whether their status as aliens did not also work to color, cloud, and even distort their view of the United States. Horkheimer and Adorno sometimes seem to be devoid of sympathy for American culture. They appear to be tone-deaf to its distinct accents; they just seem to miss the point of a Donald Duck cartoon in a way that someone native to the American scene would not.[39] Above all, their insistence on the uniformity of American popular culture is exactly the reaction of someone positioned outside a culture, someone who lacks an insider's ability to differentiate among its productions. It is ironic, then, that much of the study of American popular culture to this day is still heavily influenced by the approach developed by Horkheimer and Adorno back in the forties as displaced persons in the United States. We should not ignore their largely negative judgments about American culture, but we need to take those judgments with a grain of salt when we realize how much they were rooted in European cultural elitism and, specifically, aristocratic nostalgia.

Similar doubts arise about the validity of the film noir vision of America—and not just in the case of Ulmer's *Detour*. We tend to think of film noir as an American cultural development, and, to be sure, the classic noir films were generally made in Hollywood and have American settings.

Their plots were often derived from American detective novels, such as *The Maltese Falcon* and *The Big Sleep*.[40] But, if one views the director as central to the creation of a movie, suddenly film noir begins to look about as American as apple strudel. Many of the great noir films were directed by Europeans, including, to name just some of the most famous in addition to Ulmer, Curtis Bernhardt, John Brahm, Michael Curtiz, William Dieterle, Alfred Hitchcock, Fritz Lang, Rudolph Maté, Max Ophuls, Otto Preminger, Robert Siodmak, Josef von Sternberg, Charles Vidor, Billy Wilder, and William Wyler. Indeed, however American the subject matter of film noir may seem to be, it was often presented through European eyes behind the camera, and the formal characteristics of the genre owe more to European than to American directors, above all, to the masters of German expressionist cinema.[41]

Why is it important to stress the European roots of film noir? Many film analysts have treated the genre as indigenous to the United States and, hence, an accurate reflection of the realities of life in twentieth-century America.[42] Certainly, the dark vision and even nightmarish quality of these films give us a glimpse into the American psyche and its fears and anxieties when confronted with some of the traumatic developments of the thirties, forties, and fifties, such as the Depression, the rise of totalitarianism, World War II, the cold war, and the threat of nuclear annihilation. Yet one must be careful in talking about the "realism" of film noir when the genre is so highly stylized and so clearly involves imposing a set of narrative and other conventions on its material.[43] To the extent that these conventions were European in origin, they may have distorted the American reality that they purported to represent. In short, in viewing film noir, we may not be getting, as some critics have supposed, an unmediated look into the heart and soul of America. Rather, because in film noir we are often looking through European eyes, we may be getting an unduly negative and pessimistic view of the American way of life. Film noir may be one more example of a long tradition of European anti-Americanism, or at least a tendency to fault the United States for failing to measure up to European standards of civilization and culture.[44]

Here, the parallels between Ulmer's *Detour* and the Frankfurt school are genuinely informative since, in both cases, we can see how the very sophistication of European observers can blind them to whatever is positive in American commercial culture. It tells us something about film noir that a classic of the genre corresponds so closely to the vision of America in the work of a group of German left-wing intellectual émigrés. We can now understand the otherwise curious fact that the supposedly American genre of film noir has a European name. It is well-known that it took the French to "discover" film noir and establish it as a topic for serious aesthetic analysis. Perhaps a European sensibility was needed to appreciate film noir critically because the genre embodied a European sensibility in the first place. The fear and anxiety characteristic of film noir may be a projection—projected by European directors onto an American landscape in which they understandably did not feel at home. Ulmer may have been right in a way he did not understand. Film noir is a kind of detour. In insisting on portraying the American landscape as a vast wasteland, it may tell us more about Europe than it does about the United States.

## Notes

The epigraph to this essay is taken from W. H. Auden, *Lectures on Shakespeare*, reconstructed and edited by Arthur Kirsch (Princeton, NJ: Princeton University Press, 2000), 57.

1. For example, R. Barton Palmer (*Hollywood's Dark Cinema: The American Film Noir* [New York: Twayne, 1994], 108) calls *Detour* "undoubtedly the finest example of a purely noir thriller."

2. Alain Silver and Elizabeth Ward, eds., *Film Noir: An Encyclopedic Reference to the American Style*, 3rd ed. (Woodstock, NY: Overlook, 1992), 90.

3. See Palmer, *Hollywood's Dark Cinema*, 114.

4. See ibid., 114, 117.

5. Gregory William Mank, *Karloff and Lugosi: The Story of a Haunting Collaboration* (Jefferson, NC: McFarland, 1990), 81.

6. For a representative collection of Frankfurt school writings, see Andrew Arato and Eike Gebhardt, eds., *The Essential Frankfurt School Reader* (New York: Continuum, 1982). For a good but brief overview of the Frankfurt school, see Leszek Kolakowski, *Main Currents of Marxism: Its Origins, Growth and Dissolution*, trans. P. S. Falla, 3 vols. (Oxford: Oxford University Press, 1978), 3:341–95. For a fuller treatment, see George Friedman, *The Political Philosophy of the Frankfurt School* (Ithaca, NY: Cornell University Press, 1981).

7. On the immigration of the Frankfurt school to the United States, see Laura Fermi, *Illustrious Immigrants: The Intellectual Migration from Europe, 1930–41,* 2nd ed. (Chicago: University of Chicago Press, 1971), 332–33, and Lewis A. Coser, *Refugee Scholars in America: Their Impact and Their Experience* (New Haven, CT: Yale University Press, 1984), 90–101. On Adorno in particular, see Anthony Heilbut, *Exiled in Paradise: German Refugee Artists and Intellectuals in America, from the 1930s to the Present* (New York: Viking, 1983), 160–74.

8. See Nico Israel, *Outlandish: Writing between Exile and Diaspora* (Stanford, CA: Stanford University Press, 2000), 85–86. Israel points out that Horkheimer's home became the site of the "West Coast Institute for Social Research."

9. For a history of the reception of the German émigrés in Hollywood, see John Russell Taylor, *Strangers in Paradise: The Hollywood Émigrés, 1933–1950* (New York: Holt, Rinehart & Winston, 1983).

10. Max Horkheimer and Theodor W. Adorno, *Dialectic of Enlightenment*, trans. John Cumming (New York: Continuum, 1986), 139.

11. Theodor Adorno, *Minima Moralia: Reflections from Damaged Life*, trans. E. F. N. Jephcott (London: Verso, 1978), 43.

12. On this point, see Kolakowski, *Main Currents*, 3:377: "Whereas socialists formerly denounced capitalism for producing poverty, the main grievance of the Frankfurt school is that it engenders abundance and satisfies a multiplicity of needs, and is thus injurious to the higher forms of culture."

13. Horkheimer and Adorno, *Dialectic of Enlightenment*, 121, 124, 155, 165 (propaganda slogans), 159 (Hitler/Toscanini).

14. See ibid., 139: "If most of the radio stations and movie theaters were closed down, the consumers would probably not lose so very much.... The disappointment would be felt not so much by the enthusiasts as by the slow-witted, who are the ones who suffer for everything anyhow."

15. Ibid., 145–46.

16. Walter Benjamin, "The Work of Art in the Age of Mechanical Reproduction," in *Illuminations*, trans. Harry Zohn (New York: Schocken, 1969), 217–51.

17. For an example of this argument, see Kolakowski, *Main Currents*, 3:379.

18. Horkheimer and Adorno, *Dialectic of Enlightenment*, 143.

19. Ibid., 136.

20. For a critique of Adorno's view of jazz, see Heilbut, *Exiled in Paradise*, 127–28, 167–68.

21. Ibid., 127.

22. Tag Gallagher, "All Lost in Wonder: Edgar G. Ulmer," March 1, 2001, http://www.latrobe.edu.au/screeningthepast/firstrelease/fr0301/tgafr12a.htm (consulted April 21, 2005).

23. Mank (*Karloff and Lugosi*) reports that it was "Ulmer's idea to score *The Black Cat* with classical motifs" (56). When Carl Laemmle heard the score, he was, according to Mank, "apoplectic, hating the idea of the classical music; he wanted to rescore the entire picture" (80). Fortunately, Laemmle's son backed Ulmer, and the remarkable score was left alone. The score was actually written by the German émigré composer Heinz Roemheld. Roemheld may have provided a model for Al Roberts's musical career; according to Mank, he "had spent two almost destitute years in Washington, D.C., playing piano in the lobby of the Shoreham Hotel" (56).

24. Gallagher, "All Lost in Wonder."

25. Benjamin, *Illuminations*, 256.

26. Horkheimer and Adorno, *Dialectic of Enlightenment*, xi.

27. Gallagher, "All Lost in Wonder."

28. Mank, *Karloff and Lugosi*, 47.

29. For this view of the film, see Palmer, *Hollywood's Dark Cinema*, 110.

30. Given Ulmer's sense of alienation, it was almost inevitable that, when he turned to the genre of science fiction in the fifties, he created one of the first examples of the "lonely, misunderstood visitor from another planet" motif. In *The Man from Planet X* (1951), people from Earth fail to communicate properly with a space alien, and, in their effort to exploit his strange powers, they nearly trigger a planetary apocalypse.

31. Israel, *Outlandish*, 200 n. 37.

32. Adorno, *Minima Moralia*, 48, 49.

33. Ibid., 117.

34. See Kolakowski, *Main Currents*, 3:376, 395. For an example of cultural nostalgia, see Horkheimer and Adorno, *Dialectic of Enlightenment*, 132–33, where the Marxist authors end up praising the cultural policies of Wilhelmine Germany.

35. Adorno, *Minima Moralia*, 117.

36. Israel, *Outlandish*, 90.

37. From his daughter's description, Ulmer sounds more broad-minded than Adorno and more tolerant of American popular culture: "He loved this country, baseball, hot-dogs, Jackie Gleason, jazz, Sid Caesar, Jimmy Durante, and Bar BQs" (Gallagher, "All Lost in Wonder"). In *Carnegie Hall*, the young hero, who chooses a career as a jazz pianist over one as a classical musician, is vindicated in the end by an appearance at the famous concert hall, introduced by no less than Leopold Stokowski. The movie seems to present positively a jazzed-up version of the same Chopin waltz Roberts plays straight in *Detour*.

38. For a detailed analysis of this episode, see my *Gilligan Unbound: Pop Culture in the Age of Globalization* (Lanham, MD: Rowman & Littlefield, 2001), 172–77.

39. For the definitive Frankfurt school analysis of Donald Duck, see Horkheimer and Adorno, *Dialectic of Enlightenment*, 138.

40. Palmer (*Hollywood's Dark Cinema*, 108) stresses the roots of *Detour* in American fiction.

41. This point becomes clear if one looks at the chronological development of film noir. In the chronology in Silver and Ward, *Film Noir*, app. B, p. 333, ten of the first fifteen examples of the genre (from the period 1927–41) were directed by men born in Europe. That means that, in its crucial formative stages as a genre, film noir was shaped by European directors. For the argument that film noir was developed by European directors, see Taylor, *Strangers in Paradise*, 63, 193–205.

42. See, e.g., Nicholas Christopher, *Somewhere in the Night: Film Noir and the American City* (New York: Free Press, 1997), esp. 12: "Film noir is an utterly homegrown modern American form." In a review of *Somewhere in the Night*, I develop

further the thesis that film noir has European roots (see my "Film Noir Politics: The Ideology of a Movie Genre," *Weekly Standard,* June 30, 1997, 34–35).

43. On this point, see Heilbut, *Exiled in Paradise,* 249.

44. For a comprehensive account of intellectual anti-Americanism, see James W. Ceaser, *Reconstructing America: The Symbol of America in Modern Thought* (New Haven, CT: Yale University Press, 1997).

# Knowledge, Morality, and Tragedy in The Killers and Out of the Past

*Ian Jarvie*

> Poetry is both more philosophical and more serious than history, since poetry speaks more of universals, history of particulars.
>
> —*Aristotle*

Students of film find film noir interesting because it is a critics' rather than a filmmakers' category. Socially minded critics find interesting the pessimistic mood of so many early films noirs, coinciding as they did with wartime and the immediate postwar period.[1] The pessimism, menace, and violence of the films also clash with their prima facie status as mere popular entertainment. This leads me to my philosophical question. Perhaps these films are more than they at first seem. Are these dark films a popular extension of tragedy as Aristotle defined it, that is, dramas educing pity and terror that offer an emotional purge or catharsis to both characters and audience?[2]

Before I proceed, a methodological difficulty needs to be acknowledged. Noir is, unlike the western or the horror film, a style or way of treating a story, hardly a full-blooded genre with a locale or conventions of plot structure. This style is applied in many and various films over a long period. True, 1941–53 is the golden age, according to Borde and Chaumeton, the first critics to write on the subject.[3] But the style remains a live option available to filmmakers to this day.[4] Trying to generalize over a large number of films noirs is liable to be vacuous. The case-study method offers a partial solution to this kind of difficulty. For my case study, I have selected *The Killers* (Robert Siodmak, 1946) and *Out of the Past* (Jacques Tourneur, 1947). The solution is partial because generalizing from them need not be vacuous, but at best it may not be valid beyond the Golden Age. I shall

Exhibit 1. Synopses of Sophocles' *Oedipus Rex* and *Antigone*.

*Oedipus Rex.* Oedipus, the king of Thebes, is confronted with the problem of plague in the city. Informed by the oracles that the plague is caused by the unpunished murder of the former king, Laius, Oedipus vows to hunt down the criminal. Slowly and by degrees, he comes to the realization that he himself is the murderer of Laius, also his own father, and that he is now married to his own mother, Jocasta. Horrified at the discoveries, Oedipus blinds himself and goes into exile, while Jocasta commits suicide.

*Antigone.* Antigone, the daughter of Oedipus, disobeys the orders of Creon, now the king of Thebes, who forbids the burial of her brother Polyneices, a traitor to the city. After Antigone buries Polyneices, Creon condemns her to death and has her buried alive in a cave. Although warned by the prophet Tiresias, Creon sticks to his decree. Creon eventually yields and decides to free Antigone, but he arrives at the cave too late—Antigone has hanged herself and is already dead. Creon's son, Haemon, who had been engaged to marry Antigone, is enraged at his father and, failing to kill him, kills himself. Creon's wife also commits suicide.

argue that, although both *The Killers* and *Out of the Past* have tragic aspects, the claim that they and, by implication, other films noirs rise to tragedy is far from compelling.

## Aristotle on Tragedy

In exhibit 1, I offer synopses of two tragedies by Sophocles, *Oedipus Rex* and *Antigone*. These works are among the examples that Aristotle had in mind when he wrote his treatise *Poetics*, which deals with what he seemed to take as the three main kinds of poetry: epic, tragic, and comic. Each drama ends with horror: suicide; mutilation; exile; the visitation on those left standing of the awful things that can befall people who might be trying to act well. In their staging, these dramas from twenty-five hundred years ago little resembled what we think of as the theatrical arts. Some striking points of divergence are these. Their performance was highly stylized, with a few reciters taking all roles, using different masks. The verse was sung or chanted to music. The stage was shared with a chorus that observed the action and commented on it. And, finally, the material was mythical and well-known: several of the great tragedians wrote variations on the same plot.

Aristotle's analysis of these kinds of poetry is sometimes called *formal*

Aristotle's Classification of Three Types of Poetry

|  | EPIC | TRAGEDY | COMEDY |
|---|---|---|---|
| MEDIUM | Language<br>Rhythm | Language<br>Rhythm<br>Melody | Language<br>Rhythm<br>Melody |
| OBJECT | Agents better<br>than us | Agents better<br>than us | Agents worse<br>than us |
| MODE | Narrative | Dramatic | Dramatic |

because he was very specific about which kinds of plot, characters, and treatment were appropriate, and which were not, to each. The table above is illustrative of this, being a summary of Aristotle's views on the differences among the three kinds of poetry.

For Aristotle, all art is pleasurable representation, mimesis. While the epic and the comic present no problems for pleasure, the tragic clearly does. These grim and violent stories would seem to be no more pleasurable than dwelling on pain. One way to avoid the problem was to claim that the beauty and music of the verse, despite its often grim content, would deliver pleasure. But Aristotle went further, making an ingenious move that remains mysterious and controversial. He argued that tragic poetry arouses the emotions of pity (for those suffering undeserved misfortune) and terror (that this might happen to us) and that the aftermath is a kind of healing. Much scholarly ink has been spilled about this theory of catharsis. Scholars cannot even agree on whether it is the audience or the characters who experience it, or both. There are many uses of *catharsis* in ancient Greek texts where it scarcely resembles what Aristotle might be getting at. But, at a minimum, he expects tragedy to arouse powerful emotions in a way that has positive effects. Many scholars think he is taking issue with Plato, who expressed doubts about the value of poetry that arouses socially disruptive emotions.

A checklist of Aristotle's prescriptions for tragedy would show that the case could be made that at least some films noirs resemble tragedy (those not utterly lacking in *gravitas*). Certainly *D.O.A.* (Rudolph Maté, 1950), for example, has a pitiably undeserving hero and a terrifying premise. Allowances would have to be made for time and social context as well as the atrophy of many of the conventions of the ancient Greek stage. But my negative answer to the claim will not turn on these sorts of considerations. It will turn, rather, on certain philosophical considerations relating to questions about knowledge, who knows what and when, and about the moral behavior of the characters. I find the former difficult to fit into Aristotle's mold, the latter impossible.

## Film Noir as Tragedy

What are these questions of knowledge and morality? Noir films are seldom without an element of mystery. Principal characters, and/or the authorities, and/or we the audience are in the dark about some event, or some personal history, or some character trait. The mystery is compounded because, more often than not, appearances are deceptive. What you see is not at all what you get. The films deliver pleasure by solving the mystery, by letting us behind the appearances—however convoluted the exposition. A characteristic deceptive appearance of films noirs is that the leading man or woman is presented sympathetically, especially at first. One of Aristotle's prescriptions is that, if the protagonist is happy, the trajectory of the tragic drama should be toward unhappiness and that, if the protagonist is unhappy, the trajectory should be toward happiness.

This is not quite how things go in my two case-study films. In *The Killers*, the male protagonist, Swede, is murdered in the first reel, literally put out of his misery. But, as his backstory is pieced together, we find that it begins in misery: an injury ends his boxing career. He takes up with an alluring woman, Kitty, and seems happy. But his happiness is deluded: she is using him. In *Out of the Past*, the male protagonist, Jeff, seems very happy in the opening scenes. Then, as his backstory unfolds, we find that his starting point was neither happiness nor unhappiness but ennui. His involvement with a femme fatale named Kathy is what brings him alive enough to be happy. He is happy with a woman who tried to murder her previous lover and ran off with some of his money. His delusion is that her behavior was an aberration. In the opening scenes, Jeff appears to have put Kathy behind him and to have regained happiness. When his past catches up with him, however, he risks losing his happiness to settle matters outstanding. Neither of these trajectories conforms to Aristotle's ideals.

Yet both antiheroes are presented sympathetically. Their deaths are an end to misery (Swede in *The Killers*) and a (presumably redemptive) sacrifice (Jeff in *Out of the Past*). One is made unsure by the lack of a moral center in the films, the lack, that is, of a character or point of view through which we can assess the moral choices of their antihero and antiheroine. Their emphasis is, rather, on the antihero (or his substitute) judging the antiheroine—Kitty, Kathie—and finding her wanting. At the same time, the films invite us to accept the antihero's view of himself as victim. When the antiheroine implies that she does not want to harm the hero or claims that he is as bad as she, the film's script, direction, and, above all, casting position us so as to encourage discounting her words. Partly, this is because the films' psychology is banal or opaque. Woman as predator, man as victim, is banal. We do not know why the antihero is so vulnerable to the femme fatale; we do not know what has made the femme so fatale. No insight is offered into the psychological interior of either sex. They show what they are in action rather than words (despite films noirs being rather wordy). This accords well with Aristotle, who wrote: "Tragedy is a representation not of people as such, but of actions and life, and both happiness and unhappiness rest on action. The goal is a certain activity, not a qualitative state; and while men do have certain qualities by virtue of their character, it is in their actions that they achieve, or fail to achieve, happiness."[5]

These films, then, have a double aspect: what you see is not what you get, either in knowledge or in morals. The mystery story functions to distract us from the sleight of hand that is attractively showcasing antisocial immorality and cowardice. Thus distracted, we are reassured that the dark underworld has been kept at bay when the plot allows a semblance of normality to be restored. This seems quite removed from the aim of catharsis, of which more below.

## Knowledge and Tragedy in *The Killers* and *Out of the Past*

Pauline Kael, most philosophical of all film critics, paraphrases our two films in exhibit 2. There is, however, more going on in these films than is allowed even by the hyperintelligent Kael, first as to knowledge (which I shall discuss in this section), then as to morality (which I shall discuss below).

I begin with context. In trying to make sense of the complicated plotting and the moral confusion of Golden Age films noirs, it helps to restore them to their social and cultural contexts. Their imaginary world and their imaginary characters were ingenious means to titillate and to reassure contemporaneous audiences while remaining obedient to the general imperatives of society and culture and the specific imperatives of censorship.

Exhibit 2. Pauline Kael on *The Killers* and *Out of the Past.**

*The Killers.* Ernest Hemingway's short story about the man who doesn't try to escape his killers is acted out tensely and accurately, and, for once, the gangster-thriller material added to it is not just padding but is shrewdly conceived (by Anthony Veiller and the uncredited John Huston) to show why the man didn't care enough about life to run away. Under the expert direction of Robert Siodmak, Burt Lancaster gives his first screen performance (and is startlingly effective), and Siodmak also does wonders with Ava Gardner. With Charles McGraw and William Conrad in the opening sequence, and Edmond O'Brien, Albert Dekker, Sam Levene, Donald MacBride, Vince Barnett, and Jeff Corey.

*Out of the Past.* A thin but well-shot suspense melodrama, kept from collapsing by the suggestiveness and intensity that the director, Jacques Tourneur, pours on. It's empty trash,** but you do keep watching it. Kirk Douglas, a gangster, hires Robert Mitchum to find Jane Greer, who has run away from him. Predictably, she gets Mitchum (at his most somnolent-sexy droopy-eyed) in her clutches, and there are several killings before matters are resolved. The screenplay is by Geoffrey Holmes (a pseudonym of Daniel Mainwaring), from his novel *Build My Gallows High.* Cinematography by Nicholas Musuraca; with Rhonda Fleming and Dickie Moore.

*Excerpted from Pauline Kael, *5001 Nights at the Movies: A Guide from A to Z* [New York: Holt, Rinehart & Winston, 1982], 303–4, 440.
** *Trash*, it bears remembering, is a term of art for Kael (see Pauline Kael, "Trash, Art, and the Movies" [1969], in *Going Steady* [Boston: Little, Brown, 1970], 83–129).

Martha Wolfenstein and Nathan Leites's *Movies* is a near-contemporaneous case study of themes in the movies of the 1945–46 season, the heyday of original film noir. I find it unsurpassed for insight and careful methodology—yet underappreciated.[6] The authors, both social psychologists, argued that it was a characteristic feature of the American movies of the time that they played on the differences between reality and appearance. Thus, from comedies of this period, they identified the figure of the "comic onlooker," the nosey person who pries into and observes the action but who characteristically misconstrues as scandalous situations and gestures that are quite innocent, with hilarious results (*Sitting Pretty* [Walter Lang, 1948] is a prime example).

Not only comedy but also melodrama of this period often turns on conflicts between appearance and reality, especially dramas of false appearances.[7] Wolfenstein and Leites identified for the first time a pivotal figure of film noir, the good/bad girl. She appears to be bad only to turn out to be good and misunderstood, or she poses as good but turns out to be very bad indeed. For the first, think of Vivian Rutledge (Lauren Bacall) in *The Big Sleep* (Howard Hawks, 1946), Laura Hunt (Gene Tierney) in *Laura* (Otto Preminger, 1944); for the second, think of Brigid O'Shaughnessy (Mary Astor) in *The Maltese Falcon* (John Huston, 1941), Ellen Berent (Gene Tierney) in *Leave Her to Heaven* (John M. Stahl, 1945), Kathie Moffat (Jane Greer) in *Out of the Past,* Kitty Collins (Ava Gardner) in *The Killers,* Diane Tremayn (Jean Simmons) in *Angel Face* (Otto Preminger, 1952). Wolfenstein and Leites also explored the moral universe of the films, identifying two moralities that compete: "goodness morality," namely, the morality of winning and success, and "fun morality"—the morality of having fun.

The comic onlooker and the good/bad girl embody the disconcerting and disorienting discrepancies emblematic of the centrality of the conflicts between appearance and reality in large numbers of American movies of the time. In noir, we find heroes and others wrongfully accused, criminal policemen, honorable hoodlums, and women who are not what they seem. Wolfenstein and Leites note that the constraints of the censor and the box office are "indicative of more or less widely diffused feelings and attachments in American culture. . . . The selection of certain themes and omission of others would seem to be . . . expressive of deeper and less conscious emotional tendencies."[8]

Are films noirs, then, of the "goodness morality" or the "fun morality" genre? They are neither: they are amoral, as we will see later. Why then are they pleasurable? Why do those pleasures hold up relatively well over time? More specifically, do they invite us to broaden the notion of tragedy? That is, do these dramas of lies, violence, corruption, misanthropy, and so on transcend themselves and deliver artistic pleasure?

I chose *The Killers* and *Out of the Past* because, besides their obvious attractions as superb pieces of filmmaking, each involves a quasi suicide. This makes them challenging as they do not fit easily among the films of the period and they seem to be unpromising material for entertainment. As Wolfenstein and Leites note: "Suicides in American films tend, to a considerable extent, to express an attack against someone else, in so far as it is possible to discern a tendency in the rare instances."[9] *The Killers* does not fit this tendency; *Out of the Past* does. Swede/Ole Anderson/Pete Lund (Burt Lancaster) passively awaits his fate, which is duly delivered by the eponymous killers, and which initiates the efforts of the insurance inspector Jim

Reardon (Edmund O'Brien) to find out the whys and wherefores. Jeff Bailey/ Jeff Markham (Robert Mitchum), fearing that he will be falsely accused because of the machinations of Kathie Moffat, sets up a trap that, he has good reason to know, will kill them both. Death is the only escape from the tendrils that she has around him, the only way to protect from her the "good" girlfriend, Ann Miller (Virginia Huston), whom he really loves. The Kid, his deaf-mute sidekick, manages to convince Ann that Jeff died still in love with his femme fatale, allowing her to get over him and move on with her life.

Both films have the bad/good girl in extreme form, that is, the girl who appears sincere and needy but who is, in fact, calculating and treacherous, using and manipulating the male she has ensnared.[10] Whom she really cares for varies. Kitty in *The Killers* appears to care for her husband, although he is a thug. Kathie Moffat seems to care for no one but herself, her wealth, and her survival. Interestingly, in both cases, the casting places in the bad girl roles women of surpassing beauty: Ava Gardner and Jane Greer. Each was appearing early in her career, and each eclipsed the good girl.[11] By contrast, Swede's original girl, Lilly (Virginia Christine), and Jeff's good girl, Ann (Virginia Houston), are played by actresses whose names will not ring a bell. The male casting is more complicated. Each film matched an established star with a newcomer. In *The Killers*, Edmund O'Brien's Jim Reardon investigates the death of Burt Lancaster's Swede. In *Out of the Past*, Robert Mitchum's Jeff is trying not to let Kirk Douglas's Whit get the better of him. The use of attractive male actors as the women's victims is artful. We may envy them their looks and manners; we do not envy them their character or their fate. Both films were in the hands of expert directors. Robert Siodmak and Jacques Tourneur had each begun his career in Europe in the thirties, as had most directors of the classic noir films. Each did exceptional work in the horror genre and would go on to make further masterpieces.[12]

So what pleasures do noir films offer? First, and obviously, they were polished products of the dream factory. The American movie industry was successful at finding formulas that its public relished. Second, the film noir genre clearly grows out of a popular form of literature, the hard-boiled detective story (Hammet, Chandler) and the simply hard-boiled (James M. Cain, Cornell Woolrich). Third, the films are to be relished for the sheer skill of their filmmaking. Throughout the thirties, black-and-white film stock was improving, as was deep focus, so that, by the time noir began to gel, say between *The Maltese Falcon* (1941) and *Double Indemnity* (Billy Wilder, 1944), the only limits on atmosphere, chiaroscuro, and self-conscious framing of shots were the imagination of the director and the skill of the cinematographer.

The opening sequence of *The Killers,* taken almost word for word from the Hemingway short story, is simply breathtaking. The film begins over a shot behind the heads of two men driving at night, the only illumination the car headlights. The credits and loud music begin over a shot looking from the shadows at the illuminated windows of a diner. As the credits come toward their end, two men stroll into the shadow and try the door of the closed gas station. They then show their hard faces before entering the diner by different entrances and beginning the chilling exchanges that establish their dominance and their mission. This mood of somber menace continues until the final fusillade of bullets is directed into Swede and we move beyond Hemingway to Hollywood original.[13] This is filmmaking that would thrill any audience.

The opening sequence of *Out of the Past* is also set on a road but in daylight, in a small town. The setting is the West, whereas *The Killers* is set in the East. The dark underworld stretches from coast to coast, it seems. In broad daylight, Jeff is informed that his former client, the "gambler" Whit Sterling, wants to see him.[14] The message is delivered by Joe Stephanos. Joe's kinship with the killers in *The Killers* is more subtly signaled by his black trenchcoat, his throwing a match near the deaf-mute, and his wariness as a police car cruises by. Cue to a long flashback as Jeff narrates the backstory to Ann on the drive up to Sterling's mansion at Tahoe. His story is how he was ensnared by a fascinating woman until her acts of treachery disillusioned him. Like Swede, who seems to consider running a waste of time, if not an attempt to escape a deserved comeuppance, Jeff makes no attempt to defy the messenger and disappear again. If they find you once, they will find you again. There is nowhere to hide. The past and the underworld are everywhere.

Fourth, the plots present occasions to contemplate the forbidden or at least the unattainable. What ensnares the boxer Swede and the private eye Jeff is the woman whose sexual allure is so overpowering that their ability to judge character is switched off. The films put this allure on display to please the audience. These women are too beautiful, too desirable, and too ready to fall in with the antihero. His alarm bells fail. Sexual attraction is presented as an intense, even overwhelming basis for a relationship, but it clouds all other aspects of character and background, and the man comes to accept that his fate is destruction by this woman. Swede becomes an armed robber (the robbery, captured in one continuous shot, is another bravura piece of filmmaking); Jeff tries to evade the various traps and double crosses but fails in the end. To stop Kathie, his own life must be the ultimate bait.

Is this some sort of tragedy? In the *Poetics,* Aristotle is specific about tragedy as a form. It is "a representation of an action which is serious, complete, and of a certain magnitude—in language which is garnished in various forms in its different parts—in the mode of dramatic enactment, not narrative—and through the arousal of pity and fear effecting the *katharsis* of such emotions."[15] The characters should be neither wholly good nor wholly evil but, rather, fallible, capable of major error. They need also to have a certain weight, a dignity and standing ensuring the importance of what they undertake and undergo. One might view sexual susceptibility as an error of sorts—but only of sorts as it is not the sort of error that Aristotle appears to have had in mind. One way to bring sexual susceptibility into the classical Greek framework is to treat it as hubris. This line of thought is viable, no doubt, even though films noirs offer little context to support it, since neither Swede nor Jeff ever gets to talk about his fatal attraction. The absence of personal background information is not mythlike, as it is in the classic westerns; rather, it hints at a lonely isolation that makes these attractive males such easy victims. Still, it would be an interesting exercise, not least because it would see the subclass of noir that features the bad/good girl as in counterpoint to most other American movies, where romantic love, which always has a strong sexual component, is the mythical answer to all life's problems, including personal fulfillment.

Pity and terror are aroused when the consequences of choices are worked out. A first mistake is made, and this leads to the dire consequences that bring catharsis, provided the protagonist is serious: "A responsible moral agent ought to know that disasters can have ordinary beginnings, and to know how one mistake leads to another. The right tragic plot imparts that knowledge at the same time that it trains its audience's moral sentiments."[16] While I extravagantly admire these films and am excited by their twists and turns, I am not moved by them or by the fates of their protagonists. Still less do they educe pity and terror. They are cautionary tales. What is of desirable appearance is not necessarily good for you. Beautiful women can be dangerous. To call this banal would be an understatement. Such banality scarcely counts as knowledge, still less as material for training the moral sentiments.

Other considerations regarding tragedy are these. First and foremost, Aristotle is a formalist: he separates epic, tragedy, and comedy in a systematic way, depending on the kinds of people involved and the kinds of pleasures delivered, and he specifies restrictive structural features, such as the unities of time, space, and action and the trajectory of the characters between happiness and misery, or vice versa. This formalism is hard to reconcile with noir. As already noted, writers such as Schrader refuse to consider noir a genre just because there are no fixed rules of locale, types of characters, or structural features of plot. The logic of noir is often romantic rather than formal, and the stress on atmosphere and style would likely fall under Aristotle's category of spectacle, the lowest of the means to deliver pity and terror. Failure to preserve the unities, the absence of moral nobility in the characters, and the emphasis on spectacle strike me as quite un-Aristotelian. On the other hand, the lack of psychologizing, the emphasis on action, and the constant revelations and narrative reversals do accord with Aristotle's prescriptions.[17] So I do not deny that a case could be made, even as I choose to emphasize the differences rather than the conformities.[18] I think that the epistemology of these films can be reconciled with Aristotle; I think, however, that he would find their moral drama seriously wanting.

Tragedy or not, noir films are enthralling. They were successful in their time, they stay in the mind, and they feature in the history books. They take us into a world that seems to abut the world we normally inhabit, that perhaps undergirds some of the things in our ordinary world, yet in which people's lives and motives seldom make sense to inhabitants of the ordinary world. Two men enter a diner, and it is touch-and-go whether they execute everyone present (*The Killers*); Joe Stephanos is demonstratively genial, yet he is part of the plot to set Jeff up for a murder and later is sent to kill him (*Out of the Past*). There are rules and codes in this world—but not the familiar ones. They include the maxim that you are not safe unless you take care to have a hold over others, be it violent, sexual, blackmailing, or financial. Others are never what they seem. The more plausible and inviting the scheme, the more likely it is to be a trap, a setup. The characters face moral choices that they flub.

Before turning to the detail of morality in the two films, we can note how unpromising they are on general grounds. The best tragedy, for Aristotle, does not involve wholly virtuous or wholly villainous protagonists. It involves, rather, protagonists who mix innocence and guilt but who at least have a noble or lofty purpose. They need to be acting on principle. Then the tragedy becomes one of a clash of possibly equally worthy principles, such as between Creon's refusal to bury a traitor and Antigone's religious duty to bury her brother. The protagonists also need to make a major mistake that somehow precipitates the disaster. In general, only the first of these features is to be found in noir, namely, the mixture of innocence and guilt. There is some acting on principle, especially in noirs close to Hammett and Chandler, but, as we shall see, relentless self-centeredness and self-pity are more characteristic. As to the major mistake: as I have indicated, susceptibility to womanly wiles scarcely seems to amount to acting on principle.

## Moral Analysis of *The Killers*

*The Killers* is more morally conventional than *Out of the Past.* A crime is committed, and the film traces its solution via flashbacks. Instead of the authorities investigating the murder of Swede, however, they somehow end up playing second fiddle to Reardon, an investigator for an insurance company.[19] This allows for conflict between the sleuth, hot on the trail, and his boss, who wants him off the case. By the sheerest coincidence, Swede's gasoline supplier had insured its franchisees with the same company that insured the hat factory Swede had robbed. As the backstory of the killing is unraveled, it is the insurance investigator who is vouchsafed all the informative flashbacks. What emerges is that Swede "got in wrong," as Hemingway puts it. The film has "I did something wrong—once," which is less accurate. Swede's boxing career ended when his hand was damaged. He is smitten with Kitty and becomes a criminal in order to impress her. He is so infatuated that he goes to prison for her. In prison, he thinks about her. On his release, he is embroiled by Big Jim Colfax in an armed robbery—and not informed that Colfax and Kitty are now married. Colfax and Kitty are well aware of Swede's bewitchment and use it to make it look as though he has absconded with the take. When Kitty dumps Swede and takes the money (to join Colfax), he is despairing and suicidal. He changes his name and operates a gas station.[20] He seems to be living a quiet, "straight" life—but without a new love interest. When Colfax comes on him working at the gas station, Swede feels ill and quits work, awaiting the inevitable.

The film strongly implies that Kitty is responsible for Swede's death, as well as for that of Colfax, as well as for those of the two hoodlums Blinky and Dum Dum. It is for her that Colfax planned the big robbery and for her that he wanted to cheat the others of their share of the booty. He has used the money to set himself up in a business the legitimacy of which Kitty claims to enjoy. Swede seems not to regret dumping his original girl, Lilly, who ends up marrying the policeman Lubinsky. He seems not to regret his misconduct. He seems to mind mainly his failure of judgment, his failure to heed the warning of his cellmate, Charleston, not to listen to those golden harps (a symbol of Kitty). These failures leave him tormented, prostrate, and resigned to his fate.

The morality here is that Swede regrets mainly his own gullibility, not his crimes, and not his shielding criminals. He does not cooperate with the authorities, even though in this film they are sympathetic ("No, I wouldn't want to be a copper"). He shields Kitty from prison by telling lies and evades the police by disappearing after the robbery and the double cross. He has no family and no social background to speak of, and the beneficiary of his life insurance is the hotel maid who once dissuaded him from suicide. His resignation can be taken like this: having "got in wrong," he must now accept the personal consequences without any general obligation to the ordinary sense of righting the wrong. Society's demand for justice is met, not because of his actions, but rather because the disappearance of Swede and the money triggers a dispute within the gang. Thus, Dum Dum kills Blinky so he can search Swede's room; the police wound Dum Dum, and Colfax kills him, but not before he has mortally wounded Colfax.

Of the five, only Kitty is left standing, and we can imagine the string of charges she is going to face. Her view of herself is: "I'm poison, Swede, to myself and everybody around me. I'd be afraid to go with anyone I love for the harm I'd do them." This "poison" seems to consist of three things: she is powerfully sexually attractive; she knows this and makes use of it; and she is quite amorally interested in her own comfort. So neither she nor Swede wants to atone for wrongs done or to pay any debts to society. Swede at least does not run a second time from his comeuppance, whereas Kitty collapses at the end, desperately trying to get her dying husband to exonerate her.

Morality, then, is personal. It is about not being a sucker. It is about self-preservation. As we have seen, Wolfenstein and Leites say that it is about winning. This helps explain why we never see the story from the point of view of the authorities. The police are disinclined to investigate Swede's murder. Lieutenant Lubinsky assists Reardon rather than taking over the case when the connection to the armed robbery turns up. It becomes personal with Reardon, so much so that he ambushes and holds at gunpoint one of the hoodlums. Indeed, were it not somehow personal with him, the case would not have been cracked. Yet there is no suggestion that Reardon is fascinated by Kitty (as is *Laura*'s Lieutenant Mark McPherson by Laura), nor is he obsessed with a sense of justice or of fair play. When finally he meets Kitty, he is playing a game of cat and mouse. He knows that she will try to set him up, and he tries to get as much information out of her as he can before that. It is so personal that we are not even sure that his cracking the case will benefit his insurance company.

There are no fewer than eleven flashbacks in this film.[21] In almost every one, we are given a fragment of information that is withheld from one or more of the protagonists, all of whom are, therefore, embroiled in the drama of false appearances. Swede is unaware of Kitty's amorality and of her view of herself as "poison"; he also fails to notice that Colfax is also in thrall to her, a failure that prevents him from figuring out that Colfax might also act so as to gain her favor. Blinky and Dum Dum know that Colfax and Kitty are married but not that Kitty is manipulating Swede. This is how they fail to realize that the beneficiary of the double cross is Colfax, not Swede. Can we take it that only Kitty knows things for what they are? Can we accept her self-assessment? Does she really love Swede? The drama allows various interpretations. They all converge, however, on the idea that female sexual attractiveness is powerful and dangerous to men and to society. It is a force capable of making a man lose his moral compass (Swede was not a criminal as long as he was in the ring) and take his misjudgment as his personal failing or as his fate.

In a coda, Reardon and his boss discuss the plot endgame, minimizing the cash value of Reardon's solving it, and then, flippantly, the boss orders Reardon to take a rest but to be back at work on Monday. Things are normalized as though this was just another of the insurance company's tangled case files, all in a day's work, so to speak. The slightly cocky humor of the scene makes no sense other than as an artificially "up" way of ending a very dark tale. It encourages the audience to make light of what has gone before. If we read it as a framing chorus, then it woefully reduces the seriousness of the drama. Without seriousness, there is no tragedy.

## Moral Analysis of *Out of the Past*

In *Out of the Past,* the sequence of events narrated is more complex than in *The Killers.* This is partly because the film has no "normalizing" figure like the insurance investigator Reardon. The puzzle of the opening call by the hoodlum Joe Stephanos on Jeff Bailey both ushers in recollections of what went before (in flashbacks) and initiates what is going to happen from this point forward. Some questions are: When and how does Jeff know he has been double-crossed? How does his current love, Ann, know he is honest? The answers are opaque. Why does Jeff cover up Kathie's killing of his partner, Fisher? The answer never considered is that he is a coward; he sacrifices himself only when he can take Kathie with him and stop her. His quasi suicide is an attack on someone else.

By contrast with Swede, Jeff is on the screen a lot of the time and is given plenty of lines both in direct speech and in voice-over reflections on his situation. He too "got in wrong," perhaps inadvertently. Sent to find a mobster's absconding girlfriend, he is smitten. Instead of returning her to his client, he enjoys an idyll with her. But Fisher, his former partner in the private detective business, spots him, corners them, and demands his cut of the money she took. Fisher and Jeff fight, and Kathie shoots Fisher. She tells Jeff that he would not have done it and that they would eventually have been betrayed. She leaves him to bury the body—and to find evidence that she did, in fact, run off with the money, something she had earlier denied. Jeff's reaction is the self-indulgent "I wasn't sorry for him or sore at her. I wasn't anything." Only if he felt something would he hunt her down—or at least give Fisher a decent burial by calling in the authorities.

This is the crucial moment of error. Jeff knows that this woman is capable of murder and that he is not. He knows that she is capable of leaving him to explain the corpse even though she claims to love him. He knows that she is a flat-out liar who falsely denied having the money. With the film barely one-third over, the false appearances are gone. But Jeff is hardly the stuff of which heroes are made. He buries Fisher and changes his name and profession. Thus, he is silent about a robbery and a murder because a woman to whom he was attracted committed them. At first we do not know why: he is inactive perhaps out of chivalry and perhaps out of cowardice, of being scared that he will be suspected. He does not try to find her, much less bring her to justice. He does not go to the authorities and try to explain how Fisher met his end. Instead, he goes into hiding.

Wolfenstein and Leites note how often the protagonists of films in this period are without family or any other social context.[22] In such absence, the claims normally made on an individual are absent too. Such individuals can feel and act like free atoms, affecting only those they bump into. In the classical tragedies, family ties and responsibilities are central.

Meanwhile, the renamed Jeff has been courting Ann, whose mother objects to him precisely because no one knows who he is or where he came from. He evades Ann's questions by saying that they will be answered one day, as, indeed, they are in the major flashback sequence where he tells of his encounter with Kathie and its consequences.[23] This insouciant moral coward accepts that he must face Whit, the mobster whose girl he went off with and whose money is missing. So, again, the morality is personal. Whit does not seem inclined to punish him, instead demanding a quid pro quo, that Jeff help retrieve some incriminating documents from a tax accountant, Leonard Eels. While at Whit's mansion, Jeff encounters Kathie, now back with Whit. Although Jeff plays along, he is quite aware that he is being set up, but not by whom. When Jeff thwarts the first setup, Kathie sends Joe Stephanos to kill him. Desperately trying to extricate himself, Jeff forces Whit to see what Kathie is and to turn her over to the authorities. But she kills Whit. Earlier, Kathie had said, "I don't want to die," and Jeff had responded, "Neither do I, baby, but if I have to, I'm going to die last." With Whit dead, Jeff sees no way out. He sets them both up with the police. Very artfully, the film does not let us overhear Jeff's call to the police. After a drink, his last words to Kathie are that they deserve each other. When she sees the police roadblock, she calls him a double-crossing rat and pulls a gun from her case. He briefly struggles with her, but she shoots him and then at the police before being shot herself. Jeff does not get his wish to be the last to die.

Jeff is hardly acting morally. He tries to set things right for himself. He wants to disentangle himself from the web of crime and deception that Kathie has lured him into, not to serve justice, conventional or natural, public or private. He does not mourn Fisher,[24] he does not mourn Joe, and he coolly buries one body and moves another (Eels's), always to protect himself. He is willing to trade exonerating documents for his own skin even though Whit had him framed and had Eels murdered. His death hardly atones for all this.

Such personal morality, this kind of desperate struggle to peel back the false appearances and find who really did what to whom at the expense of any social responsibility, is the imaginary universe of a great deal of film noir. Sometimes the characters are sympathetic, sometimes not, but they are all motivated by self-protection and their wish to know. They all are in the grip of the idea that there is a plot hidden somewhere, behind the obvious plot, one that explains what everyone is up to. If they could expose this, then they would restore some kind of sense, some kind of normality to their lives. Reardon could then go back to adjusting humdrum claims; Ann could then marry the nice state official who carries a torch for her, but only after she concludes that Jeff remained enthralled to the evil Kathie. The deaf-mute, known only as The Kid, is the keeper of the secret that Jeff did love Ann to the end, a very romantic take on his death. This is confusing. Equally confusing is Lubinsky's extraordinarily antiromantic remark in *The Killers,* speaking of Lilly, now his wife: "She was always in love with him [Swede] . . . and I was always in love with her. It worked out fine for me, anyway." Normality is restored, but it continues to be predicated on lies and deception, on false appearances, and on a morality that permits those who live by society's codes to be protected from the dark truth known to those who have "got in wrong." If there is any profound moral to the story, it is that we cannot condemn those who know that dark truth, as we are hardly better, as we too live under and benefit from the tissue of lies.

The morality of "let he who is without sin cast the first stone" is not one that makes much sense in classical tragedy. We are not invited to mitigate Oedipus's crimes because he is reformed, still less because we are all guilty. Creon and Antigone clash because both act on principle. If the audience were to view principles as floating on our lies, the outcome would be not tragedy but irony.

## Knowledge, Morality, and Tragedy: The Issues Joined

The idea of personal morality is, of course, incoherent. It is a false appearance. The rules of morality are social institutions. Any claim to a personal code that is not simply internalized social rules is, by definition, amoral, if not immoral. So these films are morally incoherent. They sympathetically portray men ensnared by femmes fatales even though these men are weak moral cowards. These incoherencies in the morality of the films, including their wholesale acceptance of the "sexy woman as succubus" myth, are evidence that what drives them are the constraints of censorship, in the narrow sense, and of a culture in which puritanism and the demand for license go hand in hand.[25]

Let me elaborate. The idea that some, if not all, very attractive women are dangerous is a clear projection of fear of the power of sex. The puritan variant is that only if it is completely repressed are we safe from it. No annual bacchanalia or Sunday sport for the puritan. Hence, approved relationships, Swede with Lilly, Jeff with Ann, are low-key, respectful, headed toward pair-bonding. The ability to live those lives, however, depends on averting the gaze from, or not knowing about, the lure of powerful sexual attraction and easy money and how these associate with the underworld of immorality or amorality. The implied connection is that the one kind of transgression, fornication, is at the top of the slippery slope toward others—robbery, treachery, even murder. The connection is implied rather than stated because of its manifest absurdity. One thing simply does not lead to the other. Censorship demands only that the bad be punished. So Kitty and Kathie must get their comeuppance because they sleep with men without marrying them and manipulate them into buying them luxury lifestyles, and they do not stop short of instigating murder, even carrying it out. Justice comes to Kathie from the guns of the police, to Kitty presumably from the courts. The antiheroes who have transgressed and "got in wrong" also pay with their lives for their expiation.

But censorship is only a narrow constraint. The wider one is that the films of the period had to offer pleasures to the audience. Films that kill off almost everyone bad, that never comment on the incoherence of personal morality, that suggest that the past will catch up with you, offer some reassurance and satisfaction to the audience. Self-congratulation is something in which most people, especially those touched by the puritan spirit, take pleasure. It is reassuring to be told that, if we allowed sex free rein, it might turn all male heads. Such films allow you to contemplate seduction by a highly attractive woman, but they prevent her from harming you because she is just a movie image and because the drama shows that what she does to men is evil. So be happy that these temptations do not come your way. Such films say that respectable life floats on a magma of violence, viciousness, and evil but that this must be repressed, not acknowledged. Do not let on to the innocent and good what lurks beneath.

The two films I have discussed are in some ways limiting cases. As Wolfenstein and Leites point out:

The hero [in noir] is typically in a strange town where there are apt to be dangerous men and women of ambiguous character and where the forces of law and order are not to be relied on. . . . If he relies on no one but himself . . . he will emerge triumphant. . . . A minority . . . are cautionary tales. The hero may succumb to his attacker; this is his bad dream. . . . Out of greed and overconfidence, he may try to get away with murder; he commits the crime of which he is usually only suspected and has to pay for it. The girl may turn out to be worse than he believed. . . . He may not be able to produce anyone on whom to pin the blame for the crimes of which he is falsely accused; then he is a victim of circumstances. If circumstances fail to collaborate with his need to blame someone else, he may even end by blaming himself.[26]

Swede and Jeff blame themselves. Theirs are cases where their own impulses are the problem: their vulnerability to the sexual siren and their consequent loss of moral compass. Better we hew closely to our moral compass and eschew the power of desire; otherwise, it will undo us and possibly also our way of life. There is still room here to make a case for noir films as tragedy, but their emphases on narrative and its uncertainties and on spectacle immediately negate it.

For example, the point of view of the films differs from what one can surmise from the travails of the characters. As I noted at the beginning, the photographic style was made possible by technical advances. It helped that the directors were adept at expressionistic mise-en-scènes. Much has been written about the way the films look, how swiftly they move, and how they manage to be both exciting and detached. They are also detached in their point of view because they never settle on one. Much sophistication goes into this. The opening of *The Killers* is narrated omnisciently: we see things from the killers' view, from the diners' view, and from Swede's view. Then we switch to follow Reardon. But Reardon's drive and intensity are those of the film, not something we share. And, when it is his turn to be set up, we switch to the point of view of Lubinsky, who kills Reardon's would-be killers. The last shoot-out is offscreen, presumably as a lead-in to the prosaic final scene in the insurance office. I have already commented on its odd flippancy.

Tourneur's style in *Out of the Past* is similarly expressive, with the added touch of High Sierra settings for Ann and Jeff's idyll. Again, the point of view shifts, from omniscience at the beginning; to extended voice-over flash-back by Jeff to Ann; back to omniscience in following Jeff as he tries to disentangle himself, The Kid as he is followed in an effort to shoot Jeff, and Jimmy the game warden tailing Ann (for whom he carries the torch) and then talking to the police as they discuss tracking Jeff down. We end as we begin, by being positioned as onlookers, not mourners, as The Kid lies to Ann so as to free her from any guilt she may feel about moving on with her life.

The casting is itself an act of mise-en-scène, a way of directing our sympathies. The most alluring of the females are given the bad/good girls' roles; the protagonists' roles are handed to strong and attractive male stars. Hollywood invested talent in these films, behind the camera and in front. This itself was a way of glamorizing what it officially wanted to condemn.

The very fact that these films are invested with great skill to make them absorbing, even enticing to watch hardly fits with the script message that the whole bunch of characters and their complicated lives are low-life. Al-though Swede is a loser, he is played by an attractive, up-and-coming star, Burt Lancaster, which makes him seem a victim. Perhaps we are meant to pity him. Robert Mitchum as Jeff is even more winsome. He is calm, insou-ciant, the quintessence of what is now called *cool*. This in itself is an ad-mired trait. He also has a remarkable facility with worldly, witty, deprecating ripostes for someone who never cracks a book or even a newspaper. (James M. Cain was an uncredited writer on *Out of the Past*.) He sails through the mayhem for all the world as though he is just a put-upon regular joe. Yet, to repeat, he is utterly self-centered. Preserving his own skin is what comes first. He is played and portrayed by script and direction as a doomed ro-mantic hero. The truth that he is "no good" comes from the mouth of Kathie, at a point in the film when we have been taught not to trust any-thing she says. Like most death in noir, his is quickly set aside.[27] Death without ceremony is hardly tragic.

The philosophical balance sheet, then, is this. The solution to the mys-tery, the dark reality behind appearances, is disclosed to us as a warning. Just because bad actions are in the past does not mean that they are settled. The double aspect must be maintained. To protect the respectable, those who have knowledge must tell lies. There is no bridge. Jeff cannot escape his past but should protect Ann and her family from it; Lubinsky is happy that Swede dumped Lilly. Kathie is dead; there is no escape to respectability for Kitty. Disruption of the respectable social order has been avoided. Ann, Jimmy, Lilly, Reardon have all had brushes with the underworld, but its disruptive potential has been contained. Restoration of the respectable order is not what tragedy celebrates. The revelations, such as Swede's discovery that Kitty is not loyal to him or Jeff's discovery of the vicious side of Kathy, could be said to resemble discovery of connections in classical tragedies, as could the reversals that these discoveries trigger. But the manner of their disclosure is mainly through narrative (flashback, voice-over), not action.

Tragedies are not dramas of false appearances. The classical tragedies that Aristotle approved of were mostly set in families, often noble ones. The protagonists all acted on moral principle. Because of some fatal error, a chain of events is set in motion that leads to a situation where terrible consequences cannot be evaded—usually because two principles clash. This trajectory arouses pity and terror, and the purging effect of these emotions is some sort of artistic pleasure. Protagonists who allow romantic love to cloud their judgement, who act in self-serving and unprincipled ways, do not resemble the doomed characters of classical tragedy. Their petty affairs scarcely warrant pity and terror. In particular, Aristotle seems to have wanted his protagonists to be neither wholly guilty nor wholly innocent in order that the audience could make some connection to them. My argument has been that film noir creates a world so exotic and unprincipled that the audience makes no more than the superficial connection with it needed to sustain its involvement. Moreover, the audience is encouraged by various means to distance itself from the protagonists and the world they inhabit. This disconnection, this reassurance, is, ultimately, why I think films noirs fail as tragedy.

## Notes

The epigraph to this essay is taken from *The Poetics of Aristotle,* trans. and with commentary by Stephen Halliwell (Chapel Hill: University of North Carolina Press, 1987), line 1451b5, p. 41.

1. Paul Schrader, "Notes on *Film Noir*" (1972), in *Film Noir Reader,* ed. Alain Silver and James Ursini (New York: Limelight, 1996), 54.

2. James Ursini hints at this in his commentary on the Criterion DVD of *Out of the Past.*

3. Raymond Borde and Étienne Chaumeton, *Panorama du film noir Américain, 1941–1953* (Paris: Minuit, 1955), translated by Paul Hammond as *A Panorama of American Film Noir, 1941–1953* (San Francisco: City Lights, 2002).

4. Examples would be *Body Heat* (Lawrence Kasdan, 1981), *Blood Simple* (Joel Coen, 1984), *Into the Night* (John Landis, 1985), *Backtrack* (Dennis Hopper, 1990), *Red Rock West* (John Dahl, 1992), and *Memento* (Christopher Nolan, 2000).

5. *The Poetics of Aristotle,* line 1450a15, p. 37.

6. Martha Wolfenstein and Nathan Leites, *Movies: A Psychological Study* (1950; 2nd ed., New York: Atheneum, 1970). Wolfenstein and Leites's is a comparative study that uses British, American, and French films released in the United States in the same period to show up by contrast the characteristics of American movies.

7. Summing up the entire context of American films of this period, Wolfenstein and Leites write: "American films are preoccupied with showing events from a variety of viewpoints. We have seen what importance is attached to the discrepancies between appearance and reality; the hero and heroine in melodramas frequently appear different from what they really are. We are shown how the hero appears to the police, as a criminal, how the heroine appears to the hero, as a wicked woman. The plot is less one of action than of proof or rather disproof. The incriminating false appearance must be dispelled. It must be proved that what was supposed to have happened did not happen. The potentialities of the hero and heroine for serious action are realized only in false appearances, which indicates what they might have done if they had been carried away by false appearances" (ibid., 243–44).

8. Ibid., 14.

9. Ibid., 226.

10. Wolfenstein and Leites say that sacrificing men for her own advantage is the most "forbidding feature" of the bad girl (ibid., 37).

11. The secondary bad girl of *Out of the Past,* Meta Carson, is played by Rhonda Fleming, also a great Hollywood beauty.

12. The transfer of classic film noir to video and DVD is surprisingly spotty. To take only some examples come across in research for this article, essential works of Siodmak, Tourneur, Anthony Mann, Rudolph Maté, Otto Preminger, and Andre de Toth are unavailable, as are important works by such later directors as William Asher, Phil Karlson, Richard Quine, Don Siegel, and Richard Wilson. There are also gaps in the transfer filmographies of such major stars as Mitchum, Dana Andrews, Robert Taylor, and Richard Widmark.

13. IMDb informs us that Richard Brooks as well as John Huston was an uncredited writer (see http://www.imdb.com/title/tt0038669/fullcredits#writers [accessed May 15, 2005]).

14. Presumably, *gambler* is code for *mobster.* Sterling inhabits a luxurious mansion overlooking Lake Tahoe, owes the government perhaps a million dollars in taxes, and has various hoodlums working for him. He also controls a San Francisco nightclub.

15. *The Poetics of Aristotle,* lines 1449b24–29, p. 37.

16. Nickolas Pappas, "Aristotle," in *The Routledge Companion to Aesthetics,* ed. Berys Gaut and Dominic McIver Lopes (London: Routledge, 2001), 23.

17. Coeval with these antipsychological films was the rise of the psychological western and gangster film.

18. I am influenced here by Martin M. Winkler's "Tragic Features in John Ford's *The Searchers*" (in *Classical Myth and Culture in the Cinema,* ed. Martin M. Winkler [New York: Oxford University Press, 2001], 118–47). Winkler shows that, in *The Searchers,* we have a towering masterpiece of film that is set, like tragedy, in a semimythical landscape and that does, indeed, induce pity and terror. This is what American tragedy really looks like.

19. Hollywood's insurance adjusters are a public-spirited and responsible bunch. Think of Barton Keyes in *Double Indemnity.* Of the noir world in general, although not that of my two films, Wolfenstein and Leites write: "In American films the police tend to be ineffectual. They suspect the wrong man; they are apt to be satisfied with a hasty and incomplete investigation because they are under pressure to arrest and convict. Hence the major task of investigation is carried on by private individuals, sometimes professional private detectives, more often untrained persons whom circumstances force into the role of investigator. . . . Since the police cannot be resorted to for help or safety, and must even be avoided since they mistakenly suspect the investigator, the atmosphere of the big city becomes that of the unpoliced frontier. The self-appointed investigator must take the law into his own hands" (*Movies,* 199–200).

20. The protagonists of both my selected films run gas stations. Both are spotted there by their old cronies. It seems an unfortunate choice of job for someone who wants to disappear without trace. Such coincidences, however, make many plots work. On the other hand, the psychological commentator might say that the choice of such a job indicates an unconscious ambivalence about being caught.

21. See the entry for *The Killers* at www.filmsite.org (accessed May 16, 2005).

22. Wolfenstein and Leites, *Movies,* 101 and passim.

23. "In *Out of the Past* Robert Mitchum relates his history with such pathetic relish that it is obvious there is no hope for any future: one can only take pleasure in reliving a doomed past" (Schrader, "Notes on *Film Noir,*" 58).

24. Contrast this to *The Maltese Falcon,* in which, despite his differences with his partner, Miles, Sam Spade will not play the patsy for his murderer, Brigid, although, he admits, he loves her.

25. The United States is the land of puritanism (goodness morality) and of legal gambling and prostitution (fun morality). Each needs the other for its self-definition, perhaps even for its success (success morality).

26. Wolfenstein and Leites, *Movies,* 298–99.

27. Wolfenstein and Leites found this a feature of American films of the period: "With all the killings that occur in American films, there is little acknowledgement of death. Death is denied by furious activity and grim humor" (ibid., 233).

# Moral Man in the Dark City

## Film Noir, the Postwar Religious Revival, and *The Accused*

*R. Barton Palmer*

### The Dark Mirror

A principal problem for historians of the American film is how to explain, as Andrew Spicer puts it, "the eruption of film noir's dark, cynical, and often pessimistic stories into the sunlit pastures of Hollywood's character-istically optimistic and affirmative cinema."[1] Although influences from other cinematic traditions (primarily German expressionism) and from literature (European naturalism, native hard-boiled fiction) have custom-arily been taken into account, film scholars, Spicer among them, have for the most part relied on what we might call the *dark mirror theory* to ac-count for this surprising development. According to this view, the sudden emergence and flourishing of film noir reflects the supposedly bleak and fearful national mood that unexpectedly descended on the nation in the wake of the war's end, despite (or because of) the overwhelming victory achieved by American arms in both the European and the Pacific theaters.

Most, if not all, historians of the period endorse this notion of pro-found cultural change (something akin to a paradigm shift). The wartime consensus of what has been termed *victory culture,* based on a sublimation of racial and class tensions, is thought to have given way to a national state of mind that Hollywood could profitably metaphorize as a dark cityscape.[2] Film noir constructed a locus of entrapment, dislocation, anomie, and sexual uncertainty whose most signal quality was the dreadful solitude of its per-secuted protagonists, a state of being in stark opposition to wartime no-tions of solidarity and civic connection. Film noir was not the only cultural symptom of this new national mood. William Graebner, for example, sees the widespread anxiety of the immediate postwar years as generating, in addition to Hollywood's dark cinema, developments as diverse as the increasing popularity of psychotherapy, the enduring national preoccupation with a UFO threat after dubiously documented sightings, and the surprising adoption of existentialism by the country's leading intellectuals (including some notable theologians).

The postwar era thus became, in Graebner's formulation, a "culture of contingency." The causes, Graebner argues, are clear enough. By the end of the forties, unpredictable and destructive international events had succeeded one another for more than two decades with bewildering rapidity. Americans had, therefore, come to sense that chance, not the iron laws of economics or the inevitability of human progress, was now ruling individual and collective experience. A shooting war in which perhaps 50 million, even more, had perished raised, in Graebner's view, "the possibility of sudden, undeserved death" for one and all.[3] And, even before the Russians developed nuclear weapons of their own in 1949, a perhaps unwinnable cold war had broken out, threatening slaughter on a scale never before imagined in human history. Americans had discovered, as the theologian Reinhold Niebuhr told his fellow countrymen in 1952, that they were "the custodians of the ultimate weapon which perfectly embodies and symbolizes the moral ambiguity of physical warfare." Once invented, "the bomb" could not be renounced because no nation can justly dispense with the means to forestall a threatened destruction. Yet, if forced to use it, Niebuhr predicted, "we might insure our survival in a world in which it might be better not to be alive."[4]

The national mood, however, was not dominated simply by nuclear dread and terror. Many commentators at the time also lamented the failure or abandonment of traditional notions of human purpose and virtue, prompting what Graebner terms a *moral crisis,* for "the seminal events of the forties seemed to confirm that humanity had, indeed, been set adrift from its ethical moorings."[5] For Niebuhr, the defeat of European fascism and Oriental militarism was deeply ironic, calling into question the conventional pieties of the national creed. He opined: "We are the poorer for the global responsibilities which we bear. And the fulfillments of our desires are mixed with frustrations and vexations." Most frustrating, and morally puzzling, was the fact that "the paradise of our domestic security is suspended in a hell of global insecurity," undermining the "conviction of the perfect compatibility of virtue and prosperity which we have inherited from both our Calvinist and our Jeffersonian ancestors."[6]

The dark mirror theory proposes that noir films give narrative and visual shape to these deep doubts about national purpose and direction. Characteristically set in a murky urban tangle of bars, cheap hotels, railroad stations, and underworld dives, they construct a frightening alternative, a life of permanent impermanence, to the settled, middle-class existence that was ordinarily purveyed by a Hollywood formerly preoccupied, for sound business reasons, with picturing "sunlit pastures." Furthermore, as I have argued elsewhere, the customary forward motion of Hollywood narrative, its relentless movement toward the solution of problems and the restoration of the status quo, is fractured by story elements that come "out of the past," obviating reassuring forms of closure, and confirming feckless protagonists in their isolation from conventional values, especially a sense of regained righteousness.[7]

The rootless, morally compromised denizens of the dark city glimpse, but only briefly, the domestic inclusiveness of melodrama (arguably the most pervasive form of Hollywood fantasy) and its figuration of the protective, nurturing family as the destined end of the virtuous. In melodrama, the home is a guarantor for one and all of a stable identity established by unchallengeable notions of relatedness, a fortress against an intrusive, frightening public sphere. In the anonymous dark city, by way of contrast, all are strangers in a strange land. Noir characters find themselves embroiled in narratives that unfold in transient spaces that, like city streets, are open to everyone, yet no community, no system of values that might reflect or produce consensus, emerges to direct either their desires or their movements. Such a mode of representation finds its structural reflex in episodic narratives that, lacking little sense of determining causality, are difficult to follow (for protagonists and spectators alike) and often, in fact, lead nowhere or circle back to their beginning.

## Affirmation and Redemption in Film Noir

There is obviously much to recommend the view that what Graebner aptly terms the *age of anxiety* finds a more or less obvious cinematic correlative in film noir. Yet we should bear in mind that such general propositions (that film noir is essentially pessimistic, that the postwar era was pervaded by angst and moral doubt) are most useful as heuristics guiding, but not determining, textual analysis. Contextual approaches are most persuasive when global characterizations of a film series are nuanced by the specific connections that can be established between individual films and particular historical trends or events. In the case of film noir, such work has been significantly advanced by Paul Arthur, who demonstrates how narrowly defined postwar themes (e.g., returning veterans' difficult readjustment to civilian life) find narrative and visual form within the larger traditions of Hollywood filmmaking, thus figuring as *constructions* rather than *reflections* of contemporary reality. Arthur's detailed study confirms the general usefulness of the dark mirror theory, but it also suggests that understandings of noir films and the social contexts that inform them may have been formulated imprecisely because at too general a level.[8]

In this essay, I intend to take Arthur's approach in a somewhat different direction, with a view toward a further nuancing of the dark mirror theory. In particular, I seek to recover here an important cultural movement in the postwar world, neglected by noir historians, in order to better contextualize a considerable body of films that, although deemed noir by scholarly consensus, eschew in different ways the deep-seated pessimism about the human capacity for virtue that is otherwise such a signal feature of the series.[9] These noir films whose theme is redemption in some sense model patterns of experience that find eloquent and more reflective expression in Niebuhr's various works, especially *Moral Man and Immoral Society* (1932), a politicoreligious text that, although first published before the war, reflects and defines important terms of the spiritual revival that was such an important element of American culture in the late forties and the fifties.

The increasing concern with religiosity (and the psychological meliorism that was its secular counterpart) was a broad and complex movement, marked by a number of sometimes contradictory trends.[10] Most noteworthy, perhaps, were the dramatic rise in formal church membership, the forging of syncretic rather then strictly sectarian forms of national religion based on the perceived commonalities of the Judeo-Christian tradition, the flourishing of extraecclesial evangelism under the leadership of Billy Graham, and the spread of pop psychology religion as preached by the successful national ministry of Norman Vincent Peale.[11] This deepening interest in difficult moral experience and the possibilities of human betterment found a therapeutic reflex in the neo-Freudianism of psychologists such as Karen Horney and, especially, Erich Fromm. If Horney suggested ways in which neurotic personality formations might be overcome by an increasingly sophisticated understanding of the workings of the human mind, releasing the mentally impaired to seek self-realization, Fromm (like Niebuhr, drawing heavily on Judeo-Christian traditions) enthusiastically promoted the utopian expectation that man both individually and collectively might overcome the destructive forces within his nature and create, to borrow the title of one of Fromm's most influential books, a "sane society" in which love could triumph over self-interest.[12]

These cultural developments, I suggest, find reconfiguration in those noir films in which the descent into a nightmare world of criminality or the intrusion of the dark past into a promising present leads neither to destruction nor to some form of insincere reformation. Of course, the noir canon includes a number of essentially grim narratives, such as Billy Wilder's *Double Indemnity* (1944), to which unconvincing salvational gestures have been, perhaps somewhat cynically, added in order to satisfy the Production Code Administration's demand for compensating moral value. Here, I will focus instead on those films that trace an authentically penitential and eventually redemptive movement from sinfulness and isolation to social reintegration. In connecting this noir subgroup to its cultural moment, I shall be less concerned with either postwar evangelism or Peale's promotion of the "power of positive thinking," perspectives on the encounter with evil that, promoting what one theologian at the time termed *cheap grace,* often offer little more than a thinly disguised Pelagianism that, with its irrepressible optimism, is more closely aligned with traditional meritocratic versions of the American dream.[13]

Of more relevance to a contextual analysis of those noir films about difficult spiritual growth are the writings of Niebuhr and Fromm, who are useful figures because they gave voice to widely held views even as they exerted great influence in promoting them. Although predictably diverse in their approach to the difficult moral dilemmas posed by the postwar era for Americans (principally because of the strong influence of Marxism on Fromm's social theorizing), these two thinkers shared the view that deliverance from evil or destructiveness must acknowledge and somehow transcend, not minimize, the contradictions of human nature as expressed by the Christian concept of original sin and the Freudian notion that, if behavior was driven in part by an urge toward life, it was equally constrained by a death instinct.

## American High?

It is, indeed, a historiographic commonplace to view the forties as split between a culture of war, in which a crusade against political evil on a vast scale enabled Americans to occupy the moral high ground, and a culture of peace, in which such clarity was quickly lost, giving rise to widespread anxiety, directionlessness, and doubt. But this view ignores many significant developments that point in an opposite direction. William L. O'Neill, for example, concentrating on domestic life rather than intellectual or ideological developments, argues that the first decade and a half of the postwar period can be termed the *years of confidence,* and this assessment is echoed by others who emphasize the incredible prosperity the era witnessed, hitherto unexampled in the American experience, as a middle-class life, defined by homeownership and a bounty of consumer goods, was attained by a national (if largely white) majority.[14] Contributing to this mood of progress, Hollywood, for its part, continued to produce affirmative versions of contemporary American life.

It is a sometimes neglected fact that film noir was a substantial, but always a minority and oppositional, presence on the nation's screens at the time. The social problem film, just to take an obvious generic example, enjoyed a particular vogue in the late forties and early fifties, fueled by an enduring sense of wartime solidarity, and energized by the amazing popularity of Italian neo-realist releases with American audiences. In these texts, otherwise disturbing aspects of postwar life (racism, anti-Semitism, juvenile delinquency, the readjustment faced by handicapped veterans) are surveilled by a benevolent establishment and, ultimately, provided with heartwarming solutions that endorse consensus values, especially middle-class notions of responsible citizenship.[15]

If the mood of the postwar era was split between the celebration of family life and a desperate worry about imminent nuclear destruction, the Hollywood films of the period, it is hardly surprising, manifest a similar mix of optimism and pessimism. Yet this binary opposition should not be so starkly drawn if we are to make sense of the period's complexity. Perhaps, as Elaine Tyler May has argued, "cold war ideology and the domestic revival" were "two sides of the same coin," expressing "postwar Americans' intense need to feel liberated from the past and secure in the future." A key element in that liberation, May believes, was the hope for domestic order, which was not a return to prewar notions of family life so much as a desperate hope, especially among the middle class, for escape from the increasingly anxiety-provoking and unrewarding public sphere, defined equally by the increasing anxiety of geopolitics and the stultifying nature of postindustrial corporate labor, the discontents of the so-called organization man. As May puts it, "rootless Americans struggled against what they perceived as internal decay," and, in that struggle, "the family seemed to offer a psychological fortress that would protect them against themselves."[16]

This struggle can be seen as reconfigured within the terms made available for expression by the postwar Hollywood genre system, whose default view of human experience is found in the "sunlit pastures" of screen melodrama. Some, perhaps most, noir films confirm guilt-ridden loners as forever "in transit" because they prove unable to escape the lawlessness and moral uncertainty of the dark city that is both within and without; such characters can never transcend who they once were (although they might desire a better world), and, thus, they can inhabit only a present that is always already the past. But, in the films that I shall discuss here, the noir vision melds (if at times uneasily) with the imagery, values, and themes of melodrama. Such films focus on ultimately moral protagonists who discover that they can, in fact, transcend the past as they undergo difficult, painful moral growth into a future of rootedness, love, and integrity. The price that they are asked to pay is not inconsiderable, however. Not only must they surrender their autonomy, but they must also occupy the narrowly defined roles to which a still-constituting economy of domestication consigns them, linking themselves to others in the way that common sense (and dominant theories of human nature) at the time prescribed.

In his widely popular *The Art of Loving,* first published in 1956, Erich Fromm eloquently expressed the indispensability of togetherness, the source of security in a world rife with unseen dangers: "The experience of separateness arouses anxiety; it is, indeed, the source of all anxiety. Being separate means being cut off, without any capacity to use my human powers. Hence to be separate means to be helpless, unable to grasp the world— things and people—actively; it means that the world can invade me without my ability to react."[17] Thus, geopolitical anxiety finds a psychological reflex in apartness, which must generate its own "deterrent" (loving connectedness) in order to ward off the feared invasion of the world, defined in moral terms as "things and people." Such an attack against the inadequately attached, solitary self is an important element of many noir narratives, including William Dieterle's *The Accused* (1949), which provides us with a useful example of the noir "redemption" that exemplifies its most notable features.

## The Penitential Journey of Constructing the Domestic Sphere

For May, the notion of containment, famously formulated by the diplomat George Kennan as a strategy for countering postwar Soviet expansionism, generated a domestic version, the family home, within whose walls "potentially dangerous social forces of the new age might be tamed," enabling both men and women to obtain the "secure and fulfilling life to which [they] aspired."[18] But the process of taming implies the imposition of force, that "coercive factor in society [that] is both necessary and dangerous," as Niebuhr suggests. This question of the proper role of force in human society is "particularly insistent," he suggests, because of "the romantic overestimate of human virtue and moral capacity, current in our modern middle-class culture." In Niebuhr's view, what has been lacking in the Enlightenment tradition dominating the American self-conception is "an understanding of . . . the limitations of the human imagination, the easy subservience of reason to prejudice and passion."[19] Progress, both individual and collective, thus depends on the victory (always provisional) of reason over passion and prejudice, in the context of the acknowledgment of what May considers "potentially dangerous social forces" or Niebuhr "the ambiguity of man's strength and weakness."[20]

Such a taming process, overseen by a reason that is deeply male in several senses (legal, therapeutic, and romantic) and in which domestication emerges as the end of female destiny, is, undoubtedly, the determining element in *The Accused,* a noir film (recognized as such by the standard histories of the genre) that traces how a career woman is forced to acknowledge the dangers of sexual repression inherent in her social position and accept the prospect of love, marriage, and perpetual unemployment with a man strong enough to protect her from herself. In the postwar movement of women from the workplace back to the family home, a trend anatomized by May and other historians of the period, such a narrative is exemplary in its ambivalent portrayal of the protagonist, Wilma Tuttle, a professional, unmarried, and, hence, unattractive woman whose life choice, as we would now say, is presented as unnatural, a state of being dramatically signified by casting. Wilma is played by one of Hollywood's most glamorous actresses, Loretta Young, and so, in order to make her suitable for the part, Young's beauty needed to be restrained by a mannish wardrobe and pinned-up hair, with the inevitable result that the character's transformation into a sex object and suitable mate appears as a restoration of the real

Loretta Young to herself, the overcoming of that foolish (and socially dangerous) remaking that women must perpetrate on themselves in order to fit into the masculine world of work outside the home.

## Accusation and Deliverance

Interestingly, the movement that brings Wilma to abandon what her fiancé, in a moment of righteous protectiveness, calls her "twopenny job" results from a foolish and unthinking violation of professional decorum that can be excused in the end only because women, it is argued, are emotionally unstable, liable particularly to violent outbursts fueled by their fearfulness. Encouraged, so the story implies, by some inner sense of being unfulfilled, Wilma mismanages a relationship with a handsome male student, killing the young man more or less accidentally, and exposing herself to ruin and degradation. Because this error can be rectified only by a socially acceptable relationship with a man of her own age, it becomes proof enough that women, as patriarchal common sense would have it, lack rationality and self-control, especially in sexual matters.

Dr. Tuttle is a tenured professor of psychology at a major West Coast university who not only holds a doctorate (still a mark of special status, if increasingly less so, in the postwar collegiate world) but also has designs on becoming head of her department some day. With her education and established professional success, she represents a powerfully viable alternative to wifedom and motherhood. Coupling with the proper man thus cannot result from her working through the vagaries of the era's sexual economy, in which the principal problem for single women who wanted to be married, although they were debarred from the obvious pursuit of men if they wished to be thought virtuous, was finding a suitable mate. Only a narrative of redemption can deliver her from the spinsterly professionalism that, it turns out, has trapped her in an unhappiness of which she is initially unaware and whose figuration in the narrative is her unwilling descent into a noir world of duplicity, guilt, and persecution.

As the story begins, romance has no place in Wilma's life, a decision (if that is what it is) for which the narrative offers no explanation. But perhaps none is necessary since her devotion to her career would explain, at least in terms audiences at the time might have understood, the absence of a man. As it turns out, Wilma can banish men from her life but not sexual desire, which, because she has repressed it, sets in motion a series of events that swiftly and unexpectedly threaten her with the loss of all she has worked so hard to attain. Bill (Douglas Dick), an attractive and older male student, has been getting "fresh" with her in class, but, instead of reporting his constant and invasive flirtation to the dean, Dr. Tuttle, whose gestures and nervousness evidence the pleasure she takes in his attention, decides to "correct" him by analyzing his psychological problems. This is a process to which Bill, excited at the prospect of such easily gained intimacy, willingly submits. As Dr. Tuttle explains to Bill, he is liable to be dangerously erratic, having been raised by an overly permissive mother and a too-strict father, a combination of contradictory influences that compromises his self-control; in turn, Bill argues that she is repressed, a psychological condition evidenced in her constant, nervous checking of her pinned-up hair.

Unwisely, given what she suspects about him, and knowing now what he thinks of her, Wilma accepts Bill's invitation to dinner, and he drives her out to the Malibu coastal highway, where, so he says, he often goes diving for abalone. They share a meal, including martinis and cigarettes, and Wilma is pleased that such "daring" disputes Bill's analysis of her as a prude. Bill parks on a lonely cliff above a rocky beach, ostensibly to show her more about his hobby. Encouraged by her only-ambivalent rejection of his flirtation, Bill forces her to kiss him, and she responds with an evident passion that surprises them both. But, when he somewhat roughly tries to make love to her, she grabs a heavy piece of metal and, suddenly out of control, kills him with numerous blows to the head. Wilma convinces herself that no one will believe the truth of what happened (because she willingly went in Bill's car? because she felt attracted to him and enjoyed the power over him he seemed to invite? because she overreacted to the threat he posed?). So, fearful of exposure and subsequent professional ruin, she arranges the scene of the crime to look like an accident, pushing his body onto the rocks below, but not before drawing seawater into Bill's lungs through reverse respiration to simulate drowning.

Escaping into the night (a dark and threatening highway along which she makes her way with difficulty) but returning home undetected, Dr. Tuttle soon discovers that she cannot forget what she has done. In fact, she must undergo a kind of penance for Bill's killing, which leads to her moral restoration and the legal establishment of her innocence. As Bill's former teacher, Wilma becomes embroiled in the investigation of what the police immediately suspect is a homicide. The victim's guardian turns out to be a lawyer, Warren Ford (Robert Cummings), who, to his great surprise, falls in love with Wilma only soon to discover her involvement in Bill's death. Warren tries to convince her to leave the city and marry him. But his zealous attempt at protection fails when the police detective investigating the case (Wendell Corey), who also finds himself attracted to the shy but beautiful professor, asks Wilma to play the role of the killer in a reenactment of the crime. She is to strike a plaster model of Bill's head with the murder weapon, and, her fear and sexual passion reawakened by this reenactment, she hits out with revealing emotion.

Brought to trial as the film ends, Wilma, we are led to believe, can expect acquittal because Warren argues so successfully for her innocence, convincing the jury that everything she did was motivated by fear—of being assaulted, and, afterward, of being exposed, and, although Warren is silent on this score, of her own sexuality as well. The film's final shot shows Wilma seated at the defense table, smiling adoringly at her husband-to-be as he passionately defends her innocence (and, of course, weakness as well). She is a woman transformed by love (and the dependence that is its correlative). Dressed now in fashionable, feminine clothes (no more of her plain and unrevealing suits, all of which, as Warren remarks, look the same), the former mousy professor has been tastefully glamorized with makeup and her hair, now unpinned, attractively styled. As if to confirm that she has attained at last her natural position in the world, Wilma exudes more self-possession and confidence than before, even though she is now standing trial for her life, her character besmirched, her professional life surely ended by what is at best a shameful episode.

## Remaking Fritz Lang

As commentators have observed, *The Accused* betrays a close connection to one of the most successful noir films of the immediate postwar era, Fritz Lang's *The Woman in the Window* (1945), a much darker and more cynical *melodrama of mischance,* to use Foster Hirsch's term, in which the middle-aged and married professor Wanley (Edward G. Robinson) becomes embroiled with a beautiful and perhaps disreputable young woman, Alice (Joan Bennett), who "comes to life" beside her portrait in a gallery window and leads him back to her apartment. There, her violent lover, yet another older man, attacks Wanley in a jealous rage, and Wanley is forced to kill him and then cover up the traces of what he has done in order to prevent a scandal that would ruin his life.[21] As it turns out, one of the professor's close friends is called on to solve the murder, so he is invited to participate in the investigation, suffering constant chagrin as he must retrace the steps he took to dispose of the body. Clues begin to point toward Wanley, and an even more dangerous threat emerges when the dead man's bodyguard, attempting to blackmail the professor and his erstwhile girl-friend, cannot be scared off. Wanley is then convinced that his involvement in the killing will be exposed.

Innocent of murder, but guilty of moral indiscretions that would cost him his family and career, the professor determines to kill himself and swallows poison, not knowing that the would-be blackmailer has just been shot down by the police, who are wrongly convinced that the dead man is, in fact, the murderer they have been seeking. As the professor lies dying, the telephone starts to ring. It is Alice, who is calling to share the "good news" that they are now in the clear. But Wanley is too weak to answer and slips into unconsciousness. In a surprising finale, however, the film forsakes such fatalism and bitter irony. The story of temptation and murder is revealed to be a dream, and, thus, the film becomes something of a cautionary tale about the dangers of the surrender, however brief, to illicit desire. As, with evident relief, the professor exits the gentleman's club where he has taken his troubled nap, he passes by the gallery window he glimpsed in his dreams. Yet another beautiful woman is standing nearby, but he flees in somewhat abject and comic terror when she accosts him.

*The Accused* may share with its model a similar narrative structure, one in which a sympathetic criminal is forced by circumstances to participate, first as an interested third party, and gradually as a suspect, in the investigation of the crime he has committed, eventually manifesting his guilt. But the two films differ fundamentally in how they treat the redemption, moral and social, that allows their respectable middle-class protagonists to escape from the frightening noir alternative universe of doubleness, anxiety, and threat. In *The Woman in the Window,* Wanley experiences the consequences of his momentary failure to observe the strict sexual standards of his class and professional position, a slip that renders him vulnerable, not just to the police, but also to the blackmailing bodyguard, who exploits the professor's desire to prevent the loss of his good name. Wanley corrects his behavior after being warned by an affecting rendition of the hypothetical ruination he might have suffered, which, interestingly enough, takes shape within the theater of his own unconscious. The dream thus represents in some sense his own internalized sense of morality, the censoring of a desire that he cannot repress but that he is strong enough to punish.

Lang's pessimistic point, of course, is that the ethical sensibility that Wanley demonstrates is superficial. In both his waking and his unconscious avatars, the professor fears public shame and the loss of his position more than he regrets the immorality of what he has either done or, in some sense, desired to do. Tellingly, Wanley's wife makes only a brief appearance in both the dream and the narrative frame, deemphasizing his intended betrayal. The film's version of the noir underworld may be only a bourgeois nightmare, but that is precisely what gives *The Woman in the Window* its dark humor, its playful engagement with illicit behavior and conventional restraint. A vigilant respectability and a destructive desire for transgression reside in the same seemingly mild-mannered self, indicating the very thin line that separates criminality from obedience to the law, and, thus, disproving class-based notions of the separation of the dark city from, to continue the metaphor, its more prosperous and law-abiding suburbs. Most important, perhaps, Wanley is only chastened, not reformed, by his narrow escape from the promptings of his own id. His comically fearful endorsement of right-thinking behavior, evident in that desperate flight from the living reflex of the tempting woman of his dreams, is hardly a socially reassuring message in the mainstream Hollywood tradition.

## Becoming a Proper Woman

In *The Accused*, by way of contrast, Wilma Tuttle's misdeed is real, not hypothetical, but she is, in a sense, more innocent than Lang's professor, whose sexual urgings (a felt need for adventure and an attraction to an obviously immoral and beautiful woman) are similarly repressed. The film demonstrates the truth of what Warren Ford eloquently argues in defense of his future wife: that Wilma acted out of fear, not malice, and, thus, should be legally excused. More interesting, however, is that the narrative of investigation in which she becomes embroiled quickly becomes therapeutic, delivering her to the new self that deserves a new life, which can only be love and marriage with the same man who secures her vindication. Crucial to Wilma's transformation is Ford, who brings her "out of her shell," doing the cultural work first attempted maladroitly by Bill, whose flirtation, although ending tragically for both, does, perversely, succeed in disqualifying her professionally, a development that, in the film's terms, is positive.

Both men recognize that Wilma is, in her own psychological terms, a "psychothymiac," someone who represses her feelings. Bill inappropriately attracts her interest by his compliments and attention (which are uncomfortably aggressive yet intriguing). He eventually forces her to make love in a way that unleashes not only sexual passion but a deep-seated revulsion and dread as well. Tellingly, she never tells Bill no, only complains: "You're hurting me." In an intriguing symbolic gesture, just before his misguided attempt at seduction, Bill leads her to the edge of the cliff and shows her the wild surf below, arousing a fear and fascination that animate and excite her, even arousing what Bill, who has learned much in her class, terms her "phobicness." Bill, in other words, recognizes that beneath a deceptively prim surface lurks a woman whose transgressiveness might match his own. Wilma's overreaction to Bill's aggression (she keeps hitting him after he lets her go) indicates the dangers of her attraction to him and the power of the repressed feelings that he arouses.

In contrast, Warren courts her with gentleness and respect, responding with evident (but controlled) ardor when Wilma starts dressing more fashionably. This is, at first, an attempt to disguise her involvement in the crime, but she quickly takes pleasure in her new look and the compliments that it elicits. In any case, Warren's flattery, like that of the similarly enamored police detective, is never aggressive, and his deepening affection for the woman who he realizes killed his ward makes him increasingly protective of her vulnerability. When Warren and Wilma share their first kiss, it is chaste and brief, to be explained, Wilma blushingly admits, by her spinsterly ways. If Bill awakens dangerous passions in the repressed schoolteacher, Warren gently leads her toward an appropriately controlled and wifely affection, confirming that she is, indeed, a "nice girl." Wilma's sexual nature is thus shown to depend on what kind of man draws her out and relieves her of the burden of separateness that she has borne for so long. Wilma, then, in a deep cultural sense, is not responsible for the woman she becomes, and her "innocence" is established by the therapeutic aspects of the investigation, which, like the Freudian talking cure, makes her relive a traumatic experience in order to rid her of its destructive effects.

Two scenes are crucial to this development. In the first, Warren takes Wilma out for an evening at the prizefights after she admits that she's falling in love with him against her will. There, she sees a young man who bears an uncanny resemblance to Bill beaten brutally into unconsciousness. His body slides uncomfortably close to where she is sitting, and, suddenly, Wilma experiences a flashback to what transpired on the cliff. Reliving her own part in those horrible events, she suddenly blurts out, "I didn't mean to, I didn't mean to," in a moment of unconscious self-revelation that simultaneously makes clear to Warren not only that she is the killer but also that she was innocent of any homicidal intent. In the second scene, Wilma is also called on to relive the experience of killing Bill, but this time she does so willingly. Asked by the detective to reenact the striking of Bill with the metal club, Wilma agrees over Warren's strenuous objections. She first hits the plaster model of the young man's head timidly, but then she delivers blow after heavy blow, caught once again in the grip of the fear and terror (but also long-repressed desire) that Bill's advances had provoked. As in the boxing arena, this unreflective behavior, unlike her conscious denial of involvement, reveals the truth of her complicity—but also her innocence of any intent to harm the young man.

An important element in Wilma's therapy, of course, is the pain that she is made to suffer from facing what she has done. In an earlier encounter with the police, she had been reluctant to hold the murder weapon or do more than merely glance at the plaster head, storming out of the room with an unconvincing show of offended dignity as she declined to face what she had done. When asked to reenact the crime a second time, she refuses to refuse, mastering her distaste and fear, and brushing off Warren's attempt to protect her from herself. Wilma willingly submits to the chagrin and horror of repeating her own actions, which now can be properly surveilled by both the law and the man who loves her for (and in spite of) what she has done.

Wilma's journey toward wholeness (i.e., proper coupling with a loving mate after a restoration of her "natural" self) is truly penitential, a difficult working through of what Niebuhr considers "man's strength and weakness." The doubleness of Wilma's nature is not viewed ironically, with the cynical pessimism so evident in *The Woman in the Window*, whose professor's unthinking assumption of virtue is punctured twice: first, by the temptation to which, as a character in his own dream, he quickly succumbs; and, second, by the fact that temptation and betrayal are possibilities advanced only to be denied in extremis by his own unconscious. Unlike Wilma, Wanley is never forced to acknowledge what he has done; his own mind leads him not toward repentance and reformation but toward escape through the suicide that will forestall any proper accounting for his misdeeds. As Niebuhr writes, in a formulation of ethical purpose that seems appropriate to the spirit, if not the patriarchal fact, of Wilma's deliverance from repression and denial: "The final wisdom of life requires, not the annulment of incongruity but the achievement of serenity within and above it."[22]

## The Advent of Therapeutic Culture

Such serenity as Wilma achieves, however, comes at the expense of her character and independence, both of which must be denied. In fact, the film does show, in the terms popularized by Karen Horney, that Wilma "outgrows" the destructive forces within instead of restraining them with an "inner strait jacket," successfully disputing outmoded bourgeois notions of proper behavior and moral probity.[23] Her victory interestingly invokes the "therapeutic culture" just then beginning to be a presence on the American scene, an indication of what the sociologist Alan Woolfolk aptly characterizes as "the defeat of moralities of self-denial based upon the assumption that the path to individual salvation is through submission to doctrines of communal purpose and adherence to narratives of spiritual ascent." As Woolfolk goes on to observe: "Where once religion, morality, and custom accounted for human conduct in terms of good and bad, right and wrong, today psychology guides us towards criteria of well-being and sickness."[24] In *The Accused,* the lawyer becomes the therapist, the perpetrator the victim, the crime a symptom of maladjustment, and the court a site of transcendence. The noir city of dark desire and darker sin is left decisively behind. Stylistically, the film's most characteristically noir sequence, Wilma's escape through a shadowy and threatening night from the scene of the crime in an effort to hide the truth, rhymes with the brightly lit courtroom finale in which Wilma acknowledges the truth of her behavior and, by that acknowledgment, is set free.

Fromm observes: "To love somebody is not just a strong feeling—it is a decision, it is a judgment, it is a promise." And fulfilling that promise, he suggests, bespeaks "an attitude, an orientation of character which determines the relatedness of a person to the world as a whole, not toward one 'object' of love."[25] Wilma's deliverance from repression and fear can be understood precisely as this form of "conversion," which is the narrative movement that, Lary May suggests, characterizes the "more ideologically conservative version of film noir," a proposition that is certainly true enough. These films, he observes, "focus on authority figures . . . who cure the individual psychologically, allowing adaptation to the utopian dream of an affluent, classless American often centered on the suburban home and family."[26] Yet such narratives of psychological healing and social reintegration do not, as May believes, owe their power simply to victory culture's obsessive enactment of wartime solidarity, easily glimpsed in films such as *Casablanca* (Michael Curtiz, 1942), whose protagonists must "convert" from isolationist self-concern to collective self-sacrifice. With their foregrounding of the inner life and their prescription of an archly patriarchal therapeutic renewal that constitutes the domestic sphere, some of the so-called conservative noir films are actually avant-garde. Redemptive noir films like *The Accused* do not look backward to a historical moment in which the proper concerns of the private sphere were forced to cede to the necessity to combat the public threat posed by alien, imperialistic, antidemocratic forces. Instead, this noir subgroup is the harbinger of an emerging era that Christopher Lasch terms the *culture of narcissism,* whose first clearly perceptible symptom is that revival of faith, both secular and religious, in the difficult yet ultimately achievable perfectibility of human nature that is such a prominent feature of the postwar era.[27]

## Notes

1. Andrew Spicer, *Film Noir* (Harlow: Longman, 2002), 19.

2. Tom Engelhardt terms this change of mood *triumphalist despair* and traces its origin to the fact that "the atomic bomb that leveled Hiroshima also blasted openings into a netherworld of consciousness where victory and defeat, enemy and self, threatened to merge" (*The End of Victory Culture: Cold War America and the Disillusionment of a Generation* [Amherst: University of Massachusetts Press, 1995], 6). That "netherworld of consciousness" in which the distinction between traditional values disappeared is also an apt description of the moral atmosphere of film noir. For a useful description of the rise of victory culture, see John Morton Blum, *V was for Victory: Politics and American Culture during World War II* (New York: Harcourt Brace Jovanovich, 1976).

3. William S. Graebner, *The Age of Doubt: American Thought and Culture in the 1940s* (New York: Twayne, 1991), 19–20, 19.

4. Reinhold Niebuhr, *The Irony of American History* (New York: Scribner's, 1952), 39.

5. Graebner, *Age of Doubt,* 19–20.

6. Niebuhr, *Irony of American History,* 7.

7. R. Barton Palmer, "'Lounge Time' Reconsidered: Spatial Discontinuity and Temporal Contingency in *Out of the Past,*" in *Film Noir Reader 4,* ed. Alain Silver and James Ursini (New York: Limelight, 2004).

8. Paul Arthur, "Shadows on the Mirror: Film Noir and Cold War America" (Ph.D. diss., New York University, 1985). It is to be regretted that this fine study has never been published.

9. In this essay I discuss in detail only one example of this noir subtype, *The Accused* (William Dieterle, 1949). Other representative examples would be *Act of Violence* (Fred Zinnemann, 1949), *Abandoned* (Joseph M. Newman, 1949), *Scene of the Crime* (Roy Rowland, 1949), *On Dangerous Ground* (Nicholas Ray, 1950), *City for Conquest* (Anatole Litvak, 1941), *Somewhere in the Night* (Joseph L. Mankiewicz, 1946), *The Raging Tide* (George Sherman, 1951), *Night without Sleep* (Roy Baker, 1952), *The Man I Love* (Raoul Walsh, 1946), *Walk Softly, Stranger* (Robert Stevenson, 1950), *Shockproof* (Douglas Sirk, 1949), *Cape Fear* (J. Lee Thompson, 1962), and *Spellbound* (Alfred Hitchcock, 1945). Perhaps about 30 percent of the films customarily considered noir fall into this subtype.

10. A melioristic viewpoint, the notion that human society is progressing steadily toward some destined future state of perfection, was, of course, as popular in political as psychological polemics in the period (see esp. Eric Johnston, *America Unlimited* [New York: Doubleday, 1944]).

11. These events are usefully anatomized in two relatively recent studies, Robert Wuthnow's *The Restructuring of American Religion: Society and Faith since World War II* (Princeton, NJ: Princeton University Press, 1988) and Mark Silk's *Spiritual Politics: Religion and America since World War II* (New York: Simon & Schuster, 1988), and three notable volumes published in the era itself, A. Roy Eckhardt's *The Surge of Piety in America* (New York: Association Press, 1958), Peter L. Berger's *The Noise of Solemn Assemblies* (Garden City, NY: Doubleday, 1961), and Martin E. Marty's *The New Shape of American Religion* (New York: Harper & Bros., 1958). The formation of syncretic (or adhesional) forms of religion is, perhaps, the most significant and surprising trend of the period, as Mark Silk describes: "[Our country's] spectacular religious diversity results precisely from the historical tendency of such faiths [i.e., Christianity and Judaism] to divide and subdivide into additional, mutually hostile bodies which are, in principle anyway, equally separated from the government. Yet American society is also subject to powerful *adhesional* impulses—the desire for a common religious cause as well as for a quasi-spiritual allegiance to the religiously impartial state. In America, a church signifies at once an exclusivist body standing for itself alone, and one among many such institutions serving the public weal" (*Spiritual Politics,* 20).

12. Like other commentators of the period, Fromm noted that America, and, indeed, the Western world at midcentury, was given to "outbursts of destructiveness and paranoid suspicion," but he saw this regrettable state of affairs as little different from what "the civilized part of mankind has done in the last three thousand years of history." Even so, analyzing the varying rates of "destructive acts" such as suicide and homicide in different countries, he concluded that Freud's notion of the "comparative constancy of destructiveness" owing to the death instinct had been decisively disproved

(Erich Fromm, *The Sane Society* [London: Routledge & Kegan Paul, 1956], 4, 7–8). This meant that the kind of society that man created for himself made a difference and that "sanity and mental health can be attained only by simultaneous changes in the sphere of industrial and political organization, of spiritual and philosophical orientation, of character structure, and of cultural activities." Noting the present call from the Christian church for spiritual renewal, he regretted that religious leaders had neglected "the changes in the social order without which spiritual renewal must remain ineffective for the majority of the people" (271–72). For Fromm, ever the idealist, this change could come about only through "humanistic communitarianism," which will mean that man can be "restituted to his supreme place in society, never being a means, never a thing to be used by others or by himself" (361).

In *Neurosis and Human Growth* (New York: Harper, 1950), perhaps her most influential text of the period, Karen Horney also argues for the priority of self-realization, indebted, like Fromm, to one of the central concepts of ancient Greek culture. The way to deal with the "destructive forces in ourselves," she argues, is to outgrow them through "an ever increasing awareness and understanding of ourselves," which is not "an aim in itself, but a means of liberating the forces of spontaneous growth." Such a cultivation of the self, then, is "not only the prime moral obligation, but at the same time, in a very real sense, the prime moral privilege" (15).

13. As the theologian A. Roy Eckhardt observed at the time: "Much of our modern revivalism faces the temptation of the ancient Pelagian heresy in the Church, the fancy that men somehow determine their eternal salvation by their decision of will" (*Surge of Piety*, 100).

Examples of such thinking are easy to find. A chapter in Peale's bestselling *The Power of Positive Thinking* (New York: Prentice-Hall, 1952) is entitled "Expect the Best and Get It," and therein Peale admonishes his readers: "Learn to expect, not to doubt. In so doing you bring everything into the realm of possibility. This does not mean that by believing you are necessarily going to get everything you want or think you want. . . . When you put your trust in God, He guides your mind so that you do not want things that are not good for you or that are inharmonious with God's will." Success is, thus, simply a question of mind over matter: "If you believe in your job and in yourself and in the opportunities of your country, and if you believe in God and will work and study and put yourself into it . . . you can swing up to any high place to which you want to take your life and your service and your achievement" (91, 99).

A similar form of "happy Christianity" was to be found in the evangelical movement as well. In his *Peace with God* (New York: Doubleday, 1953), Billy Graham typically calls on those who would be saved to "renounce the principle of sin" but then observes that "when you fall in love completely and absolutely with Jesus Christ you will not want to do the things that he hates and abhors" (113–14), thereby providing a quick and easy solution to the ambiguities of a human nature perverted by original sin.

14. William L. O'Neill, *American High: The Years of Confidence, 1945–1960* (New York: Free Press, 1960). A similar view is offered by Joseph C. Goulden, *The Best Years, 1945–50* (New York: Atheneum, 1976). Of works written at the time expressing an unapologetic optimism in the American future, none, perhaps, was more popular or influential than Johnston's *America Unlimited.* In it, Johnston observes: "We Americans are optimists. . . . It is one of our spiritual dimensions, and therefore stronger than any statistics. . . . Defeatism does not suit our national character. We yield to it only rarely and briefly" (15).

15. Important examples, some of which, interestingly, contain noir elements, are *Crossfire* (Edward Dmytryk, 1947) and *Gentleman's Agreement* (Elia Kazan, 1947) (anti-Semitism), *Home of the Brave* (Mark Robson, 1949) and *Lost Boundaries* (Alfred L. Werker, 1949) (racism), *Blackboard Jungle* (Richard Brooks, 1955) and *Knock on Any Door* (Nicholas Ray, 1949) (juvenile delinquency), and *The Best Years of Our Lives* (William Wyler, 1946) and *The Men* (Fred Zinnemann, 1950) (the problems experienced by injured veterans).

16. Elaine Tyler May, *Homeward Bound: American Families in the Cold War Era,* rev. and updated ed. (New York: Basic, 1999), xxi.

17. Erich Fromm, *The Art of Loving* (New York: Harper & Row, 1956), 8.

18. May, *Homeward Bound,* xxiv–xxv.

19. Reinhold Niebuhr, *Moral Man and Immoral Society* (New York: Simon & Schuster, 1932), 20, xx.

20. Niebuhr, *Irony of American History,* 3.

21. Hirsch identifies an important subgroup of noir films as melodramas of mischance. In these films, the protagonists are, at least at the outset, respectable, law-abiding members of the middle or professional class who, losing control of their desire or violating moral law in some way, find themselves involved in crime, descending into a noir world from which escape proves difficult or, more often, impossible (see Foster Hirsch, *The Dark Side of the Screen* [New York: A. S. Barnes, 1981]).

22. Niebuhr, *Irony of American History,* 63.

23. Horney, *Neurosis and Human Growth,* 15–16.

24. Alan Woolfolk, "The Dubious Triumph of the Therapeutic: The Denial of Character," in *Therapeutic Culture: Triumph and Defeat,* ed. Jonathan B. Imber (New Brunswick, NJ: Transaction, 2004), 70, 71.

25. Fromm, *Art of Loving,* 56, 46.

26. Lary May, *The Big Tomorrow: Hollywood and the Politics of the American Way* (Chicago: University of Chicago Press, 2000), 220.

27. Christopher Lasch, *Culture of Narcissism: American Life in an Age of Diminishing Expectations* (New York: Norton, 1991).

# On Reason and Passion in
# The Maltese Falcon

*Deborah Knight*

An elegant, dark-haired woman in a fur wrap enters the office of the private detective firm of Spade and Archer. Sam Spade's secretary has already told him that he'll want to see her because "she's a knockout." Miss Wonderly, as she initially identifies herself, wants to hire Spade to find her younger sister, Corinne, who has apparently run away to San Francisco with a man named Floyd Thursby. Miss Wonderly insists that Thursby is dangerous and will stop at nothing. Spade's partner, Miles Archer, arrives during the interview, obviously finds Miss Wonderly quite attractive, and agrees to tail Thursby that evening. When Miss Wonderly leaves, Spade and Archer agree that her story is suspicious but that she has certainly paid well, perhaps too generously, for their efforts. Later that night, Spade is awakened by a telephone call from the police telling him that Miles Archer has been shot and killed. At the scene, Spade learns that Miles was shot at point-blank range in a dark alley with his gun still buttoned down in his pocket. Still later that night, Floyd Thursby is shot to death. The police suspect that Spade killed Thursby in retaliation for Miles Archer's murder. Spade must now resolve Miss Wonderly's case while finding out who killed his partner and, in particular, must solve the murder of Thursby to get the police off his back. Even though he wasn't particularly fond of Miles Archer, Spade is fully and ironically aware that, being a private detective, it is bad for business if your partner is murdered and nothing gets done about it.

In this essay, I examine what I take to be the philosophical core of *The Maltese Falcon* (John Huston, 1941), namely, its examination of the relation between reason and passion as exemplified by the two central protagonists, Sam Spade (Humphrey Bogart) and Brigid O'Shaughnessy (Mary Astor), who initially calls herself Miss Wonderly. My approach is to start from certain distinctive conventions and structures of the hard-boiled detective genre.[1] These include the defining characteristics of the hard-boiled detective, the central female character and her relationship to the detective, how the detective enters a story partway into its development, and the strategies used by the detective to uncover the criminals and solve the crimes. With respect to the philosophical status of the emotions, I am a cognitivist and will briefly explain what that position entails. Part of my concern is to debunk the view that hard-boiled detectives are dispassionate reasoners, solving crimes through a detached rationality. Several key scenes from *The Maltese Falcon* will help me make this point. But my ultimate goal is to indicate that there is something special about the hard-boiled detective, as opposed to the classic detective, something that has to do with his personal and emotional investment in the events and people he is investigating, an investment that requires that he act to ensure justice is done even after the crime has been solved. This final step could not be taken, I argue, if the hard-boiled detective were simply a dispassionate reasoner.

## The Private Detective and the World of Film Noir

Private detectives have a privileged place in the world of film noir, a genre itself identified with stories that take place down dark streets, skirt the edges of the law, and involve deception and double-crossing. Film noir private detectives typically operate among a host of morally dubious characters pursuing their own gain at whatever cost. They are hard-boiled—that is, they are tough, cynical individualists who have a history of ill-will toward more obviously legitimate, although invariably plodding, representatives of the law, such as police detectives and district attorneys. They must inevitably—considering the petty criminals and other lowlifes with whom they associate—look out for themselves. Their self-interest is understandable. Given their clientele and their clientele's particular problems, staying alive and out of jail is not for them as straightforward a process as it might initially appear.

\ Film noir private detectives typically enter a situation in media res, which is to say that they become involved partway into an ongoing course of action that predates their involvement. Therefore, the most immediate job for them is to figure out just what course of action they have gotten themselves into\This is different from the situation in which classic detectives find themselves, one in which the central crime has typically already been committed and the only questions left to answer are who did it and how. The film noir detective, by contrast, must first discover what the real situation is. A central task for him is to avoid being the dupe of his client, who usually has good reasons not to communicate everything she knows about the situation. Not all clients are duplicitous—one need only think of General Sternwood (Charles Waldron) in *The Big Sleep* (Howard Hawks, 1946). But there is always some risk since even a nonduplicitous client typically does not fully understand the situation she wants sorted out. Thus, the film noir private detective must critically analyze everyone involved: not only his client, but also the people he is investigating. This is where toughness and cynicism pay off. For private detectives, cynicism is more than an attitude; it is something of a life skill, keeping them properly suspicious of those who might try to take advantage of them. The consequences of miscalculation here are dire, something Miles Archer (Jerome Cowan) plainly should have learned before going down that dark alley. Not understanding the situation can lead to arrest and imprisonment and even, sometimes, death.

Because the private detective enters the situation in media res, he must figure out, from the minimal information that he is originally given, precisely what is unfolding. This means that he is, in effect, operating hermeneutically.[2] Frank Kermode correctly observes that detection narratives feature "a specialized 'hermeneutic' organization."[3] The detective's goal is to piece together the real story from the range of story fragments that he learns about or discovers. One thing he discovers is that the initial object of investigation invariably turns out not to be the central crime or puzzle, although solving this initial situation is necessary if what will later emerge as the main crime is to be properly resolved. So, in *The Maltese Falcon,* the initial object of investigation is Miss Wonderly's sister Corinne and her association with Thursby. But it turns out that Corinne is merely a fictional pretext invented by Miss Wonderly to cause Archer to trail Thursby in order to throw suspicion on Thursby for Archer's murder. Nevertheless, solving Miss Wonderly's involvement with Thursby is an important step in Sam's progress toward finding out who killed Miles.

It is generally agreed that the private detective must have exemplary reasoning skills. This assumption is understandable since his job is to figure out "whodunit," that is, to solve a complex situation, usually a crime, by means of sorting out who has done what to whom. There is obviously good reason to think that the private detective has particularly well-honed skills and that skill at reasoning is high in his repertoire. But we must acknowledge that the sort of reasoning exemplified by a classic detective such as Sherlock Holmes is very different in kind from the sort of reasoning exemplified by a hard-boiled detective such as Sam Spade. As John Cawelti persuasively argues in his analysis of the main differences between classic detective fiction and its hard-boiled variant, classic sleuths such as Holmes are typically upper-class amateurs whose chief satisfaction derives from the demonstration of "superior intellect and psychological insight" in solving the crime. The hard-boiled detective, by contrast, is much more directly involved, and his participation in the investigation of a crime quickly becomes something more like a personal mission. First, he becomes "emotionally and morally committed" to certain figures at the center of his investigation. Second, his involvement in solving the crime typically requires that he extract himself from a threat to his own life or career. For these reasons, it is not just the solution of the crime that is important to him. Rather, he "remains unfulfilled until he has taken a personal moral stance toward the criminal." Unlike the classic detective's work, the hard-boiled detective's work does not stop with the solution of the crime; instead, there is an important further step, which Cawelti describes as "some kind of personal choice or action," that brings closure to his mission.[4]

While both hard-boiled detectives such as Sam Spade and classic detectives such as Sherlock Holmes rely on guesses and hunches and use the progress of their investigation to test their best guesses, the nature of their involvement with the crime and its investigation is decidedly different. One way to see this difference is to note that Spade is involved emotionally and morally in the progress of his investigation, whereas no comparable emotional or moral commitment is required of Holmes as he sorts out the facts of the case and draws his conclusions. Yet it might initially seem a peculiar thing to emphasize the role of emotion in the hard-boiled detective's investigations, given that we typically think of him as a dispassionate reasoner rather than as a passionate one. In fact, noticing his passionate side allows us to ask what the proper relation between reason and the emotions might be and how that question is resolved in the case of the film noir private detective. Philosophers have often argued that reason is locked in a perpetual struggle against the negative influence of the emotions. This idea has roots that date back at least to Socrates and Plato. Roughly, Plato argues that reason must take precedence over the emotions since, obviously, the emotions corrupt good reasoning.[5] This view has recently been contested by a number of philosophers who argue that emotions are integral to sound reasoning.[6]

The view that the emotions are themselves rational is known as *cognitivism about the emotions*.[7] The basic claim of cognitivism is that our emotions contribute positively to, rather than inevitably distracting from, our understanding of the world. Furthermore, our emotions are centrally involved in our decision making, since they help us determine what we desire and value. This means that the emotions are prerequisites, not only for right judgments, but also for right actions. Proper moral agency does not result from reasoning conducted in isolation from the rich resources that our emotions provide for us.

Anyone doubtful about this claim should consider the description by Antonio Damasio, the noted neurologist, of the remarkable aftermath of a devastating accident that befell a man named Phineas Gage in 1848. An iron rod with a lot of force behind it pierced Gage's head and in fact traveled straight through, exiting the other side, permanently damaging a quite specific part of his brain, that which is responsible for feelings and emotions. Astonishingly, Gage survived the accident, but crucial aspects of his personality changed as a result of it. Most important from Damasio's point of view, Gage's ability to make decisions and, in particular, to make good choices was completely annihilated. Although "attention, perception, memory, language, intelligence" were all undamaged, Gage's decisions no longer took into account his own best interests or advantage. Worse yet, his respect for social conventions and for ethical matters more generally construed disappeared. Damasio uses this case to illustrate the deep interconnection among our emotions, our judgments, and our ability to operate as moral and social beings.[8]

Still, it is not commonly recognized that emotions play a formative role in at least some key decisions made by film noir detectives. We tend simply to assume that private detectives exhibit a paradigmatic sort of rationality, and this assumption tends to obscure the role that emotions play in their reasoning. Yet philosophers such as Robert Solomon argue that emotions just are judgments about situations that we face, and private detectives are first and foremost figures who must make good judgments, since the consequence of bad judgment could, as mentioned above, very well be death. Private detectives are practical reasoners in the sense that they are professional problem solvers. This means that, in any situation, they must be able to juggle competing answers to the main "whodunit" question. And they must be able to track the implications of various equally plausible answers to that question, at least until they have focused in on the real target of their investigation, the person who really did it. But emotions need not be absent from any of these undertakings.

## The Private Detective and His Client

Let us look at two key exchanges between Sam and his attractive client after Miles Archer's murder. These two interviews introduce various key concepts that help us see how detective and client negotiate their relationship with one another. The concepts I am thinking of include trust and confidence and the sort of loyalty that is appropriate not only between a private detective and his client but also between lovers. Trust, confidence, and loyalty all seem to be products of the conjunction of reason and emotion. I could judge you to be trustworthy—that is, I could arrive at this judgment through reasoning—but still not trust you. For me to trust you, there seems to be a necessary emotional component to my judgment. The same seems to be true of confidence and loyalty. Given that Sam is still largely in the dark about his client's actual plans, it is little wonder that his trust in her is based partly on his feelings. Of course, Sam doesn't need to trust her to continue his relationship with her. In fact, he needs to know more about the scheme she's involved in if he's going to be able to prove that he didn't kill either Archer or Thursby. But Sam opts to trust Brigid.

The first exchange occurs the day following Miles Archer's murder. After learning of Archer's death, Sam tries to phone Miss Wonderly at her hotel, only to learn that she has checked out and left no forwarding address. The next day, she phones him and gives him her new address and another name, Miss Leblanc. At the new apartment, she confesses her "real" name to Sam—Brigid O'Shaughnessy. She begs for his protection and support. She insists that she is alone and needs help and swears that she was not involved in the two deaths the previous night. Sam isn't satisfied with her story. He isn't satisfied with its content, which may or may not be factual, but, just as important, he isn't satisfied with its presentation as a plea for his help. The combination is a potent one. He says, "Now you *are* dangerous!" by which he means that her plea for help is a ploy to make him overlook the irregularities of her situation and the omissions and contradictions of the stories she has thus far told him. He realizes that her plan is to make him feel sorry for her and to feel responsible for her, a plan that, if successful, might compromise him as a private detective.

Sam admits in this conversation that he and Miles had not believed Brigid's initial story about a missing sister, although, as Sam says, they believed her two hundred dollars. She had paid too much, but enough too much to "make it all right." This is meant to show Brigid that he has not been taken in by her story, that he realizes she is up to something, and that at the very least it is not obvious that he should trust her. But Brigid puts a different spin on the question of trust, saying that she needs to be able to trust Sam completely. His response is that Brigid does not need to trust him so long as she can persuade him to trust her.

The very idea that someone must be persuaded to trust signals the relation between the emotions and reason. Sam is working from a limited amount of information, and he doesn't yet know what part of that information is reliable—in fact, important parts turn out not to be reliable, which will have important consequences later on. Brigid is asking him to trust her in spite of many facts he has learned about her, for example, that she has lied in hiring him, has used false names, has changed addresses without informing him beforehand, has paid too much for the work she hired him to do, and in situations of apparently straightforward intimacy between them has described her own situation in ways that Sam cannot believe.

Brigid pleads with Sam to help her, asking him to share some of his strength, but Sam suspects a con: "You're good, chiefly your eyes, I think, and the throb you get in your voice." Brigid admits she deserves the rebuke. "The lie was in the way I said it, not at all in what I said." All this tells Sam that she has confessed again to lying. Whether what she has said is true—for instance, that she was not involved in the death of Miles Archer— remains to be determined. But, at the same time, by admitting to the lie in the way she spoke to him, Brigid has confessed that she is trying to manipulate Sam, trying to make him pity her, or be sympathetic, or worry on her behalf. The way she said it was, as she confesses, an attempt to entrap him emotionally. Sam resists, but this isn't necessarily because he is dispassionate; rather, he seems to want another sort of emotional relationship altogether.

The second meeting again takes place at Brigid's apartment. In the meantime, Sam has met with Joel Cairo (Peter Lorre) and learned of the existence of the black bird, the object desired by all the main criminals in the film. He guesses that Brigid is also interested in the whereabouts of this valuable statue. Moreover, he thinks that Brigid is involved in a situation much more complex than the one she has so far disclosed to him. "You aren't exactly the sort of person you pretend to be, are you?" Sam says to her. He means that the weakness and innocence that she projects is an act. She admits that she hasn't led a good life, that she has been bad. This strikes Sam as a good thing since, if she were really as innocent as she pretended to be, they'd never get anywhere.

In the first interview, Sam told Brigid that she needed to tell him enough so that he would know what was going on, but Brigid would not reveal the specifics of her situation. Sam manages to get some information out of her in the second interview by mentioning Joel Cairo and watching her response. Cairo had offered Sam five thousand dollars for the black bird. This is far more money than Brigid has available if she has to bid for Sam's loyalty. This angers Sam, who reminds Brigid that so far she hasn't given him "any of [her] confidence, any of the truth." He also accuses her of having tried to buy his loyalty with money and nothing else. Brigid asks what else she can buy him with, after which they kiss. What was initially a professional relationship now becomes a personal relationship, complicating things still more. Sam isn't interested in knowing Brigid's secrets, he tells her, but he insists that he has to have more confidence in her than he has at the moment. Brigid wonders whether he couldn't trust her a little longer.

## The Question of Trust

The question whether the private detective can afford to trust the principal female character is a recurring theme in film noir. To take another example, in *The Big Sleep,* Philip Marlowe (Humphrey Bogart) is hired by General Sternwood to solve a blackmail plot targeting the general's younger daughter, Carmen (Martha Vickers). During the investigation, Marlowe becomes attracted to the general's elder daughter, Vivian (Lauren Bacall), but her involvement with a notorious gangster, Eddie Mars (John Ridgely), makes trusting her difficult. Ultimately, Marlowe does trust her, and his trust is rewarded, but again the decision to trust is partially based on his feelings for her.

But anyone familiar with the conventions of film noir knows that there is a major difference in the types of female characters represented, on the one hand, by Brigid O'Shaughnessy and, on the other, by Vivian Rutledge. Brigid O'Shaughnessy is recognizably a femme fatale, whereas Vivian just as obviously is not. Characteristically, the femme fatale lures men with her sexuality and apparent vulnerability, manipulating them so as to achieve some goal or other, usually involving money. *The Big Sleep* refashions the femme fatale since the seductive and vulnerable figure in this film is Carmen, yet in Carmen the two key aspects of the genuine femme fatale, namely, sexuality and cold reasoning intended to promote ulterior motives, are disassociated.

At her first meeting with Marlowe, Carmen tries to sit in his lap while he is standing up (to paraphrase Marlowe). Carmen has the sexual allure of the typical femme fatale, but she lacks the brains. By contrast, Vivian is sexually attractive to Marlowe, but she does not lure him. Ironically, Brigid is sexually attractive to Sam but not on the basis of overt flaunting of her sexuality. Rather, Sam falls for Brigid while she is using what he describes as her "schoolgirl manner," even though he doesn't believe that this manner is anything more than an act. In fact, Brigid initially presents herself to Sam as clinging and needful, as weak and uncertain, and as emotional, specifically, as alone and fearful. Sam is cast in the role of protector and defender. Vivian, by contrast, is Marlowe's equal—their verbal sparring is reminiscent of the repartee between two other pairs of Howard Hawks's classic protagonists, Walter Burns (Cary Grant) and Hildy Johnson (Rosalind Russell) from *His Girl Friday* (1940) and Harry Morgan (Humphrey Bogart) and Slim (Lauren Bacall) from *To Have and Have Not* (1944). Vivian associates with various crooks, gamblers, and blackmailers and appears to move confidently in their midst. Her cool independence is what attracts Marlowe to her, yet it also raises questions of trust between them. As Marlowe eventually figures out, she is being forced to lie to him by Eddie Mars, who is blackmailing her. Marlowe has already become, to recall Cawelti's words, "emotionally and morally committed" to Vivian, as he is also committed to Vivian's father, General Sternwood.

So, even though there is a question of trust, it is not because Vivian is intentionally misleading Marlowe. This is different from the situation between Sam and Brigid. Although both Vivian and Brigid lie, Vivian does so because she believes this will help her sister, whereas Brigid lies because she is trying to help herself. Vivian is not a femme fatale, although she is certainly enigmatic. One thing is clear: as viewers familiar with the conventions of film noir, we doubt that Vivian is a real threat to Marlowe, yet we know that Brigid is likely to be a threat to Sam. Given that Sam is a private detective operating in the film noir world, we understand that Sam realizes, just as Marlowe does, that any situation in which he has less information than he needs in order to make reliable judgments is one where he is potentially at risk. In fact, Sam is more than potentially at risk: in the course of the film's action, he is held at gunpoint more than once, tailed, drugged, blackjacked, and beaten, not to mention suspected of being the murderer of Floyd Thursby.

## Spade's Decision

So far we have been considering *The Maltese Falcon* as a hermeneutical process in which we are initially introduced to a private detective and a client and are then immediately thrust into the midst of an ongoing series of actions that Sam Spade must sort out as they develop. These events involve deceit, lies, murders, and more. Given that this is a film noir, there is a central female character who invariably functions as a femme fatale or an enigmatic woman—in this case, a femme fatale. We have thought about the private detective in terms of the role played by reasoning, the emotions, and the detective's personal, social, and moral stake in the crimes under investigation. It is time to draw these themes together.

One standard way of thinking about detection narratives, especially those featuring a male detective, is to say that the male detective operates on the basis of reason against a variety of antagonists whose motivation is based on desire, lust, craving, or even coincidence, happenstance, or being in the wrong place. I have been arguing that even in the most unlikely of situations, namely, hard-boiled detective fiction, we find much more than dry rationality at work. I have also sketched a way of thinking about hard-boiled detective fiction—a view that is, I think, mistaken—that associates maleness and reason, in the case of the detective, and femaleness and the emotions. But *The Maltese Falcon* and *The Big Sleep* show that it is mistaken to assume that the hard-boiled detective is simply a dispassionate reasoner, let alone that the central female character is working primarily on the basis of emotion rather than some long-range plan. The final scenes of *The Big Sleep* and *The Maltese Falcon* make this case clearly.

Up to this point, I have had little to say about the Maltese Falcon itself and the sorry crowd of criminals on its trail, including the now-deceased Thursby as well as Joel Cairo, Kasper Gutman, known as "The Fat Man"

(Sydney Greenstreet), and the gunsel, Wilmer (Elisha Cook Jr.). The question raised earlier about Brigid's (a.k.a. Miss Wonderly's) relationship to Thursby is slowly revealed. The two have been tracking the priceless Maltese Falcon, as have Cairo and Gutman. One of the most compelling moments of the film occurs when the bunch of criminals brought together in Sam Spade's apartment think that they have finally found their prize. The thing they believe to be the Falcon arrives bound up in newspaper, is unwrapped, and is proudly stood up on a tabletop. Then, to make sure they have the right object in their hands, Gutman takes a knife to the Falcon, aiming to slice off its black surface covering to reveal the jewel-encrusted statue that should be beneath. They find that they have all been duped. The statue in their possession is just lead, nothing more, certainly not the treasure they had all been pursuing. The only one who sees the humor in this situation is Sam Spade.

The time that Sam has spent with Gutman, Cairo, Wilmer, and Brigid has apparently been entirely focused on the black bird, although of course Sam has in addition been watching the others interact. At a particularly tense moment before the arrival of the black bird, when Sam has made it clear that he knows its whereabouts and that, if the others want it, they will have to deal with him, Wilmer takes it on himself to hold a gun to Sam and challenge him. Sam reasons with Gutman: if the others want the black bird, they won't dare kill him, since he's the only one who knows its whereabouts, and, if he knows they can't afford to kill him, why would any threat they make be persuasive? Gutman, tellingly, remarks: "In the heat of action, men are likely to forget where their best interests lie and let their emotions carry them away." Still, Gutman persuades Wilmer to put away his gun and a little later allows Sam to convince him that, of the various candidates, Wilmer is the one they ought to hand over to the police as Thursby's killer.

The realization that the object they have been pursuing is a fake is of course initially a disappointment, but, like anyone engaged in a grand quest, Gutman quickly recomposes himself and suggests a way to carry on. He even asks a flattered Cairo to accompany him. Wilmer has fled, fearing that he will be handed over to the police as the fall guy. So Gutman and Cairo happily leave Sam and Brigid as they go off to pursue their fetishized prize. And, with their departure, it seems that everything should have been worked out, most important, the crucial issue of who killed Thursby, since it has been concluded that Wilmer, in fact, committed that murder. It would seem that Sam and Brigid are now free and clear, assuming that Sam can convince the police about Wilmer's role in the whole affair.

But not so. While Sam and Brigid are left together, this is not the typical happy ending that unites the correct romantic couple, a conclusion seen so often in Hollywood movies, including even some films noirs, for example, *The Big Sleep*. In fact, we are left with the only plausible romantic couple that this film could produce, but it is not, in Hollywood terms or in film noir terms, the correct one. For Hollywood cinema has its own morality with regard to romantic couples, ensuring that those who eventually unite are in some important sense worthy, and at the same time ensuring that those who are kept apart are kept apart for good moral reasons.

I speak broadly here, but the point can be illustrated, once again, through a comparison of *The Big Sleep* with *The Maltese Falcon*. Despite the fact that Vivian Rutledge has lied to Philip Marlowe, her deception has been justified because of her desire to protect her younger sister. This ultimate purpose clears the way to her reconciliation with Marlowe. Brigid, by contrast, has used Sam throughout to further her own ulterior motives. This is what Sam has finally realized throughout his involvement with her and her nefarious coconspirators. In the final confrontation between private detective and femme fatale, Sam presents his best reasoning about why, after all, he is going to hand Brigid over to the police for the killing of his partner, Miles Archer. But his best reasoning is importantly informed by his awareness of the emotions that this decision calls for.

In this decisive moment, we recognize that what Cawelti warned us to watch for, namely, the detective's moral commitment to some character or other in the film, has actually and unexpectedly been a commitment to his dead partner, despite the fact that he didn't like him and that Miles wasn't particularly smart. The right thing, in Sam's situation, is to find out who killed your partner; anything else would be "bad for business, bad all round, bad for all private detectives everywhere." The facts as Sam has reconstructed them point unfailingly to Brigid as Miles Archer's murderess. After all, as Sam has known from his initial visit to the site of the murder, Miles was found down a dark alley with his gun undrawn and buttoned down. It is improbable that Miles went so incautiously down a dark alley with Thursby, the reputedly dangerous man he was tailing. However, as Sam realizes, Miles would have "licked his lips" and gone down that same dark alley with Miss Wonderly. She is the only one in the entire case who could have lured Miles to his death.

But Sam has also already said that he isn't worried about Brigid's secrets. He has accepted that she has a dark past, that she isn't "innocent," that she has had at least some relationships with men he regards as dubious, if not downright dangerous. Despite this seeming trust in Brigid, Sam must now face the consequences of what he has learned about her. And he must also resolve the problem he himself faces as the person the police believe killed Floyd Thursby. The core problem pits reason against passion yet, in a way that is oddly characteristic of the film noir detective, unites reason and passion in the detective's ultimate verdict. Sam's final decision about Brigid requires that he take a personal moral stand about her and what she has done. It means that he must acknowledge the full implications of what he has learned about her through his investigations. And it means that he must confront his own feelings for her, the fact that he might, as he says, love her. Here is his conclusion: "I have no earthly reason to think I can trust you, and if I do this and get away with it you'll have something on me that you can use on me whenever you want to. Since I've got something on you I couldn't be sure you wouldn't put a hole in me sometime."

What Sam is saying is that he realizes that Brigid killed his partner, that she lured Miles down a dark alley, and that she has lied to him about her involvement in Miles's death. In a case such as this one, there is no question of forgiving and forgetting, since Miles was Sam's partner. The problem is trust—and, as we have seen, trust is a judgment at the intersection of reason and the emotions. Up to this point, Sam has allowed his emotional involvement in this case to shape his response to it, and his emotional response has not, so far, let him down. He has discovered the identities of those involved in the Maltese Falcon caper, and he has concluded who is responsible for his partner's murder. That said, he faces a serious choice. The choice focuses on whether, knowing what he knows, he can trust Brigid. And, at this particular intersection of reason and passion, he realizes that he cannot in fact trust her. Whether he loves her, and whether she loves him, is an issue to the side of the main one, whether they can trust each other, or, rather, whether he can trust her. The question of trust is put on one side of the scale, and the question of their possible love for one another is put on the other. Sam's conclusion illustrates the connection between reason and the emotions in this difficult decision. The question is whether he will protect her from disclosure to the police, a question that has been a running theme throughout their brief relationship, and, in answer to that question, Sam says: "I won't because all of me wants to, regardless of consequences, and because you counted on that with me." This statement might seem as though Sam is rejecting emotion in favor of reasoning, insofar as he is sending Brigid over. But, in fact, Sam is letting emotion inform his rational decision making.

What Sam realizes is that he and Brigid have very different sorts of investments in their mutual relationship. Sam is not someone bound by the niceties of legal conventions; he could harbor a criminal, possibly even a murderer, if he had good reason to. The problem that he faces with Brigid, as he explains, is that she has counted on him to play the sap, expected him to take whatever fall would allow her to escape unharmed; in short, she has been manipulating him from the start. The fact that maybe she loves him and maybe he loves her simply doesn't stand a chance against the fact that he can't trust her. And it surely hasn't escaped Sam's attention that, if he had gone with Miss Wonderly that first night, she would have killed him instead of Miles.

Sam has recognized all along that Brigid has consistently presented herself in a stereotypically "feminine" manner—as Sam says, lisping and blushing, or, as we might observe, as someone trying to ensure that a stronger, more intelligent, more practical man could protect her. In fact, Brigid has chosen Sam to be a dupe in her broader scheme—the scheme of killing Thursby and trying to acquire the Maltese Falcon for herself. Brigid, as it turns out, has used the stereotypical view of femininity as a disguise. She has hidden herself and her motives behind the surface appearance of weakness, passivity, indecision, and neediness. She has calculated Sam's emotional attachment to her, but she has used this against him, believing that she has found the best possible fall guy. In fact, Brigid has been *The Maltese Falcon*'s best exemplar of dispassionate reasoning. However counterintuitive it might seem, Sam as the hard-boiled detective has used his emotions in conjunction with his reason to do the morally right thing, namely, to let Brigid assume responsibility for what she has done. By contrast, Brigid has tried to use pure calculation and the affectation of emotion to manipulate Sam. He has combined emotions and reasons to reach the best conclusion about how he should treat her. His decision to turn her over to the police is the right one, both personally and morally. In coming to this decision, the hard-boiled detective has let reason and emotion inform one another, whereas the femme fatale seems never to have let emotion enter her mind at all.

# Notes

1. For further discussion of the hard-boiled detective, see Jerold J. Abrams, "From Sherlock Holmes to the Hard-Boiled Detective in Film Noir" (in this volume).

2. The hermeneutical aspect of detection narratives is described in more detail in Deborah Knight and George McKnight, "The Case of the Disappearing Enigma," *Philosophy and Literature* 21, no. 1 (April 1997): 123–38.

3. Frank Kermode, "Secrets and Narrative Sequence," in *On Narrative*, ed. W. J. T. Mitchell (Chicago: University of Chicago Press, 1981), 83.

4. John Cawelti, *Adventure, Mystery, and Romance: Formula Stories as Art and Popular Culture* (Chicago: University of Chicago Press, 1977), 143.

5. One of the main statements of Plato's views on the emotions is to be found in the *Republic*.

6. For example, Ronald de Sousa, *The Rationality of Emotion* (Cambridge, MA: MIT Press, 1987), and Robert Solomon, *Not Passion's Slave: Emotions and Choice* (New York: Oxford University Press, 2003).

7. Within the philosophy of mind, some, including de Sousa, want to claim that they are not, technically, exponents of cognitivism. For my purposes here, *cognitivism* refers to all those views that maintain that emotions have a rational dimension.

8. Antonio Damasio, *Descartes' Error: Emotion, Reason, and the Human Brain* (New York: Avon, 1994), 3–10.

# RIDE THE PINK HORSE

## Money, Mischance, Murder, and the Monads of Film Noir

*Alain Silver*

> The holidays
> go around and around
> The merry go-round brings them
> and takes them away.
>
> —*Federico García Lorca*

> Every man takes the limits of his
> own field of vision for the limits
> of the world.
>
> —*Arthur Schopenhauer*

The history of film noir is simple enough. Despite occasional squabbling over the identity of the first film noir, it is clear that, after some early prototypes, the classic period of film noir transpired over a mere two decades. While most commentators would agree on the key motion pictures that constitute the body of noir films, beginning with John Huston's *The Maltese Falcon* in 1941 and ending with Orson Welles's *Touch of Evil* in 1958, there is certainly no consensus about the philosophy of noir. That the noir phenomenon exists is indisputable. Although some of the critical analyses that have followed in its wake have attempted to muddy the waters, most agree that film noir is defined not only by its visual style but also by its relation to the psychological and philosophical developments of the first half of the twentieth century.

From a simplistic Freudian perspective, the imagery of film noir—its dark corridors, wet streets, and figures lurking in the shadows—reflects the underlying apprehension, even paranoia, of many of its protagonists.

Many observers have perceived in the deterministic narratives of film noir a reflection on the concepts of existential anguish and despair. The defining comment of Bradford Galt in *The Dark Corner* (Henry Hathaway, 1946) is cited as a prime example of existential anguish: "There goes my last lead. I feel all dead inside. I'm backed up in a dark corner, and I don't know who's hitting me." These characters who reflect on the uncertainty of their situation, who don't know who's hitting them but must make choices nonetheless, are mired in existential despair. But, as a film cycle or movement[1] that incorporated many generic indicators, film noir is not simply about Freudian or existential motifs, about characters forced to make impossible choices. If there is a noir prototype, it must be approached from a broader base, something more akin to Bateson's analysis of the "transcontextual" double bind: "Exogenous experience may be framed in the context of dreams, and internal thought may be projected into the contexts of the external world."[2] Taken in transcontext, these issues so prevalent in film noir, fate and free will, existential anguish and despair, are not such clear-cut expressions, not instances, as Bateson often noted, of being "just that and nothing more."

There is no clear line from any preexisting epistemology to film noir, not from Freud or Kierkegaard, not from German expressionistic film or American hard-boiled fiction. Being neither philosophy nor aesthetics but fiction, what film noir does take from these sundry influences is a dynamic that uses different character perspectives to create dramatic tension. These differing viewpoints of narrative events are defined with a transcontextual expressive code; that is, some images and events are rendered subjectively using point-of-view shots or voice-over narrative, while others are staged objectively with the camera recording events from the position of a detached observer. Because the aesthetic or system of visual and aural meaning in film noir is fluid or relative, Einstein's paradigm of the railway carriage and the embankment, from which positions observers witness very different behavior from a falling stone, could also apply to the universe of film noir.[3] The problem of Bradford Galt and of many noir protagonists can be taken as one of perspective. From his dark corner, Galt can see only straight lines; he cannot envision the parabolic narrative arc that has entrapped him.

In his or her quest for the knowledge that promises salvation, the noir protagonist conducts a metaphoric search for an absolute truth, for the thing-in-itself. In an existential or transcontextual world, in any system of values that does not accept the concept of a simple, a priori truth, such a quest is doomed to failure. Despite this, or because of this, most of these figures actually survive their immersion in an unstable noir underworld.

## Arthur Schopenhauer and *Ride the Pink Horse*

What this essay proposes to briefly consider is *Ride the Pink Horse* (Robert Montgomery, 1947) as a prototypical noir film and also as an embodiment of aspects of the worldview/aesthetics of Arthur Schopenhauer (1788–1860). In Schopenhauer's major work, *The World as Will and Representation,* revised over the course of four decades, the interplay of will, representation, religion, and aesthetics defines an uncertain universe much like that into which the noir protagonist ventures. As Schopenhauer's first words assert: "The world is my representation: this is a truth valid with reference to every living and knowing being, although man alone can bring it into reflective, abstract consciousness. If he really does so, philosophical discernment has dawned on him."[4] For Schopenhauer, the Kantian thing-in-itself is undiscoverable; but the will to find it is not. What also imperils or destroys any man is not misperception but that same will. Will causes discord, suffering, and evil. Its relentless and compulsive grip on a rational being renders most human action pointless and, ultimately, absurd: "A man can do what he wants, but not want what he wants."[5]

Beyond any philosophical perspective on absolute truth, Schopenhauer's discourses probe the meaning of suffering and suggest that life is substantially without higher purpose. Rather than accept the belief in any absolute, Schopenhauer accepts the world as what each man sees or wills it to be. Ironically for Schopenhauer, although man has free will, he is imprisoned by its pointlessness. The only escapes from will are through sacrifice, through helping others and self-denial, and through an aesthetic experience. In fact, for Schopenhauer, art is more important than knowledge, in that it helps man transcend his situation, for a person listening to music or watching a drama is at moments free from self-consciousness and will.

In the world of film noir, these same contradictions dog the characters. For Schopenhauer, mitigation of will is possible through denial, through the arts, through transcendence, through religious conviction; but, in the end, there is no escape. Action, even self-immolation, is an expression of will that defeats the man who seeks escape. As Schopenhauer noted: "The ancient wisdom of the Indians declares that 'it is Maya, the veil of deception, that covers the eyes of mortals, and causes them to see a world of which one cannot say either that it is or that it is not, for it is like a dream, like the sunshine on the sand that the traveler at a distance takes to be water, or like the piece of rope on the ground that he regards as a snake.'"[6] In film noir, the dream, the mirage, the slightest mistake, are typical expressive factors that embroil its protagonists in the struggle to survive. For Aquinas, Kant, Leibniz, and other rational theists, God and truth exist to prevent man and morality from being meaningless. Hence, a righteous man can navigate a world of shifting monads without fear of running aground on a shoal of misperception. For Schopenhauer, a rational atheist, his answer was plain enough to be frequently co-opted by religion and nowadays is even sold emblazoned on T-shirts: "Compassion is the basis of all morality."

If Schopenhauer believed that truth traveled a bumpy road to validation,[7] he could embrace a Keatsian view that equated truth with beauty.[8] As with most ironic drama, the narratives of film noir revolve around the distinction between belief or perception and truth. It is in that nexus, where who people are and what events represent may be confounded, that lines between good and evil, between malice and morality, are blurred and that noir figures grapple with their antagonists for survival.

The postwar film noir *Ride the Pink Horse* is based on a 1946 novel by Dorothy B. Hughes. Hughes's main character, known only as Sailor, who travels from Chicago to a fictionalized Santa Fe, New Mexico, during a fiesta week, is intent on blackmailing his mentor, "the Sen," the former Illinois senator Willis Douglass. The screenwriters, Ben Hecht and Charles Lederer, had worked individually and as a team on such earlier noir films as *Cornered* (Edward Dmytryk, 1945), *Gilda* (Charles Vidor, 1946), *Notorious* (Alfred Hitchcock, 1946), and *Kiss of Death* (Henry Hathaway, 1947). The star and director, Robert Montgomery, had just finished directing *Lady in the Lake* (1947), adapted from Raymond Chandler's 1943 novel. Together, the filmmakers transformed the thoroughly venal Sailor into Gagin, a war veteran with more ambiguous motives for extorting the petty mobster Frank Hugo. In changing the self-aggrandizing Sailor into Gagin, who is likelier to deprecate himself, and the elitist Douglass into the petty mobster Hugo, whose cynical attitude is almost proletarian, the filmmakers define characters that are prototypically noir.

One striking element of the novel that was retained is the high point of the annual festival in Santa Fe, the burning of Zozobra, a god of anxiety or gloom created by the local artist Will Shuster in 1924. While most of the picture was shot on the Universal back lot—much of it centered around an authentic *tío vivo,* or carousel, that the studio rented from another New Mexico town, Taos—several scenes were shot on exterior locations in and around the plaza of Santa Fe.

## Themes and Characters

Although he is referred to only by his last name during the course of the movie, the lead character, the main title announces, is named "Lucky" Gagin. Gagin himself does nothing to explain his sobriquet. Aside from the burning of Zozobra, who the carousel owner, Pancho, explains to Gagin is the god of bad luck, the only pointed references to luck, good or bad, come from Pila, the young Indian girl who befriends Gagin. In their first meeting, she gives him a good luck charm, a small carving of Ishtam, to "protect" him. Like Sailor in the novel, Gagin comes to town carrying a gun, and, for him, that is the "best charm in the world. Keeps away the boogeyman." Of course, for Gagin, it is not Pancho's boogeyman Zozobra but Hugo that concerns him. Gagin, fixated on money and revenge, and taking the limits of his own field of vision as the limits of the world, firmly believes that "you make your own luck." For Pancho or Pila, who cryptically remarks, "It is a sign of good luck when you find a new bucket," one should take what the world offers. For them, fate and irony are as invisible as Leibniz's monads or the shadows at the back of Plato's cave,[9] but beauty and compassion are not.

   The interaction of the primitive and the sophisticate is a dialectic that Schopenhauer could endorse. Balancing the willfulness, suffering, and pessimism of Gagin are the suffering and kindness of Pancho. Balancing the rationalism and evil of Hugo are the morality and asceticism of FBI Agent Retz. Transcending it all is Pila, whose instinctive and unaffected behavior epitomizes the selflessness that Schopenhauer valued so highly.

   Among the various portraits of weary veterans in postwar film noir, Gagin is most literally devoid of identity. Since Lucky is an ironic moniker confined to the main title, he has no real first name. The surname Gagin is clipped, guttural, appropriate to Robert Montgomery's taciturn portrayal. Pancho gives him a sort of epithet when he observes: "That's the kind of man I like, the man with no place." When asked his identity on his first visit to Hugo's, Gagin says: "Just tell him Shorty's pal called and will call again." Gagin comes from nowhere in particular, has no stated destination, and, as he offhandedly remarks to the inquisitive Pila, is "nobody's friend."

Initially, the mise-en-scène supports this self-image. Gagin descends from the bus, and the camera tracks him through the small terminal as he deposits an envelope in a locker, conceals the key, then exits and enters the town proper. The actions are direct enough, but the unbroken moving shot in which they are inscribed rivets the audience's attention. The use of a long take instills suspense in the otherwise ordinary acts. From his silent, methodical activity the concentrated staging also distills for the viewer a sense of the tenacity in Gagin's character. At the same time, the sustained camera "imprisons" the protagonist temporarily within the unattractive limits of the bus depot, giving a subtle hint of some underlying fatality even as he emerges and takes the dusty road to town.

Gagin is not a mere cipher. The typical qualities of the embittered loner in film noir, which the figure immediately evokes through this visual inscription, combine with the narrative development of his hatred for Frank Hugo to create a more complex character. The initial assertion of Gagin's generic identity is grounded in understated conflict with both the environment, in which he is stranger, and the imminent clash with the unseen criminal presence, Hugo. San Pablo itself offers nothing other than the promise of finding Hugo within its confines, nothing to mollify the alienation that Gagin sports so visibly, no alternate reality to the naturalistic images of the terminal, the town, or the crowded hotel lobby. Only after Gagin's quest to even the score for his dead pal, Shorty, is necessarily suspended because of Hugo's absence does he discover Pancho, Pila, and the *tío vivo*.

From his demeanor and his statements, Gagin is clearly a willful and determined man; yet, remarkably, all the supporting characters in *Ride the Pink Horse* want him to embrace their point of view. This is expectedly the case with Hugo, who wants the incriminating letter that Gagin holds over him, and with Retz, who wants the same item with which to prosecute Hugo. In their first meeting, Hugo lectures Gagin at length about his own beliefs, about what makes his world turn: "[Shorty] got himself all crumbed up looking for easy money. . . . Don't kid yourself; you're doing it for Shorty. You're doing it for you. We eat out of the same dish. You used to think if you were a square guy, worked hard, played on the level, things would come your way. You found that people are interested in only one thing, the payoff. There are two kinds of people in this world: ones that fiddle around wondering whether a thing's right or wrong and guys like us." At the end of *Ride the Pink Horse*, when an injured and insulted Gagin is on the brink of cooperating with Retz, Hugo offers a last, disdainful assessment of guys like Gagin, who "work all your lives and end up with enough money to buy yourself a hole in the ground."

Compare Hugo's attitude to Schopenhauer's profession: "Money alone is absolutely good, because it is not only a concrete satisfaction of one need in particular; it is an abstract satisfaction of all. . . . Money is human happiness in the abstract; he, then, who is no longer capable of enjoying human happiness in the concrete devotes himself utterly to money."[10] Gagin would likely agree that "money . . . is absolutely good." As he ruefully explains when Pancho asks him why he hangs around with Pila, why he doesn't have a princess with more flesh on her bones: "I've had princesses. I got one now back east, but she's busy with another guy. He's got what it takes: dough." Although at odds with the statements of Hugo and Gagin, Pancho's attitude is also aligned with Schopenhauer's in that he expresses a preference for happiness that is not abstract. In his first meeting with Gagin in the Tres Violetas bar, Pancho intervenes when Gagin pays with a twenty-dollar bill for which the barkeep has insufficient change. In an unselfish manner, Pancho suggests that Gagin take ten dollars and that he and the others drink the rest of his change: "You want to make everybody happy, *sí?*" Later, after he offers Gagin his own bed to sleep in, Pancho refuses additional payment and adds: "Some people only happy when they got money. Me, I'm only happy when I got nothing. Nothing and a friend . . . they can keep everything else. Keep the whole world."

Shortly after he meets her, as she leads him to the La Fonda hotel and bumps into a post, Gagin tells Pila: "You should look where you're going." In his unenlightened state, he does not yet realize that he should take his own advice. His hatred of Hugo is matched by his distrust of institutions. Of Retz, who represents social morality and the "government," Gagin contemptuously inquires: "Doesn't the government work for Hugo? It did all during the war." When Hugo's girlfriend, Marjorie, proposes a complicated double cross involving an honest attorney, his derisive retort is: "Hugo buys them all—even the honest ones." He is equally scornful of women, or, rather, of "dames": "They're not human beings. They're dead fish with a lot of perfume on them. You touch them, and you always get stung. You always lose."

While the filmmakers cannot express what goes on inside Gagin's head as directly as can the novelist Hughes, Montgomery's direction and performance go beyond the purely laconic prototype. His reaction to Pila is the cornerstone of his character's development and hints at the perception of which Hughes wrote explicitly: "She was young, young as a kid, and she was old, old as this country. . . . She was unreal, alien; yet she belonged, and he was alien. [There was] something deep and strong and old under the tawdry trapping, under the gimcracks. Something he did not understand because he was a stranger."[11]

## Visual Style and Symbolism

While Hughes's novel is not written in the first person, her original prose is imitation Hammett, full of offhanded racism and sexism reflecting the main character's prejudices and fears. Her overt symbolism is restricted to figures such as Zozobra: "Made of papier maché and dirty sheets, yet a fantastic awfulness of reality was about him. He was unclean, he was the personification of evil." But, as Sailor realizes moments later: "The evil was manmade; it wasn't real."[12]

For the filmmakers working with viewer expectations associated with film noir, symbolic construction is much easier. The opening shots of the bus moving along the highway end at the local station where Gagin descends and define a real, that is, nonstudio, environment. Montgomery uses his own presence as the lead actor to draw the audience's focus, then stages his first appearance, the intricate sustained shot already mentioned. Although the viewer may not be aware that there is no cut, the unbroken shot creates both suspense and figurative meaning. Since there is no alternate shot, no sudden shift of angles, permitted, the implication is that there is no alternate possible outcome. In the next sequence, Gagin walks alone down a porch toward an open area at upper frame center. He moves down a narrow passageway, hemmed in by a wall on one side and a dark wooden post on the other. Again, besides a sense of visual constriction, the staging makes the pathway at frame center the only one available, the only course to follow.

In their first meeting, balanced against the reaction shots of Gagin is the physical aspect of Pila portrayed by eighteen-year-old Wanda Hendrix. Although she was four years older than the fourteen-year-old Indian girl created by Hughes, Hendrix's aspect, while conforming to a Hollywood stereotype of an Indian, is striking. Because it is a movie, the contrast between that aspect and Montgomery's is visually palpable and makes an immediate impact not possible in Hughes's prose: "scrawny . . . black fathomless eyes . . . brown face . . . strong black hair." At the beginning and end of the film, the black-and-white, Hollywood Pila has a dusky face with black hair, parted in the center and braided on each side; but, after enduring Gagin's jibes, being called "Sitting Bull" and hearing that she should fix herself up to "look like a human being," Pila visits the beauty salon in the hotel and gets her hair done. In the most perilous moments of the movie, she sports an incongruous permanent wave with spit curls across her forehead and a flower on top.

Although the first encounter between the two is on a false exterior—the soundstage containing the carousel set—the next sequence takes them into the veritable Santa Fe plaza, just outside the genuine La Fonda hotel. By using location here and in the night exteriors when Zozobra is paraded to his pyre, Montgomery seamlessly imbues the studio sets with a portion of their reality. Within this noir landscape, under the pull of some predetermined inclination, Montgomery/Gagin goes to the Tres Violetas that first night, and Pila is there waiting in the darkness. How did she know he would come to the bar? And, if she knew, why does she say: "I thought I would never see you anymore"? There is another long take when an inebriated Gagin and Pancho leave the bar. As the drunken men stumble away, Pila comes up, then leaves. When they exit the shot, she returns, crossing in the background to frame center, then coming forward. Although she has offered Gagin a totem and now follows in his wake, Pila feels unable to shield him from the deadly fate that she has foreseen, for, as she later will admit to Retz, she has had a vision of Gagin lying dead.

A last long take is used when Gagin goes to a restaurant to exchange the letter for Hugo's money. En route, Gagin weaves through the crowd of onlookers gathered for the parade and burning of Zozobra, and a dissolve momentarily superimposes the effigy of Zozobra on a close-up of Hugo, revealing the true face of Gagin's god of back luck. Gagin appears at the table like a waiter, asking: "Everything all right Mr. Hugo?" Marjorie leads Gagin from the table onto the dance floor, and they waltz around the corner to the door. Montgomery ends the long take and cuts as they exit into darkness. Outside, he holds on the silhouetted two-shot as Marjorie's purported warning is revealed as treachery and Gagin gets stung by a dame—that is, knifed in the back.

Despite being wounded, Gagin overcomes his assailants, and then Pila leads him back to the sanctuary of the carousel. It is not merely because it gives the film its title that the *tío vivo* is the central image of *Ride the Pink Horse*. Like other havens in film noir, like Rica's apartment in *Thieves' Highway* (Jules Dassin, 1949) or Doll Conovan's place in *The Asphalt Jungle* (John Huston, 1950), the carousel offers refuge to the spiritually and physically wounded hero. But, in *Ride the Pink Horse*, Gagin is never fully at ease around it, never understands the emotional relation between it and its patrons. On his first night there, he insists that Pila have a turn on it, and she asks which horse she should ride. Approaching the merry-go-round, Gagin uncovers the horse nearest and suggests tersely, "Why don't you ride the pink one?" To Gagin it makes no difference which horse is chosen. They are all essentially the same, all traveling in the same circle, all taking their riders nowhere and ending up in the same spot. To Pila, who understands instinctively the significance of choice, it makes all the difference. The carousel is at once one of the most stylized objects in the movie—both by nature as a theatrical "amusement" and also because it is photographed on a soundstage under neutral gray light that differs subtly from the "real-world" location shooting—and the one object that is most free of artificial restraints. By its very artifice, by the aspects of ritual that its patrons attach to circling a finite space on the small wooden horses, the *tío vivo* becomes a quintessentially noir set piece. Gagin, who comes to it burdened by the complex codes of behavior imposed by the noir universe, focused on the belief that he must even the score, cannot see its broader dimensions.

The symbolism of the carousel as Lorca and others have perceived it is simple: you go a long way in a circle and end up in the same place as you started, a pessimistic metaphor for life, or, as Schopenhauer observed: "After your death you will be what you were before your birth."[13] On one level, the enclosed world and the totemic horses are somewhat Platonic, idealized representations of the actual universe, as stylized as shadows on a cave wall. On another, more primitive level, the carousel is a wellspring of primordial energy, or, as Lorca elaborated:

On ponies
disguised as panthers
the children devour the moon
as they would a cherry.[14]

Like ropes disguised as snakes, Lorca's poetic imagery pierces the veil of deception with symbolic language.

While long takes and low angles can underscore a sense of fatalism, Montgomery also used montage for phenomenological effect, relating the perceptual awareness of the characters to the visual style, as in the first meeting between Gagin and Hugo. Both shot selection and set pieces color the process. Hugo is hard of hearing, and, early in the scene, he holds the phone upside down so that the earpiece is next to an oversized microphone/amplifier clipped to his shirt pocket. The symbolism of this unsettling inversion is ambiguous. When Hugo and Gagin are speaking alone, close-ups and over-the-shoulder shots alternately isolate and link the two figures; but Hugo continues to sidestep. "Your pal Shorty wasn't as tough as he thought he was," Hugo ingenuously clarifies.

GAGIN: So you had him killed.
HUGO: Let's just say that he lost the argument.
GAGIN: To three guys with blackjacks.
HUGO: Were there three?

Shorty's dead, so what difference does it make how many killers there were? Displacement and indirection are part of Hugo's modus operandi, the warp and woof of his veil of deception. At midpoint in the scene, Hugo even walks around Gagin in a circle, a menacing variant on the movement of the *tío vivo*.

In the narrative progression of *Ride the Pink Horse,* Pila's totem Ishtam overcomes the bad luck god, as Gagin survives his encounter with Zozobra's personification in Hugo. In the symbolic and stylistic progression of the movie, Gagin leaves as he began. Like Nick Garcos in *Thieves' Highway,* who learns to trust based on instinct, or Dix in *The Asphalt Jungle,* who refuses to die until he gets home to the ranch in Kentucky, the lessons learned in the sanctuary are critical. Only after he accepts the *tío vivo* as a beneficent "uncle" does Gagin begin to comprehend its meaning. Conditioned as he is to living with his estrangement, even taking solace in that emotion as part of his role, Gagin alone cannot resolve his conflict. Only after the sacrifices of Pancho and Pila can he make the right choice, reject evening the score, and save himself in the process.

Perhaps the most telling interaction of the carousel, noir stylistics, and the principles of Schopenhauer is in the beating of Pancho. Moments after he conceals a wounded Gagin next to Pila in one of the *tío vivo* chairs, two of Hugo's thugs arrive. Pancho keeps several children aboard the carousel by offering a free ride. In several angles, the camera is mounted on the carousel, focused on a young boy and girl, another boy alone, and Pila wearing a blanket over her head like a mantilla with a covered Gagin beside her. While the children's heads turn to watch the men walk up in the background, Pila does not move. As the shadows of horses fly across their bodies, the men stand on each side of Pancho, hemming him in. Their verbal interrogation about the man Pancho met in the bar, the man whose name he does not know, quickly gives way to a more severe approach. As they beat him, Pancho's cries and groans and the dull thud of a clenched fist are mixed with the repetitive carillon sound of the carousel. The cutaways to the moving camera reveal closer shots of the now terrified children, trapped on the merry-go-round, and unable to run away, grimacing and whimpering as the relentless motion of the mechanism takes them past the wall where the men beat the prostrate Pancho over and over. Finally, as Pancho moans, "Oh, my, you hurt Panchito," the thugs relent, convinced he knows nothing.

Pancho crawls over to the lever that starts and stops the *tío vivo*, and, as it slows, the children finally jump off and run away. Although his kindness had already been demonstrated the night before, Pancho is not resentful. Instead, he offers an aesthetic evaluation of the beating that echoes Schopenhauer's belief in validation and redemption through suffering: "They want to know, where is Gagin. Hit me in the nose, I don't know. Hit me in the mouth, I don't know. I fall down, and I don't know." Pancho re-creates it vividly, almost gleefully, for Gagin, a man who conversely exemplifies that particularly pointless striving that Schopenhauer believed was the real root of human suffering. Where a simple thank-you would have sufficed, Gagin's response is to offer to cut Pancho in, to give him $5,000— when he gets it. Pancho had already voiced his casual acceptance of violence when he bandaged up Gagin's wound: "Knife is good. More easy to fix. I got knifed three times. When you're young, everybody sticks knife in you." Just as casually, he shrugs off the possibility of a fortune that he doesn't need: "Lots of people gonna get lots of things, but they don't." Kindness and friendship are their own rewards.

## The Ideal Truth

Gagin's self-deprecating remark to Hugo, "There are a lot of people in this world smarter than me, and they aren't sitting up nights figuring out how to help me," neatly mirrors an observation of Schopenhauer's: "The more unintelligent a man is, the less mysterious existence seems to him."[15] Indeed, the ending of Ride the Pink Horse reaffirms that an instinctive behavior can be more effective than a more purely analytic one. The extortion plot is resolved when a dazed and confused Gagin goes to confront Hugo. Pila catches up to him at Hugo's door but cannot prevent him from being captured. After Gagin is slapped and loses consciousness, Pila is beaten. A low-angle close-up frames Hugo leering like Zozobra over the shoulder of a henchman as he tells him to "keep it up." Then Retz intervenes, and Gagin is saved. In a semicomic "afterword," Gagin worries that Pila will be quite upset when he goes to say good-bye. In a moment that recapitulates his lack of understanding, he awkwardly makes small talk, returns her totem of Ishtam, and is confounded by her easy acceptance of the fact that their relationship is ending.

Two core beliefs of Schopenhauer could arbitrarily be linked to many different movies or other works of art: that the world is a personal representation and that what Schopenhauer calls *unwillful perceptions of art* can help man escape the tyranny of self. But, in many noir films, as in *Ride the Pink Horse,* the characters' attitudes toward money and power, the striving for a needless wealth that Schopenhauer compared to "sea-water: the more you drink, the thirstier you become," reflect a moral alignment between the attitude of the filmmakers and the seminal values expressed in *The World as Will and Representation.*[16]

From both an aesthetic and a philosophical perspective, Gagin remains relatively unenlightened at the conclusion of *Ride the Pink Horse.* His final, puzzled look as he glances back at Pila confirms this. Gagin still takes the limits of his own field of vision for the limits of the world. Pila transforms the moment at the Tres Violetas when she knocked out a Hugo minion with a whiskey bottle. As she animatedly recounts it in Spanish and reenacts it for her friends, Pancho standing by nodding his approval, she turns the event into art. As Schopenhauer observed: "The picture or the poem will thus emphasize its idea, and give us that ideal truth which is superior to nature."[17] The final shot of the picture fades out, not on Gagin, but on the smiling face of Pila. As does Pancho, she realizes that the risks that she took and the beating that she endured were the compassionate and moral thing to do—and that a good story shared with friends is all the reward anyone should need.

## Notes

The epigraphs to this chapter are taken from Federico García Lorca, "Tio-Vivo" (http://home.tiscali.be/ericlaermans/cultural/lorca/canciones/teorias/tio-vivo.html; translation by Linda Brookover), and Arthur Schopenhauer, "Psychological Observations," chap. 5 of *Studies in Pessimism,* trans. T. Bailey Saunders, in *The Essays of Arthur Schopenhauer* (Champaign, IL: Project Gutenberg, 2004) (http://www.gutenberg.org/files/10732 [accessed June 14, 2005]). The text of the Spanish original of the Lorca poem is as follows: "Los días de fiesta / van sobre ruedas. / El tío vivo los trae, / y los lleva."

  1. For extended discussions of film noir as a cycle or movement with beginning and end points, as opposed to an open-ended genre such as the western, see my introductions to *Film Noir: An Encyclopedic Reference to the American Style,* ed. Alain Silver and Elizabeth Ward (New York: Overlook, 1979); *Film Noir Reader,* ed. Alain Silver and James Ursini (New York: Limelight, 1996); and *The Noir Style,* by Alain Silver and James Ursini (New York: Overlook, 1999).

  2. Gregory Bateson, *Steps to an Ecology of Mind* (New York: Ballantine, 1972), 272–73. Bateson coined the word *transcontext* to describe a situation in which autogenous, or internal, perception gives one meaning and exogenous, or external, factors create another.

  3. "The stone traverses a straight line relative to a system of coordinates rigidly attached to the railway carriage, but relative to a system of coordinates rigidly attached to the ground (the embankment), it describes a parabola. With the aid of this example, it is clearly seen that there is no such thing as an independently existing course, but only a course relative to the particular body of reference" (Albert Einstein, *Relativity—the Special and General Theory,* trans. Robert W. Lawson, 15th ed. [New York: Crown, 1952], 10).

  4. Arthur Schopenhauer, *The World as Will and Representation,* trans. E. F. J. Payne, 2 vols. (New York: Dover, 1966), 1:3.

  5. Quoted in Albert Einstein, "The World as I See It," in *Ideas and Opinions,* ed. Carl Seelig, trans. Sonja Bargmann (New York: Bonzana, 1954), 8: "I do not believe in human freedom in the philosophical sense. Everybody acts not only under external compulsion but also in accordance with inner necessity. Schopenhauer's saying, 'A man can do what he wants, but not want what he wants' has been a very real inspiration to me since my youth; it has been a continual consolation in the face of life's hardships, my own and others', and an unfailing well-spring of tolerance. This realization mercifully mitigates the easily paralyzing sense of responsibility and prevents us from taking ourselves and other people all too seriously: it is conducive to a view of life which, in particular, gives humor its due."

  6. Schopenhauer, *The World as Will and Representation,* 1:8.

  7. "At times we fancy that people are utterly unable to believe in the truth of some statement affecting us personally, whereas it never occurs to them to doubt it; but if we

give them the slightest opportunity of doubting it, they find it absolutely impossible to believe it any more" (Arthur Schopenhauer, *Counsels and Maxims,* trans. T. Bailey Saunders, in *The Essays of Arthur Schopenhauer* [Champaign, IL: Project Gutenberg, 2004] [http://www.gutenberg.org/files/10715 (accessed June 14, 2005)]).

8. "Beauty is truth, truth beauty,—that is all / Ye know on earth, and all ye need to know" (John Keats, "Ode on a Grecian Urn," in *Introduction to Literature: Poems,* ed. Lynn Altenbernd and Leslie L. Lewis [New York: Macmillan, 1963], lines 49–50, p. 302).

9. Plato's allegory of the cave is described in bk. 7 of the *Republic.* Men cannot see a monad, the elemental or ideal truth from which material truth derives but a semblance; it is as if they were chained inside a cave and able to "see only their own shadows, or the shadows of one another, which the fire throws on the opposite wall of the cave" (*Republic,* trans. Benjamin Jowett [Adelaide: University of Adelaide Library Electronic Texts Collection, 2004], bk. 7, lines 515a–b [http://etext.library.adelaide.edu.au; e-text p71r]).

10. Arthur Schopenhauer, *Parerga and Paralipomena* (1851), trans. T. Bailey Saunders, excerpted in *The Oxford Book of Money,* ed. Kevin Jackson (Oxford: Oxford University Press, 1995), 317.

11. Dorothy B. Hughes, *Ride the Pink Horse* (Edinburgh: Canongate, 2002), 33.

12. Ibid., 18.

13. Arthur Schopenhauer, "On the Doctrine of the Indestructibility of Our True Nature by Death," essay 10 in *Parerga and Paralipomena: Short Philosophical Essays,* ed. and trans. E. F. J. Payne (New York: Oxford University Press, 1974), 2:268.

14. "Sobre caballitos / disfrazados de panteras / los niños se comen la luna / como si fuera una cereza" (García Lorca, "Tio-Vivo"; translation by Linda Brookover).

15. Quoted in Tom Morris, *Philosophy for Dummies* (New York: Hungry Minds, 1999), 172.

16. Arthur Schopenhauer, "Property, or What a Man Has," chap. 3 of *The Wisdom of Life,* trans. T. Bailey Saunders, in *The Essays of Arthur Schopenhauer* (Champaign, IL: Project Gutenberg, 2004) (http://www.gutenberg.org/files/10741 [accessed June 14, 2005]).

17. Arthur Schopenhauer, *The Art of Controversy,* trans. T. Bailey Saunders, in *The Essays of Arthur Schopenhauer* (Champaign, IL: Project Gutenberg, 2004) (http://www.gutenberg.org/files/10731 [accessed June 14, 2005]).

# Contributors

Jerold J. Abrams is director of the Program in Health Administration and Policy and assistant professor of philosophy at Creighton University (Omaha, NE). His research focuses on aesthetics, film, semiotics, and ethics. His publications include "Art and Voyeurism in the Films of Woody Allen," in *Woody Allen and Philosophy*, ed. Mark T. Conard and Aeon J. Skoble (Open Court, 2004); "Cinema and the Aesthetics of the Dynamical Sublime," in *Film and Philosophy*, 2003; "Aesthetics and Ethics: Santayana, Nietzsche, and Shusterman," in *The Modern Schoolman* (forthcoming); and "Aesthetics of Self-Fashioning and Cosmopolitanism," in *Philosophy Today* (summer 2002).

Paul A. Cantor is the Clifton Waller Barrett Professor of English at the University of Virginia. He is the author of *Gilligan Unbound: Pop Culture in the Age of Globalization* (Rowman & Littlefield), which was chosen by the *Los Angeles Times* as one of the best nonfiction books of the year in 2001. Portions of the *Simpsons* chapter of that book appear in *The Simpsons and Philosophy* (Open Court, 2001).

Mark T. Conard is assistant professor of philosophy at Marymount Manhattan College in New York City. He is the coeditor of *The Simpsons and Philosophy* (Open Court, 2001) and *Woody Allen and Philosophy* (Open Court, 2004). He is the author of "*Kill Bill: Volume 1*, Violence as Therapy," "*Kill Bill: Volume 2*, Mommy Kills Daddy," and "*Pulp Fiction*: The Sign of the Empty Symbol," all published on Metaphilm.com. He is also the author of the novel *Dark as Night* (Uglytown, 2004).

Jason Holt is assistant professor at Acadia University. He is the author of a number of scholarly articles, the book *Blindsight and the Nature of Consciousness* (Broadview, 2003), the novel *Fragment of a Blues* (Famous Thursday, 2001), and three books of poetry, including *Memos to No One* (AB Collector, 1999) and *A Hair's Breadth of Abandon* (AB Collector, 2003). His popular writings include "The Costanza Maneuver: Is it Rational for George to 'Do the Opposite'?" in *Seinfeld and Philosophy* (Open Court, 2000), "Springfield Hypocrisy," in *The Simpsons and Philosophy* (Open Court, 2001), and "Woody on Aesthetic Appreciation," in *Woody Allen and Philosophy* (Open Court, 2004).

Ian Jarvie is Distinguished Research Professor of Philosophy at York University, Toronto, where he has taught philosophy of science for many years.

His film publications include *Movies and Society* (Basic, 1970), *Window on Hong Kong* (University of Hong Kong Press, 1977), *Movies as Social Criticism* (Scarecrow, 1978), *Hollywood's Overseas Campaign* (Cambridge University Press, 1992), *Children and the Movies* (with Garth S. Jowett and Kathryn H. Fuller; Cambridge University Press, 1996), and many papers. He is also the author of "Arguing Interpretations: The Pragmatic Optimism of Woody Allen," in *Woody Allen and Philosophy* (Open Court, 2004).

DEBORAH KNIGHT is associate professor of philosophy and Queen's National Scholar at Queen's University, Kingston, Canada. She has published numerous articles on topics such as aesthetics, philosophy of film, philosophy of literature, and philosophy of mind. In addition, she is the author of "Popular Parody: *The Simpsons* Meets the Crime Film," in *The Simpsons and Philosophy* (Open Court, 2001), and coauthor of "Actual Genre and Virtual Philosophy," in *The Matrix and Philosophy* (Open Court, 2002).

R. BARTON PALMER is Calhoun Lemon Professor of Literature at Clemson University. In addition to numerous articles and book chapters on film noir, he has published *Hollywood's Dark Cinema: The American Film Noir* (Twayne, 1994) and edited *Perspectives on Film Noir* (G. K. Hall, 1996). His current work on noir directors includes *Joel and Ethan Coen* (University of Illinois Press) and the forthcoming *After Hitchcock: Imitation/Influence/Intertextuality* (with David Boyd; University of Texas Press).

ROBERT PORFIRIO received his B.A. in history from Yale University in 1960, his M.A. in motion pictures from UCLA in 1966, and his Ph.D. in American studies from Yale University in 1979. His dissertation was "The Dark Age of American Film: A Study of American Film Noir, 1940–1960." He was professor of American studies at Cal State Fullerton from 1972 to 1980. He has published numerous articles on film in various periodicals, including his seminal "No Way Out: Existential Motifs in the *Film Noir*" (*Sight and Sound* 45, no. 4 [autumn 1976]: 212–17). He was coeditor of *Film Noir: An Encyclopedic Reference to the American Style* and *Film Noir Reader 3*; he also contributed essays to *Film Noir Reader* volumes 1, 2, and 3 and to *The Noir Style* (all edited by Alain Silver and James Ursini).

STEVEN M. SANDERS is emeritus professor of philosophy at Bridgewater State College in Massachusetts. His work in ethics, epistemology and political philosophy has appeared in *Philosophia*, the *Personalist*, the *Southern Journal of Philosophy*, the *Journal of Social Philosophy*, and elsewhere. He is the author, most recently, of essays on the films of Alfred Hitchcock and Stanley Kubrick and on postmodernism and politics. He is currently writing a novel titled *Phenomenology of Me*.

READ MERCER SCHUCHARDT is assistant professor of international communications at Franklin College Switzerland and the publisher of Metaphilm.com, the cult-film interpretation Web site. His writing on film has appeared in the collections *Taking the Red Pill: Science, Religion and Philosophy in* The Matrix (BenBella, 2003) and *The Science Fiction Film Reader* (Limelight, 2004).

ALAIN SILVER holds a Ph.D. in theater arts/motion pictures from UCLA and is the coeditor of *Film Noir: An Encyclopedic Reference to the American Style* (Overlook, 1992) and coauthor of *Film Noir* for the Taschen film series (September 2004). His other work on noir includes editing the four *Film Noir Readers* (Limelight, 1996, 1999, 2002, 2004) and an analysis of the film noir movement's visual motifs, *The Noir Style* (Overlook, 1999). His other books include the photo-odyssey *Raymond Chandler's Los Angeles* (Overlook, 1987), *What Ever Happened to Robert Aldrich?* (Limelight, 1995), and *More Things Than Are Dreamt Of* (Limelight, 1994). He has also produced nine independent feature films, most recently, an adaptation of Dostoyevsky's "White Nights," which he also wrote and directed.

AEON J. SKOBLE is associate professor of philosophy at Bridgewater State College, in Massachusetts. He is the coeditor of *Political Philosophy: Essential Selections* (Prentice-Hall, 1999), *The Simpsons and Philosophy* (Open Court, 2001), and *Woody Allen and Philosophy* (Open Court, 2004) and the author of the forthcoming *Freedom, Authority, and Social Order* (Open Court, 2006). He writes on moral and political philosophy for both scholarly and popular journals.

ALAN WOOLFOLK is professor of sociology and director of the core curriculum at Oglethorpe University in Atlanta, Georgia. He has published extensively on the sociology of culture and intellectuals. Recent articles include "An Impossible yet Necessary Ethic of Resistance" (*Journal of Human Rights* [June 2003]), "The Therapeutic Ideology of Moral Freedom" (*Journal of Classical Sociology* [November 2003]), and "Impossible Counter Cultures" (*Society* [May/June 2004]) as well as recent book chapters and articles on such intellectual figures as Albert Camus, Hannah Arendt, Christopher Lasch, and Thomas Masaryk. He has twice been a National Endowment for the Humanities Fellow and is an advisory editor at *Society*.

# Index